Farm Size and Marketing Efficiency
Pre and Post-Liberalization

About the Author

Dr. Parmod Kumar obtained his M.Phil. and Ph.D in Economics from the Jawaharlal Nehru University, New Delhi. He has taught under-graduate classes in Delhi University for around three years. He held the positions of Consultant and Economist at the NCAER, New Delhi. Presently, he is a 'Visiting Fellow' (Sir Ratan Tata Fellow) at the Institute of Economic Growth, Delhi. He has co-authored a book and published several research articles in the national and international journals.

Farm Size and Marketing Efficiency

Pre and Post-Liberalization

Parmod Kumar

CONCEPT PUBLISHING COMPANY, NEW DELHI-110059

Cataloging in Publication Data—DK
Courtesy: D.K. Agencies (P) Ltd. <docinfo@dkagencies.com>

Kumar, Parmod, 1966-
Farm size and marketing efficiency : pre and post-liberalization / Parmod Kumar.
p. cm.
Revision of the author's thesis (Ph. D.)—Jawaharlal Nehru University.
Study conducted at Kaithal and Sirsa districts of Haryana, India.
Includes bibliographical references (p.)
Includes index.
ISBN 8180693430

1. Farms, Size of—India—Kaithal (District). 2. Farms, Size of—India—Sirsa (District). 3. Farm produce—India—Kaithal (District)—Marketing. 4. Farm produce—India—Sirsa (District)—Marketing. I. Title.

DDC 338.160 954 558 22

ISBN 81-8069-343-0

First Published 2007

Published and Printed by
Ashok Kumar Mittal
Concept Publishing Company
A/15-16, Commercial Block, Mohan Garden
New Delhi-110059 (India)
Phones: 25351460, 25351794
Fax: 091-11-25357103
E-mail: publishing@conceptpub.com

Dedicated to My Son

JIVITESH PUNJ

Foreword

In today's globalising world, trade is becoming increasingly important. In such a scenario, one pertinent question to ask is: can farmers of less developed countries survive and progress? The increasing nearness to global markets demands that the present day farmer becomes efficient, competitive and innovative in both production and marketing. The future farmer of India needs new skills, new perceptions and a new commercial understanding if he is to do well in marketing just as he has to become a more efficient and well-informed producer. The trends in the field of marketing of agricultural produce in India need therefore to be studied intensively and with care. These issues become even more important given the fact that there exists an immense potential for trade in the area of agriculture and related activities.

This book examines issues related to farmers approach to the market and farm level efficiency in marketing farm products. The author has calculated marketing efficiency at the aggregate, using data from wheat, mustard, paddy and gram markets in Haryana with the techniques of cointegration and error-correction. A comprehensive study of market structure, market surplus and price analysis provides information about marketing efficiency of different farm size categories.

The book reveals that agricultural *mandis* in Haryana in general are well integrated in the long run while in the short run price transmissions are lacking because of paucity of information and lack of its quick dissemination. This finding holds true for wheat and paddy markets in both the pre-liberalization and post-liberalization periods. Further, inter market linkages in pulses (gram) were less efficient during post-reform period. In oilseeds (mustard) no long run integration existed in the post-liberalization period.

The study also analyses marketed surplus and related issues using primary data sets and information. It confirms the existence of equitable market access of farmers of all size classes and the disappearance of the practice of excess market charges. The main strength of the book lies in the fact that it provides crop and farm size level information related to market surplus, farmer's price and measurement of marketing efficiency at the farm level. The study finds that farmers of this region are, by and large, well-situated with respect to markets. At the policy level, the study suggests that there exists a scope for raising the level of short run integration of markets by improving communication through better information services and by providing incentives to the farmers to produce more quality products. The question of differences in post-liberalization situation for different crops also throws up issues for further studies.

This book is a revised and updated version of the author's Ph.D. dissertation and was completed during his tenure as Sir Ratan Tata Fellow at the Institute of Economic Growth, Delhi during 2004-06. The SRTT Post-doctoral Fellowships were designed for just such ventures by scholars who took some time off from their regular positions. It gives me great pleasure to see it published. I am sure it shall be of immense value to researchers, academicians, planners and policy-makers besides catering to the needs of post-graduate university students.

Kanchan Chopra
Director,
Institute of Economic Growth,
University of Delhi Enclave,
Delhi-110 007

Preface

Development of agricultural marketing is considered as imperative for sustaining the growth of agricultural production. An efficient marketing system must ensure the best possible returns for the produce to the farmer, minimum incidental costs as also reasonable prices to the consumer. The system must be capable of mopping up the increasing market surplus, developing a systematic mechanism for price determination and of fostering competition. It is generally believed that India's indigenous private marketing system for agricultural products is exploitative, economically inefficient and operates with high profit margins. The recent investigations conducted into the performance of the system, however, unanimously confirmed that the private foodgrains marketing in India operates quite efficiently by the standard economic criteria of a perfect market. However, the statistical tools used in most of these studies to calculate marketing efficiency consisted of the most ambiguous bivariate correlation and regressions of the time series data, which were employed without taking care of autocorrelation and other time series properties.

The present study aims at the objective of calculating marketing efficiency by using the recent developments in time series, namely the 'Cointegration Technique'. An analysis of the regulated markets in the state revealed that Haryana has successfully implemented the regulated marketing system in the state. Farmers generally sold their produce in the regulated *mandis* through the services of commission agents. The empirical evidences of cointegration suggested that markets in Haryana exhibited a long run relationship during both pre and post-liberalization periods. The farmers transferred their produce form one market to the other according to the price changes and arbitrage through trade tied their prices together.

The primary data revealed that wheat, paddy, cotton and fodder were the main crops in terms of area devoted to these crops by the households. On the marketed surplus, it was observed that all size of farmers fully participated in the market and could be termed as commercial farmers. The analysis revealed that on an average 87 per cent of aggregate output was marketed by farmers. The study shows that cultivators with small families, other things being equal, contributed more to the marketed surplus than did those with larger families. In the case of net price obtained by the farmers, the study revealed that an extra mileage covered to search for a better *mandi* by the farmers yielded them a higher net price. Similarly, those farmers who avoided sales immediately after harvest and delayed their sale by a month or more, generally obtained higher net prices. Regarding marketing efficiency at the farm size level, it was observed that there was market participation by all size classes of farmers. The net prices obtained by marginal and small farmers were not lesser than those obtained by large farmers. There was no price discrimination against the marginal farmers. Rather, if any discrimination was prevalent, it was against the large farmers who obtained less than the average price.

A major part of this study is based on the author's thesis prepared under the supervision and guidance of Professor R.K. Sharma and approved by the Jawaharlal Nehru University for the degree of Doctorate of Philosophy. Discussions with Professor R.K.Sharma at all stages of this work were an unfailing source of intellectual stimulation. My debt to him, therefore, is immense.

The thesis has been revised and updated for publication. A major part of the revision was done during my tenure as 'Sir Ratan Tata Fellow' at the 'Institute of Economic Growth'. I am extremely grateful to the 'Sir Ratan Tata Trust' for giving me this wonderful opportunity. Thanks are also due to the Institute for providing me infrastructural support. I have benefited enormously from discussion with Professor Kanchan Chopra who was always generous in sparing her precious time for me. I am also grateful to the faculty members of the institute for their valuable help and advise. I record my thanks to Dr. Ramesh Chand, Officiating Director NCAP for the help provided by him in clarifying various issues pertinent to my work. I also thank Mr. Devendra Pratap and Mrs. Seema Bathla for their constructive suggestions and help provided by them.

I am also profoundly grateful to my parents and family members, whose good wishes and support have been a source of strength during this period. I cannot express in words my feelings to my wife, Nutan, whose interest was instrumental in the completion of this book. I am also grateful to her for reading the manuscript and correcting the mistakes.

Parmod Kumar

Contents

List of Tables

List of Figures

1

Introduction

Performance of Indian Agriculture

Indian agriculture has metamorphosized from a largely subsistence orientated activity to full-fledged commercial farming since the advent of the Green Revolution in the mid-1960s. The introduction of scientific technology in agriculture has resulted in a tremendous increase in the output of food-grains and cash crops. As a result, many farmers for the first time are able to generate surplus at the farm after meeting their consumption requirements. Spectacular increase in production has been realized, particularly after the adoption of Mexican wheat and Philippine rice along with other agricultural inputs and the resultant marketable surplus has touched new heights.

This is evident from the fact that the production of foodgrains during 2001-02 touched an all time high of 211.9 million tonnes from a mere 72.0 million tonnes in 1965-66. Cereal production increased from 62.2 million tonnes to 198.5 million tonnes in this period. In the absence of any technological breakthrough the production of pulses increased marginally from 11.1 million tonnes in 1965-66 to 13.4 million tonnes in 2001-02. Production of oilseeds has more than tripled from 6.4 million tonnes to 20.7 million tonnes during the same period. Production of fibres such as cotton increased from 4.8 million bales to 10.0 million bales and jute and mesta from 5.7 million bales to 11.7 million bales during this period. Sugarcane production increased from 119.6 million tonnes in 1965-66 to 298.4 million tonnes in 2001-02. Production increase in fruits and vegetables has also been impressive.

The growth performance of Indian agriculture in the pre- and post-green revolution periods is presented in Table 1.1. The post-green revolution period is further devided into three phases, *i.e.*, 1966-67 to 1979-80; 1980-81 to 1989-90; and 1990-91 to 2002-03. These three phases earmark three different trends in the crop production. The first phase signifies a rapid increase in the output of foodgrains, especially of rice and wheat. The second phase, witnessed a fractional shift in area and production growth from foodgrains towards oilseeds. Finally, the third phase connotes a declining trend in area and yield of foodgrains as well as other traditional cash crops.

Looking at the growth performance crop-wise during the pre and post-green revolution periods, it is clear from Table 1.1 that in the pre-green revolution period, *viz.*, 1950-51 to 1965-66, growth in output was generally attributed to the expansion in area under crops. All food crops namely, wheat, rice, jowar, bajra, maize, gram and other pulses and cash crops such as groundnut, rape seed, mustard, other oilseeds, cotton and sugarcane observed a significant expansion in area during this period. The scope for area expansion, however, diminished considerably in the green revolution period.

In the mid-sixties, the country adopted HYV seeds for wheat and rice, which entailed a considerable use of irrigation and chemical fertilizers. The strategy manifested in a quantum jump in the yields of these two crops. Consequently, wheat and rice production in a short span of 6 years between 1965-66 and 1971-72 witnessed an increase of 30 million tonnes, which was 168 per cent higher than the achievement of the

15 years following 1950-51 (Chand 2004). The quantum jump in production of wheat and rice led by HYV seeds marked the beginning of the green revolution in the Indian agriculture. Thus, the remarkable increase in production of foodgrains and other cash crops during the next two phases (1966-67 to 1979-80 and 1980-81 to 1989-90) were primarily due to increase in the yield rates (see Table 1.1).

As a result of the extensive growth strategy of the pre-green revolution period and Borlaug seed fertilizer led intensive growth strategy in the post-green revolution period, foodgrain production registered an overall annual growth rate of 2.75 per cent during 1950-51 to 1989-90. However, the technology that heralded the process of green revolution during the 1970s and 1980s started showing signs of deceleration during the 1990s. Technological stagnation is clearly evident from the stagnating levels of productivity growth of almost all the crops. For instance, the yield of food-grains grew at a trend growth rate of 2.22 per cent during the 1970s and 2.92 per cent in the 1980s while it went down to 1.67 per cent in the 1990s. Similarly, all the major oilseeds saw significant positive growth in productivity in the 1980s, while they experienced a fall and insignificant growth in productivity in the 1990s. Total oilseeds production that went up by an impressive growth rate of 5.31 per cent during the 1980s, however, experienced a negative growth rate of –0.35 per cent in the 1990s. Similar trends were observed in the case of cotton lint and sugarcane (see Table 1.1).

Technological stagnation is paralleled by increasing evidences of stagnating productivity of food and other cash crops even in many potential growth areas. The trend in productivity is not one of consistent increase in many states of India during the 1990s. The growth has been flat and even started declining in some of the progressive as well as

Table 1.1: Trend growth rate of area, production and yield of principal crops (All India).

Name of the crop		*Pre GR (%)*	*Post-Green Revolution (%)*			
		1950-51 to 1965-66	*1966-67 to 1979-80*	*1980-81 to 1989-90*	*1990-91 to 2002-03*	*1966-67 to 2002-03*
Rice	P	3.63*	2.55*	3.55*	1.28**	2.71*
	A	1.36*	0.84*	0.41	0.25	0.54*
	Y	2.26*	1.71*	3.14*	1.03*	2.17*
Jowar	P	2.42*	1.94***	0.28	-3.64*	-0.25
	A	0.77*	-1.16*	-1.01**	-3.24*	-1.76*
	Y	1.65**	3.11*	1.28	-0.39	1.51*
Bajra	P	2.29**	-0.15	0.00	0.10	0.93**
	A	0.93**	-1.21*	-1.05	-1.57*	-0.95*
	Y	1.37**	1.06	1.06	1.67	1.88*
Maize	P	5.95*	0.63	1.90	3.11*	2.26*
	A	2.57*	0.51***	-0.18	1.00*	0.34*
	Y	3.39*	0.12	2.08	2.12*	1.92*
Wheat	P	3.73*	6.52*	3.51*	2.41*	4.34*
	A	2.29*	3.57*	0.45	0.80**	1.46*
	Y	1.44*	2.95*	3.06*	1.62*	2.87*
Total coarse cereals	P	2.24*	0.98	0.35	-0.30	0.49*
	A	0.70*	-0.92*	-1.35*	-1.94*	-1.45*
	Y	1.33*	1.90*	1.69	1.65**	1.94*
Gram	P	1.73	0.06	-0.80	-0.02	0.23
	A	1.27***	-0.27	-1.43	-0.74	-0.62*
	Y	0.47	0.33	0.64	0.73	0.85*
Total pulses	P	1.60**	0.36	1.48	-0.72	0.72*
	A	1.46*	0.50***	-0.10	-0.88*	-0.05
	Y	0.14	-0.13	1.57**	0.16	0.77*
Total food-grains	P	2.92*	2.77*	2.70*	1.27*	2.51*
	A	1.22*	0.54*	-0.23	-0.41**	-0.02
	Y	1.70*	2.22*	2.92*	1.67*	2.53*
Rapeseed-mustard	P	3.30*	1.49	7.04*	-1.64	4.51*
	A	2.58*	1.07**	1.93***	-2.27**	2.14*
	Y	0.71	0.43	5.12*	0.63	2.38*
Groundnut	P	3.48*	1.61***	3.69	-2.41***	1.12*
	A	3.72*	-0.18	1.63***	-2.59*	0.03
	Y	-0.23	1.79**	2.06	0.17	1.08*
Total oilseeds	P	2.89*	2.34**	5.31*	-0.35	3.49*
	A	2.50*	1.18*	2.41*	-1.09**	1.63*
	Y	0.39	1.16***	2.91**	0.73	1.85*
Cotton lint	P	3.63*	2.76*	2.76	-0.41	2.34*
	A	1.65*	-0.03	-1.27***	1.23***	0.29**
	Y	2.00*	2.82*	4.01**	-1.63**	2.05*
Sugarcane	P	6.22*	3.24*	2.67**	1.99*	3.06*
	A	3.35*	2.06*	1.45	1.61*	1.74*
	Y	2.86*	1.51*	1.22*	0.38	1.37*
Fruits and vegetables	P	7.67*	4.19*	3.64*	3.59*	3.93*
	A	5.69*	2.48*	1.02*	2.81*	1.93*
	Y	1.90*	2.01*	2.07*	1.37*	1.80*

Note: *** *** Significant at 1, 5 and 10 per cent levels respectively.

Source: Agricultural Research Data Book, 2001 & Agricultural Statistics at a Glance 2003, Min. of Agriculture, Govt. of India.

upcoming states (Ramasamy 2004). The declining trends in productivity are also reflected in declining total factor productivity. Total factor productivity grew at an average annual rate of 1.37 per cent per annum in the 1970s, grew faster at 1.99 per cent in the 1980s and since the 1990s, its growth has slid downwards at the rate of –0.9 per cent per annum (Fan 2002). A host of factors responsible for stagnating technology/productivity includes differential levels of adoption of new technologies and high yielding seeds, varying degrees of water control, imbalances in infrastructure development and use of various inputs (Ramasamy 2004), rapid decline in public investment in agriculture (Chand and Kumar 2004), irrigation and research and development (Rao 1997) and rising input subsidies leading to inefficient use of scarce resources like power, water, fertilizer and credit (Gulati 1999).

Agricultural Marketing

Production and marketing of produce are interdependent in the sense that products in the field have no value unless they are converted into a consumable form and reach the ultimate consumer at his convenience. Since the greater part of farm output in many countries is not consumed by the people who produce this, it must, like industrial products, be sold to satisfy the consumers' demand (Cohen 1965; p.75). There is an increasing awareness that it is not enough to produce a crop; it must also be marketed. Marketing of agricultural products is a process, which starts with a decision to produce a saleable farm commodity. It involves an integrated market system, both functional and institutional based on techno-economic considerations (Rajagopal 1989). According to Cohen (1965; p. 77), "In its essence, the marketing process is the mechanism for fixing prices, just as a market is a place where buyers and sellers together arrive, by bargaining, at the current price". Thus agricultural marketing is a process whereby prices of agricultural commodities are determined, either by the forces of demand and supply or by some other mechanism. The process also involves assembling, grading, storage, transportation and distribution activities apart from the pre and post-harvest operations.

Ruttan and Hayami (1971) stressed that market structure reforms are an important pre-requisite for successful agricultural development. Functional improvement relating to the science and craft of agriculture may result in increased productivity in general, and may delay the operation of the law of diminishing returns in the farming business. Increased agricultural productivity, however, will not be translated into a proportionate increase in the level of real income in an economy in which the distributive system is inefficient. Hence, the economic need for an efficient marketing set up is imperative. Agricultural planners should realize that unless there is an efficient marketing system, the economic incentives cannot reach the producers. The basic aim of an orderly marketing system should be to ensure that the producer realizes a reasonable price for his produce, is not subjected to traditional malpractices and pays as little as possible for services in the marketing of his produce. Unless these basic criteria of marketing are met and an orderly marketing environment is built, the majority of agricultural producers, who are mainly small and marginal farmers, will remain deprived of their just share of the final price of the their produce.

With development, marketing gradually becomes more a complex operation than a simple producer-consumer relationship. Various intermediaries come in between these two extremes to facilitate marketing. This complex marketing system operates and functions in an orderly society, which sets the rules and norms for the system (Kohl and Joseph 1985). The effectiveness and efficiency of the marketing system depends on how these rules and norms are obeyed. Producers are the people who feed the marketing system and as such they are the people most affected by its inefficiency. According to Thomsen (1951) from the producers' viewpoint an efficient marketing system is one that gives maximum returns from products sold after a deduction of the minimum market charges so as to induce further production of these products.

Marketing Efficiency

It would be useful to distinguish between 'technical efficiency' and 'economic efficiency'. Technical efficiency relates to such matters as mechanization and rationalization of individual work processes. To be technically efficient, a marketing structure would have to utilize the best method available for every marketing job and to use these methods with maximum effectiveness. Economic efficiency, on the other hand, reflects the efficiency of the functioning of the marketing system. An economically efficient marketing system will ensure that the physical savings realized in improvements in the handling of the product are transmitted to producers as well as consumers in the form of reduction in money costs (Subbarao 1989). It involves the elimination of wastes, high costs and exploitative profits. The principal means of ensuring this elimination is the pressure of competition. The more nearly perfect a market is, the closer it is to an economically efficient one and the stronger would be the possibility for minimizing wastes and exploitation. An economically efficient marketing system therefore must ensure the highest possible returns for the produce to the farmer, minimum incidental costs and reasonable prices to the consumers.

In general, economic efficiency implies operational and pricing efficiency. Operational efficiency refers to the input-output ratio and focuses on reducing costs in the performance of physical marketing functions, *e.g.*, storage, transportation, etc. The state of pricing efficiency refers to a situation where the sellers get the value of their produce and the consumers receive the value of their money (Sidhu 1986). Pricing efficiency improves the buying, selling and pricing aspects of the marketing process so that it remains responsive to consumer directives. Uniform pricing over the entire market area is an important attribute of pricing efficiency. Over the years, policy-makers have laid a greater emphasis on the presence of pricing efficiency to protect both the producers and consumers from the exploitation of the middlemen.

In India, the view that agricultural markets are imperfect, exploitative and unhelpful to the development of agriculture has been gradually changing over the years. However, the general belief that traders in these markets manipulate prices through malpractice and reap excessive profits has not changed much. Contrary to such common belief, researchers have found that most agricultural markets are benefiting farmers and contribute substantially to the economic development process (Jasdanwala 1966; Lele 1968; Bhide *et al.* 1981; Patnaik and Shankar 1985; Rajagopal 1985, Chatterjee and Bhattacharya 1986). However, it has been observed that the agricultural commodity market, though, it appears to be competitive, is however restrained by recurring uncertainties. These uncertainties are related to the supply and demand of agricultural commodities, especially in seasonal periods when supplies are not sufficiently available to carry out necessary adjustments after demand changes are recognised. As a result, the short run prices may be above or below the expected levels, which cannot be achieved under pure competition. It is imperative that arrangements should exist for efficient movements of the farmers' produce to the consumers and for adequate and timely supply of superior inputs to the farmers.

In terms of farmers' economic benefits from the operations of the marketing system, it is essential that an efficient marketing system be brought about by regulation through rules and norms formulated by society. Where society itself is unable to ensure the operation of these norms, government has to play a vital role (Abbott 1972). Government attention has been focused on agricultural marketing reforms since 1897 (Joshi 1971). However, the creation of an orderly and efficient marketing system has received particular attention from various state governments and the central government since the inception of formal national planning in 1951.

Regulated Marketing

The setting up of the Agricultural Price Commission (now, Commission for Agricultural Costs and Prices) was a first step towards the initiation of efficient marketing through a positive price policy for the farmers' production. Fixation of procurement and minimum support prices by the government on the recommendations of the Agricultural Price Commission provided the necessary assurances to producers to further augment their production. Obviously, this was a different ball game than what existed earlier wherein prices could fall to an unprecedented low level in the post harvesting season in the eventuality of a bumper crop. Further, the buffer stocks of foodgrains have played a positive role in stabilizing returns to the farmers in face of fluctuations in production. They have prevented a fall in the prices to un-remunerative levels during the years of bumper production and kept a check on an undue price rise during the years when domestic output declined sharply.

However, a major breakthrough in agricultural marketing reforms took place after the creation of regulated markets in most of the states. These regulated markets function with clear rules and regulations with regard to open auctioning and fixed marketing charges including those for various operations. These markets generally provided adequate infrastructure in terms of marketing yards and succeeded in reducing many illegal exactions earlier charged by the traders.

The regulated marketing system was further strengthened by the significant development of rural credit. With the nationalization of banks, cooperative and other institutional credit options have become an important component of the total credit available in rural areas. The development of regulated marketing supported by such institutional credit has resulted in the weakening, if not breaking of the credit-marketing nexus, which earlier gave the trader a competitive advantage and a visible edge over his competitors. Likewise, with the setting up of regulated *mandis*, market sales by farmers have increased and physical losses during handling, storage and transportation have been reduced along with the rationalization of market charges. The process of price settlement in most of the markets has become quite transparent and backward and forward linkages of wholesale *mandis* have been considerably strengthened. Owing to a widening of the production base of the agricultural sector, the market orientation of the farm sector has considerably increased. The overall impact of the working of these institutions on agricultural marketing has decidedly been positive and has helped to increase its competitiveness and efficiency.

However, these institutional reforms have not been successful in terms of coverage over the whole of India. These regulated markets are generally more successful in agriculturally advanced areas and have relegated the importance of the trader-cum-moneylender to a secondary position mostly in areas of the green revolution. Market imperfections continue to operate in most of the areas where an agricultural breakthrough has not taken place (Bhalla 1991). In the backward areas, the number of these markets is limited and further, the markets continue to be dominated by the trader-cum-moneylender nexus. In the agriculturally advanced regions, the market infrastructure is fairly developed resulting into efficient marketing. In the agriculturally underdeveloped parts of India, it is highly inadequate and consequently, the marketing system continues to be non-competitive and dominated by monopolistic interests.

Other Aspects of Marketing

The factors, which affect the marketed surplus and the nature of flow from producers to the ultimate consumers over time, space and form, affect the marketing efficiency to a great extent. Nevertheless, merely the creation of infrastructure in agriculturally backward regions is of no help if sufficient marketed surplus does not accrue. The developmental programmes to increase production will not be a stimulus to economic development, if the total production is consumed by the producers themselves. If the marginal propensity to sell is low and the income elasticity of demand for foodgrains is high, the additional increase in foodgrains will be consumed by the producers. Marketed surplus needs to be accelerated to pull the agricultural economy out of trap. Agricultural marketing problems start only after there is a generation of sufficient surplus on the field. Such marketed surplus, if is generated by farmers of all size of holdings would help in creating a market infrastructure in the rural areas and thus fasten the process of efficient marketing.

The differences in infrastructural facilities also create marketing problems in particular areas for the same commodity. As infrastructural facilities undergo change over time in the same area, there can be differences in the problems faced between two periods of time. The price differentials thus found between markets can be taken as a yardstick for measuring the efficiency and dimensions of marketing performance.

There is also a need to examine the various elements, which influence the net prices received by various categories of farmers for the same quality and quantity of goods at the same point of time. The small volume of produce of the small farmers is relatively uneconomic and costly to handle in the market and so may fetch a lower net price to the producer. Those farmers who borrow from the moneylender-cum-traders on the understanding of repaying the loans by selling the produce to them, loose their bargaining power in the open markets and become victims of exploitation both as borrowers as well as sellers. Finally, the rise and fall of the seasonal pattern of prices can help in testing the hypothesis of exploitation by traders by comparing the seasonal rise in prices with the storage costs. Due to the pressure of such discrimination existing in the market, the marketing system becomes inequitable and hence inefficient. The present study is an attempt to identify the marketing problems of farmers. This study examines the participation of farmers in the market and the pricing and operational efficiency of marketing at the aggregate as well as at the farm size level.

Objectives of the Study

The study is undertaken with the following objectives:

(i) To measure marketing efficiency by estimating market integration;
(ii) To study the participation of farmers in marketing by size class of holdings;
(iii) To examine the factors affecting the marketed surplus across farm size;
(iv) To find out the seasonal pattern of marketed surplus by farm size;
(v) To study the marketing channels or intermediaries for selected agricultural commodities; and
(vi) To examine the factors affecting the price received by farmers across the farm size.

Main Hypotheses

With the given objectives, the following hypotheses are tested in the study :

H_1: Agricultural commodity markets in Haryana are integrated;
H_2: Proportion of output marketed is directly related with the farm size;
H_3: Marginal propensity to sell rises with the rise in output;
H_4: Marketed surplus and distance of the village from the market are inversely related;
H_5: The larger the size of holdings, the larger the time lag in marketing the produce;
H_6: Price obtained by farmers is directly related to the farm size; and

H_7: Higher proportion of produce is sold to intermediaries by small farmers as compared to large farmers.

Data Base and Methodology

The relevant data used in this study have been collected from both secondary as well as primary sources. The secondary data like market arrivals of important agricultural commodities in the regulated *mandis* of Haryana for the various years were collected from the Haryana Agricultural Marketing Board, Panchkula. Monthly wholesale prices of the commodities, which were used for cointegration analysis, were collected from the Economic and Statistical Organisation (ESO), and the Department of Food and Civil Supplies (Haryana), Chandigarh. In addition the other relevant secondary data were taken from Haryana Statistical Abstracts, Statistical Handbook of Haryana and Agriculture Statistics at a Glance. The primary data were collected from the farmers through a field survey with the help of a structured questionnaire, keeping in view the objectives of the study. This questionnaire was pre-tested before going for the interviews. The data relates to the agricultural year 1993-94, *i.e.*, 1 July, 1993 to 30 June, 1994.

Selection of Markets

The basic purpose of the primary survey in the present study is to analyse the market participation of farmers and the pricing efficiency of the produce they sell in the market. Therefore, for the selection of households, those *mandi* areas were chosen where the arrivals of products to the market were the highest. As the main cropping pattern in Haryana consists of wheat, paddy and cotton, two districts were intentionally selected for the study. It is seen from agricultural point of view that in the two main regions of Haryana, namely first constituting,

Ambala, Karnal, Kurukshetra and Kaithal is dominated by wheat and paddy crops, while the other region constituting Sirsa and Hisar has wheat and cotton as the predominant crops. From the market arrival data collected from the Agricultural Marketing Board, it was evident that in the Kaithal-Karnal region, the Kaithal *mandi* was one of the largest *mandis* in paddy arrivals. In the Sirsa-Hisar region, the Sirsa *mandi* was the largest *mandi* for cotton. Therefore, for the present study, Kaithal and Sirsa districts were selected for the survey.

Sample Design

The sample design of this study was of two-stage sampling, with the village as a first stage sampling unit and farmers or households as the second and ultimate unit. The selection of the sample broadly involved the following stages.

Selection of Villages

Before selecting villages for the field survey, all the villages around these *mandis* were classified into four groups. The first group included all villages situated within a radius of 6 kms. Villages within the radius of 6 to 12 kms. were included in the second group. The villages located between 12 and 18 kms. from the *mandi* centre were placed in group three, whereas villages beyond 18 kms. from the market centre were placed in the fourth group. From each group, one village was chosen randomly by a 'Lottery Method'. Thus, four villages each were selected from Kaithal and Sirsa districts for this study. The basic aim of choosing different villages at different locations was to find out the differences in marketed surplus and price received by the farmers at different locations to the *mandis.* The following table shows the selected villages from each district and their distance from the main market.

Table 1.2: Selection of villages and their distance from the market centre.

Kaithal District		*Sirsa District*	
Name of the village	*Distance (Kms.)*	*Name of the village*	*Distance (Kms.)*
Manas	5	Bamboor	5
Sewan	10	Bajekan	10
Mohna	16	Randawa	15
Taragarh	22	Barokhan	20

Selection of Farmers and Formation of Size Groups

A list of all the farmers of each selected village was prepared along with the records of their operated area. For the selection of households, all households were further categorized into five sub-classes following the categorization given in the Agricultural Census, 1986. These five sub-classes are as follows:

1. Marginal farmers having an operational holding up to 2.50 acres;
2. Small farmers with operational holdings from 2.51 acres to 5.00 acres;
3. Semi-medium farmers with operational holding from 5.01 acres to 10.00 acres;
4. Medium farmers with operational holdings from 10.01 acres to 25.00 acres; and
5. Large farmers with operational holdings above 25.00 acres.

A systematic random sampling method was adopted for the selection of households. Tippett's random numbers table was used for the random start for the selection of households in each category. This method is very simple and easy for operational purposes and selects sample households that are a near approximation of their probability proportions. For example, the number of households in village Manas in the category of marginal farmers were 60 while 12 households were to be selected from this category. One starts with the random number drawn from the random number table (*i.e.*, random start) and adds to it the random interval, which is obtained as 60/12 = 5. The random start was 29 in this category and selected households were numbered as 29th, 34th, 39th, 44th, 49th, 54th, 59th and 64-60=4th, 9th, 14th, 19th and 24th. The same procedure is followed to select all the other category of households. However, if a household cannot be surveyed due to any reason, in that case, it is substituted by the household with the next sampling serial number.

Table 1.3 gives the details of the households selected in each category and from each village. However, appropriate weights have been used in the text, wherever necessary, to make the averages of the field data representative at the state (aggregate) level.

Other Aspects of Methodology

The principal findings in this study are based on a cross-section field data of 400 households surveyed from eight villages in two districts of Haryana, namely Kaithal and Sirsa. The household data are used to study the marketed surplus by farm size and prices received by different categories of farmers and the factors affecting them. However, households in each category are pooled together and no separate study is done at the village or district level. Tabular analysis is carried out to examine the effect of specified factors on marketed surplus and net prices received by the farmers. The tabular analysis is done across farm size categories. Subsequently, the multiple linear regression analysis has been undertaken as an analytical tool. For regression analysis, all classes of farmers have been

Table 1.3: Distribution of sample households village-wise.

Name of the village/district	*Marginal farmers*	*Small farmers*	*Semi-med. farmers*	*Medium farmers*	*Large farmers*	*Total*
Manas	12	12	12	9	5	50
Sewan	9	11	13	10	8	51
Mohna	14	12	11	8	3	48
Taragarh	13	12	12	11	2	50
Kaithal district	48	47	48	38	18	199
Bamboor	7	9	10	7	3	36
Bajekhan	9	11	13	8	6	50
Randawa	17	15	14	11	8	65
Barokhan	12	12	12	10	4	50
Sirsa district	48	48	48	36	21	201
Grand total	96	95	96	74	39	400

pooled together and no separate regressions are run for different farm size categories. Finally, to search out the relationship between the marketed surplus and output, quadratic regressions have been used and MPS and elasticity of marketed surplus are calculated. The main procedures adopted in the study are discussed in the chapters wherever necessary.

An important limitation of the household data collected was that only one agricultural year was taken into account. The reference year was a normal year in terms of the monsoon. However, paddy in Kaithal district suffered due to floods in some areas and there was some loss to the cotton crop by pests in Sirsa district. The area under these two crops was dropped from the analysis wherever these anomalies were observed. Generally, the responses of the farmers were based on memory. However, an attempt was made to check these data by cross questioning so that some conclusions could be drawn from the data without losing the accuracy.

Overview

The study is divided into eight chapters. Chapter 1 presents the introductory notes and sets out the main objectives of the study along with the hypotheses to be tested. Database Methodology and Concepts used in the study are also presented in this chapter. The second chapter is divided into two sections: Section I presents a brief review of the studies on market surplus and price received by the farmers and related aspects, while Section II presents a review of the studies on market structure, price spread and market integration.

Chapter 3 deals with the regulated market structure in Haryana and agricultural production in the two surveyed districts, namely Kaithal and Sirsa, in relation to state of Haryana as a whole. A detailed discussion is undertaken about the functioning of regulated *mandis* and their functionaries in Haryana. The development in agricultural production in the districts and the state is sought to be explained in terms of growth of production and productivity, availability of irrigation facilities, HYV seeds, etc.

In Chapter 4, market integration is calculated for the nine wheat, four paddy, six mustard seed and four black gram wholesale markets in Haryana. The time series cointegration technique has been used for this purpose. Chapter 5 presents the economic profile of the surveyed households with reference to household composition, cropping pattern, output and cost structure of different farm size categories.

Chapter 6 deals with marketed surplus, cropwise and at the aggregate level of the households surveyed. Tabulation and regression analysis has been used for working out the factors affecting the marketed surplus for the aggregate as well as individual crops. In addition, the functional relationship between marketed surplus and output, APS, MPS and elasticity of marketed surplus with respect to output is calculated crop-wise and at the aggregate level.

The marketing efficiency of the households is examined in Chapter 7 in three sections. The first section presents the nature of market structure in the regions surveyed. Second section gives details about the marketing cost according to farm size. In the third section, analysis of prices received by farmers is presented through tabular and regression techniques. Lastly, Chapter 8 presents the main conclusions of the study.

ANNEXURE—1A

CLASSIFICATIONS OF AGRICULTURAL MARKETS IN INDIA

The market organization means the whole economic structure involved in marketing functions. There exists an elaborate and interconnected system of agricultural produce markets through which the produce flows from producer to the consumer. These agricultural markets may be classified into different categories according to their functions and seller-buyer participation potential. In nutshell, the agricultural markets can have a three-order classification: Primary Agricultural Village Markets, Secondary Markets, and Terminal Markets.

Primary Agricultural Village Markets

These are periodical markets, locally known as *haats, painths* or *shandis*. These markets are generally held once or twice a week, sometimes over longer intervals. The place where these markets are held is generally in open on the roadside at important and centrally situated localities. The days on which these markets meet are fixed so that itinerant merchants can visit the area. As these markets are situated in the producing areas, commodities produced in the surrounding neighbourhood are sold in these markets. Producers sell their surpluses and purchase supplies for their daily requirements. Most of the transactions in these markets involve very small quantities. Generally, cultivators, labourers, small retailers and itinerant traders deal in these markets.

Village markets are very poorly equipped, generally uncovered and are without drainage and storage facilities. On account of their location in the interior, roads approaching these markets are *kachha* and rough. Under such circumstances, the important means of transportation are head loads, pack animals and bullock carts. Some markets lack even a proper *kachha* road. There is hardly any modern facility like the telephone, postal or banking facility available. On an average, a primary village market serves an area 16 kms in radius. There are about 30,000 such markets located in the rural areas of the country (Rajagopal 1988, 44; Nayyar and Ramaswamy 1995, 28, Acharya and Chaudhri 2001, 131).

Secondary or Wholesale Markets

Unlike the primary village markets, these markets also known as *mandis*, are regular wholesale markets. These markets are held in fixed places where business is transacted daily, with the help of intermediaries. Some wholesale markets also serve as assembly points for distant producing centres. These markets are generally situated in all the small and big towns, cities and other important trading centres. Some of these *mandis* have their sub-yards also, located in the villages or in production areas. These sub-yards serve the purpose of assembling the produce of the farmers and supplying it to these wholesale markets working under the network of these *mandis*.

Most of the wholesale markets are better equipped with telephone, telegraph, postal and banking facilities. These markets are not specialized and business is done in all kinds of foodgrains, oilseeds, cotton, jute and other agricultural products. These secondary markets are generally connected to distant consuming and terminal markets by *pucca* roads. Many of these markets are situated on railway lines. These markets serve an average of 500 square kilometres. There are about 7,000 agricultural wholesale markets in the country (Nayyar and Ramaswamy 1995, 28).

Terminal Markets

Terminal markets are those markets in which the produce is either finally disposed of direct to the consumer or processor or assembled for shipment to foreign destination or for redistribution to the surrounding areas. In terminal markets transactions take place mainly among traders, instead of between cultivators and traders. In these markets traders are well organized and use modern methods of marketing. Such markets are situated at all the big cities like Mumbai, Delhi, Kolkata, Chennai, Kanpur, etc.

A market cannot function in isolation. It influences other markets in the market circuit and, in turn, gets influenced by other markets. The primary, secondary and terminal markets are also interrelated. The markets in rural areas for agriculture are generally of primary nature where the assembling of produce is the dominant function. Such markets should have a link with the secondary markets where the grading, standardization and redistribution of the produce takes place. The produce is supplied to the terminal market from the secondary market where it is exported to inter-country and intra-countryside markets. If these markets are not linked to higher order markets by appropriate transport and communication network, the market system may undergo many undesirable business effects pertaining to demand, supply and price. As a result, interruption in the mobility of goods and services would cause monetary loss both to the producers and traders and high price to the consumers.

ANNEXURE—1B

CONCEPTS AND DEFINITIONS

It is always desirable to clearly define the various concepts used in the study so as to avoid any ambiguity in understanding the analysis. Although standard definitions and concepts have been used, a brief description of these concepts is given below:

Household

Household is a unit in which all the members of the family carry out joint operations for their livelihood. Some members may be engaged in cultivating activities and others in non-farming activities, but there is a single decision-making body for the household. In some cases, the members of the family jointly operate their farm and non-farm activities but have a separate kitchen. In this study, such cases are taken as single households. For a household to be a cultivating household, s/he need not own but must operate some land.

Size of Operational Holding

Operational holding here refers to net land operated by a household. It comprises of land owned minus uncultivated land plus land leased in minus land leased out. It includes land taken on mortgage and excludes land given out under mortgage. Addition or subtraction must be during the year of the survey, *i.e.*, the reference year.

Gross Output

Gross output includes the value of gross output from all the crops plus their by-products in the form of straw, stalks, etc.

By-products are converted into value after multiplying their respective prices prevailing in the village at the time of threshing. Main products are converted into value terms by using the respective prices received by the farmers at the time of selling of their produce in the market or otherwise the prices prevailing in the market. However, neither the by-products nor the fodder crops like jowar, barseem, etc. are sold in the market. Therefore, for the marketing analysis, while dealing with marketed surplus as well as prices received by farmers, the value of output is calculated by subtracting the imputed value of fodder crops and by-products from the gross value of output.

Marketing Cost

Marketing cost here includes, the transportation cost incurred in transferring the produce from the field to the *mandi* (only the paid out cost is included and no imputed cost in case of transportation by own tractor is included); Marketing charges in terms of unloading, cleaning and weighing; storage cost and the other cost incurred in terms of refreshment, etc. in the duration of sale in *mandi* are also included.

2

Market Surplus, Market Structure, Price Spread and Market Integration

A Review

Backdrop

A market may be defined as a sphere within which price making forces operate and transfer of ownership is consummated (Waite and Trelogan 1951). Marketing has become essential for farmers as they are no more subsistence producers and generally produce more than their home requirements. The market provides them with an opportunity to review their production system and specialize in those crops, which offer them the best returns. Farmers cannot avail of the opportunity to produce a specialized crop unless marketing techniques and organizations are available to take this product to the consumer.

The interest in marketing can be traced back to 1897, when the first legislation of the Government of India, *viz*., 'Berar Cotton and Grain Marketing Law' empowering the government to open bazars and regulate markets was enacted (Shah 1971). The farmer's inability to benefit from the marketing of crops and hence, the need to protect their interest provided the impetus for this law. Since then the problems relating to the marketing of field crops have been studied extensively and from various angles.

Before independence, the Directorate of Marketing and Inspection, a government agency created specially for this purpose, organized major studies on the marketing of crops. However, their surveys were not based on any scientific sampling designs and hence, the estimates were not fully reliable. After independence, economists have carried out an enormous amount of research on the problems of agricultural marketing. A wide range of research studies are available on different aspects of marketing such as market surplus and market supply; Price structure and factors influencing the farmer's price; Pattern of market arrivals; Structure of marketing; Price spread, Channels of distribution and cost of marketing; and Efficiency of marketing and market integration.

The review here is limited only to those studies that have a bearing on the aspects of marketing that are analysed in this study. Various aspects of marketing are, however, inter-linked and it is difficult to separate them and make a review of each category separately. Therefore, the present review is divided into two broad categories, namely, first, the Marketed Surplus, Farmer's Price and Related Aspects and second, the Market Structure and Price Spread and Margins, Market Integration and Marketing Efficiency.

Marketed Surplus, Farmer's Price and Related Aspects

The major focus of the studies conducted in the fifties and early sixties was on the relationship between marketed surplus and different farm size holdings. The emphasis of these studies was to investigate whether the marketed surplus was confined to a particular size category of farmers or was it spread across all categories of farmers. The studies on marketed surplus can be grouped under two categories. The first category consists of those studies, which look into the distribution of marketed surplus by different size of farmers based on indirect estimation from secondary data, covering the whole of India. The second category of studies is based on direct estimation from micro-level data analysing the relationship between the marketed surplus and size of land holdings. Both sets of studies are briefly examined here.

Before examining the studies on marketed surplus, it is essential to bring out the theoretical distinction between the two concepts of 'marketed surplus' and 'marketable surplus'. Marketed surplus represents that part of farm produce which is actually marketed irrespective of the fact whether the domestic needs have been met or not. The marketable surplus, on the other hand, refers to that part of farm produce which is the excess or balance left with the farmer after meeting his farm family consumption requirements, seeds and kind payments of different types on the farm. In the present context, the term 'marketed surplus' has been used in the discussion except where there is an attempt to measure the exact quantity of marketable surplus.

In his pioneering study, Narain (1961) estimated marketed surplus across different size classes of farmers for the period 1950-51. He generated data for total output at the all-India level based on a number of sources, namely: NSS data on land holdings and consumer expenditure; National Income Accounts, Farm Management Surveys, All India Rural Credit Surveys of the Reserve Bank of India and Reports of the Agricultural Labour Inquiry. The marketed surplus was defined as the difference between total agricultural produce and the retentions of cultivating households, the latter including consumption at source, rent on leased in land, wages, seed and animal feed and payments to artisans. For analytical purposes, land holdings were divided into nine size classes.

The estimated marketed surplus from Narain's study worked out to around 33 per cent of the total produce of

1950-51. It was estimated that in the total value of marketed surplus, the lower three classes of holdings (those operating up to 15 acres) contributed as much as 54.4 per cent. The larger holdings operating 15 acres and above, accounted for the remaining 45.6 per cent. Even within the lower classes, the contribution of lowest two classes (operating up to 10 acres), accounted for 46.5 per cent of the total value of marketed surplus. He also found that the marketed surplus as a proportion of output declined as size of holdings increased up to the size class of 10-15 acres and rose steadily thereafter along with the size of holdings, thereby giving it a U shape curve.

Narain interpreted the higher proportion of sale by the lower size classes up to 10-15 acres as indicative of distress sales, which presumably had a perverse relationship with output and contributed more than half of the marketed surplus. Since the smaller farmers were forced to make distress sales for cash requirements, they later purchased a part of that product from the open market at higher prices. Thus, in this study the quantity of marketed surplus was composed of: (i) Distress Surplus with a backward sloping curve; and (ii) Commercial Surplus with a forward sloping curve. While, small farmers supplied mostly their distress surplus, large farmers supplied their commercial surplus of agricultural produce.

However, the pioneering study by Dharam Narain suffered from a number of shortcomings and was criticized by many scholars. A serious draw back of his findings was that his estimates were not obtained from any direct observations and many of the assumptions that he made and statistical devices that he adopted might not be valid under all circumstances. The diverse sources of data used by him had made the indirect estimates very unreliable. Each data source of the study suffered from a distinct set of limitations. For example, the distribution of the value of agricultural produce for the entire country was obtained from the FMS data collected from a few districts of Uttar Pradesh. Similarly, the NSS data used by him were not given according to the size class of holdings but according to size classes of total per capita expenditure. It appears that the published data used in the study were manipulated for producing a particular set of results. Given the structure of ownership of land holdings in the country, Dandekar (1964) and others expressed strong doubts about the validity of the findings that more than half of the total marketed surplus came from smaller size classes of farmers. The U shape curve of marketed surplus has also been questioned.

As a strong reaction to the study of Dharam Narain, Patnaik (1975) re-estimated the distribution of marketed surplus by size class of holdings for the year 1960-61 and also for the year 1950-51 (re-estimated). She used the same database of secondary sources as used by Dharam Narain but adopted a number of improved methodologies and corrections to the secondary data before using them in her estimates of marketed surplus. Patnaik observed from her re-estimates of marketed surplus that the farm holdings of up to 10 acres contributed 32.2 per cent and those up to 15 acres contributed only 44.4 per cent to the total marketed surplus of all size of holdings. In addition, she did not find any perversity as the proportion of marketed surplus increased steadily from 20 per cent in the lowest size class of one hectare and below to 63 per cent in the highest size class of 20 hectares and above. Among the ascending ordered size classes of farmers, Patnaik found no fluctuations in proportions of marketed surplus. Further, her study results were not consistent with the dominant role of small farmers in output and marketed surplus, as found by Dharam Narain. Utsa Patnaik observed that her estimated proportions of marketed surplus for 1960-61 held good for the year 1950-51, the period for which Dharam Narain made his estimates.

Rastyannikov (1975) compiled the data from the All India Rural Debt and Investment Survey (1961-62) of the Reserve Bank of India and classified this data based on the value of assets to estimate the behaviour of marketed surplus. Rastyannikov found that the behaviour of marketed surplus was fairly the same as found in Patnaik's study. The proportion of marketed surplus to total product increased steadily from 19.8 per cent in the lowest asset group of less than Rs. 1,000 to 41.4 per cent in the highest group of Rs. 20,000 and above. For all households together, the value of marketed surplus amounted to 31.4 per cent of total value of farm produce. The lowest two asset groups (up to Rs. 2,500) amounted for only 10.7 per cent of the marketed produce. The corresponding figure for the two largest asset groups stood 56.3 per cent.

However, both the studies by Patnaik and Rastyannikov have a similar limitation in that they used the gross sales, which were overestimated. In both the studies, none of the size classes had a negative marketed surplus because of non-inclusion of the purchased quantities of foodgrains. Moreover, both the studies used the gross values of output. In a detailed study, Sharma (1972) carried out an indirect estimation of marketed surplus. He analysed a mass of secondary data, collected through household schedules of the 1961 population census. After careful examination of the 1960-61 data, Sharma presented his findings separately for the country as a whole and for the 15 states individually. The analysis had shown that size class of up to 5 acres had a negative marketed surplus at the national level and also in all the states except, Andhra Pradesh, Kerala and Tamil Nadu. Even the next size class of 5 to 10 acres was found to be deficit in Gujarat and Maharashtra. The proportion of marketable surplus to net production of foodgrains also increased consistently with the increase in size of holdings. Unlike the earlier studies, which used gross output, Sharma used net production as the basis for calculating the proportion of marketed surplus. In addition, Sharma also fixed a minimum desirable level of consumption as the cut-off point for the determination of consumption retention. The proportion of marketed surplus to net production of foodgrains for all the classes together was estimated at 37.4 per cent. However, this study also suffered from the same deficiencies and limitations as encountered by earlier studies using indirect estimates of marketed surplus. The next section presents a brief review of micro level studies as stated above.

Bhattacharjee (1960) examined the marketed surplus by using the household level data in a survey of six villages conducted by the Agro Economic Research Centre of the Visva Bharati University. A detailed analysis of the marketed surplus with respect to size of holdings was made for the three states of Bihar, Orissa and West Bengal for the two year period from 1955-56 to 1956-57. The study revealed that during 1955-57, the small farmers operating less than five acres of land contributed less than one-fourth of the total marketed surplus of paddy. The relative shares of medium and large farmers, operating above 5 acres, were found to be dominant in all the selected villages. The variations in the proportions of marketed surplus of different villages reflected differences in the stage of development of the respective villages. He also compared the above-mentioned marketed surplus data of West Bengal with the village level data of the Institute of Rural Reconstruction, Sriniketan for the period of 1942-45 for paddy crop. It was observed from the comparison that there was a tremendous increase in the relative share of marketed surplus of large farmers, between the early forties and the middle fifties. The relative share of medium and small farmers, on the other hand, declined by 16 and 25 per cent, respectively. Comparing the quantity of sales per acre of land holdings, Bhattacharjee found that the extent of cash sales of small farmers decreased, that of medium farmers remained more or less the same, while for large farmers their figure increased considerably during the above-mentioned period. He concluded that the speculative and precautionary motives of the medium and large farmers added to the problems of frequent price rises and seasonal price variations and suggested for government price policy to control the anti-seasonal elements.

Muthaiah (1964) analysed the data from six selected villages of Rajasthan and two villages of Madhya Pradesh for jowar and wheat crops. The study found the marketed surplus of wheat as a proportion of net produce steadily increasing from 24 per cent in the holding size of less than five acres to 64 per cent in the highest size of more than hundred acres. Corresponding percentages for jowar were 18 and 50, respectively. Further, the study revealed a positive relationship between the per capita annual income of cultivators and the proportion of marketed surplus to total production. Parthasarathy and Rao (1964) examined the production and marketed surplus data for another set of six villages selected from the Godavari, Krishan, Pennar and Cauvery delta regions of Southern India. The data for paddy crop related to the triennium 1958-61. The study found that the large majority of small and marginal farmers accounted for only a small proportion of marketed surplus, while a few large and medium cultivators contributed a major chunk of marketed surplus of paddy. However, the marketed surplus was found to be positively related to the level of production among all size classes of farmers. Further, the marginal propensity to market paddy was much higher by big farmers than by the small farmers.

Another important and controversial study by Krishna, Raj (1965) used a wide range of data drawn from eight states of India for a sample of 23 farmers to study the marketed surplus in a partially monetized economy. Raj Krishna introduced family size as an additional factor among the explanatory variables. All disposals other than family consumption were treated as the marketed surplus in the study. Working out the functional relationship between the quantity of marketed surplus and level of output, linear as well as non-linear relationships were observed by Krishna.

The most important findings of Raj Krishna's study include the following: (i) There was constancy of marginal propensity to sell over a wide range of output above the minimum subsistence level; (ii) The average propensity to sell increased as the output increased above the minimum subsistence output, but at a decreasing rate; and (iii) The elasticity of sale with respect to output was positive and high ranging 1.04 to 1.60 for wheat and 1.04 to 1.36 for rice. Raj Krishna observed that 17 out of 23 samples had a positive price elasticity with a linear functional relationship and only six samples depicted significant deviations from a linear relationship. These six samples consisted of either very rich or very poor farmers. These observations led him to draw the policy conclusion that it was best for government to concentrate on encouraging higher farm output without any special discrimination in favour of small or large farmers. Even with the farm size structure remaining what it was, increase in output would lead to more than a proportionate increase in marketed surplus without any discriminatory or coercive policy.

Raj Krishna's study is not free from limitations and has been widely criticized. His observation of a linear relationship in most of the samples might be due to the unique definition of marketed surplus taken by him. His assumption that all produce disposals should be considered as the real components of the marketed surplus was unrealistic. If kind payments were deducted from the defined marketed surplus, the results would have shown non-linear zones in a greater number of samples. Criticizing Raj Krishna's study, Rao (1965), Majumdar (1965) and Prasad (1965) expressed the view that a linear marketed surplus function did not appeal to them as satisfactory and that linearity violated a matter of common sense and general observations that marketed surplus was concentrated among the bigger size class of holdings.

In their study on Punjab, Kahlon and Vashishtha (1968) analysed 43 selected farm households of Ludhiana district to study the marketed surplus by size class of holdings. The study identified six key factors, namely volume of produce, size of family and holdings, consumption habits of people, relative prices of different farm products and the accessibility to markets as important factors, which determined the proportion of marketed surplus of different products and farmers. No definite relationship was found between the size of holdings and the marketed surplus of cash crops like cotton, groundnut and sugarcane. As these crops were grown primarily for the market, their proportion of marketed surplus to total produce ranged from 71 per cent to 92 per cent. They used the tool of partial correlation coefficient and observed that the coefficient between marketed surplus and volume of production (when the size of holding remaining constant) was positive and significant for maize and positive and non-significant for wheat. The correlation between the size of the family and the proportion of marketed surplus as well as between distance from the village and marketed surplus were found to be negative. Thus, the other important factors in the determination of marketed surplus were highlighted in this study.

Bardhan (1970) used the village level cross-section data of 27 villages of Punjab and Uttar Pradesh for the period 1956-61. She ran a regression of the marketed proportion of production (Y) on the production of foodgrains in quantity per adult (X_1). The other explanatory variables taken in the regression were, the average price of foodgrains for cultivators (X_2); the value of production of commercial crops other than foodgrains per adult unit (X_3); average income of cultivators from sources other than the crop production (X_4); index of concentration of cultivated area (X_5); other disposals of food-grains (other than sale) *minus* other receipts of foodgrains (X_6).

Bardhan observed from her study that the volume of marketed surplus was a quadratic function (with positive first and second order derivatives) of the average level of food-grain production. However, the regression coefficients of Y on X_3 were positive in some cases and negative in others, though insignificant throughout. Coefficients of Y on X_4, X_5 and X_6 had expected signs of negative, positive and negative, respectively. Output elasticity of marketed surplus was found to be positive with an estimated value of 1.8 while the price elasticity of marketed surplus was negative with an estimated value of –0.6. It may be noted that the marketed surplus in her study was equal to gross sale, which is always non-negative as repurchase during the lean season is not subtracted from the marketed surplus.

Hati (1976) analysed the relationship between marketable surplus of paddy and farm size for the period 1971-72 to 1972-73 for the Hooghly district in West Bengal. He defined marketable surplus as marketed surplus net of repurchases and fitted two non-linear equations and grafted them into one. The results when plotted on a graph gave a curve with three distinct parts. Each part represented a particular group of land holdings. Marketable surplus was found to be negative for the first part of the curve up to the size class of 0.66 hectares. The curve rose sharply upwards till it crossed the zero line. For holdings between 0.66 and 1.98 hectares, the curve flattened at about 5 per cent of marketable surplus and an increase in farm size practically had no effect. In the case of farm holdings above 1.98 hectares, the proportion of marketable surplus grew at an incremental rate as farm size increased.

In his micro level study, Nadkarni (1980) made use of Farm Management Survey data of 1969-70, 1970-71 and 1971-72 for 143 farm households spread over 15 villages in Ahmednagar district of Maharashtra. He made an in depth study of marketed and marketable surplus in a predominantly millet region. It was observed that the net marketed surplus was negative for jowar and bajra and for total foodgrains in the smallest two size classes of below 2 hectares and 2 to 4 hectares and in the case of jowar even for the next size class of 4 to 6 hectares. The net marketed surplus as a percentage of output for jowar, bajra and wheat was respectively, 16, 20 and 30 per cent for all size of holdings. In case of all food-grains, the figure stood for 21 per cent. It was observed in the study that the percentage of net marketed surplus to net output for wheat remained positive even for the lowest size of holding which indicates that in this millet region, wheat was treated as a cash crop and the smallest size of cultivators were forced to sell superior grains (wheat) for purchasing relatively inferior cereals (jowar and bajra) for consumption.

Talukdar (1984) following Hati's model (1976) in a field study of Assam found that factors like family size, size of holdings, gross income, total consumption, kind receipts of the crop, level of debt and total production of substitute crop significantly affected the marketed surplus of rice and arecanut. He observed that small and semi-medium farmers were below the subsistence level and a major amount of marketed surplus was contributed by medium and large farmers.

Chattopadhyay and Sen (1988) used Farm Management Survey data on paddy for West Bengal and Andhra Pradesh for the period of 1970-71 to 1972-73 and Tamil Nadu for the period of 1968-69 and 1970-71. They fitted a regression between per capita marketable surplus and average farm size, per capita farm size and per capita land cultivated under a specific crop. They analysed the data separately for the above-mentioned three states and observed that the distress sale of rice among the smaller farms were pervasive in West Bengal. In the case of Andhra Pradesh, the phenomenon of distress sales as well as negative marketable surplus were prominent. In the case of Tamil Nadu the phenomenon of distress sales was not prevalent, rather small farmers were found to be the primary source of marketable surplus of rice.

In determination of marketable surplus, family size was found to be the most important factor, having a negative relation with marketable surplus even in case of big size class of farmers. The outstanding finding of their study was that, "per capita availability of cultivated land among the larger farms is certainly higher compared to the smaller ones, but per capita availability of land under a specific crop need not be higher in the larger size groups than the smaller farms. The phenomenon of marketable surplus should be examined not in terms of size classes of holdings but with the average of individual crops separately against each size class." Following the same data and methodology as that of Chattopadhyay and Sen, a subsequent study by Sen and Banerjee (1995) concluded that yield was the more important determinant of the volume of marketable surplus than population for non-major food crops in Uttar Pradesh and Punjab. For major food crops, population pressure on land played a dominant role, specifically if the average farm size was small and fragmented.

In order to arrive at detailed estimates of marketed surplus for different crops for the major states, NCAER (1990) surveyed 58 agro-climatic regions selecting 36,818 households from all over India following the two stage stratified random sampling method. The survey period was 1988-89. The average estimates of marketed surplus as a proportion of output at the all-India level were estimated as: 59 per cent for rice; 54 per cent for wheat; 55-60 per cent for coarse grains; 53-75 per cent for pulses; 64-94 per cent for oilseeds; 95 per cent for cotton; 87-97 per cent for jute and senn-hemp; 93 per cent for sugarcane; 96 per cent for tobacco; and 70-90 per cent for fruits and vegetables.

To find out the marketing problems of hill state farmers, Thakur *et al*. (1997) made a primary survey of 145 farmers in the Kangra and Mandi districts of Himachal Pradesh during 1992-93. The authors observed that the marketed surplus of different crops in the case of large farmers ranged from 21 to 43 per cent and for small farmers from 9 to 28 per cent in the case of food crops. In the case of vegetables, the marketed surplus was much higher: 90 to 96 per cent for large farmers and 86 to 91 per cent for small farmers. Supply response was positive in the case of all categories of farmers and all crops. The elasticity of marketed surplus with respect to output was positive and greater than unity for all crops. In the event of marketing problems faced by hill farmers they recommended that they should be provided with the facilities of regulated markets, low cost transport, mechanical grading and packing facilities, remunerative markets and support prices and early establishment of co-operatives. Maheshwari (1998) in her study of market regulation concluded that while regulated markets may be called upon to provide for larger quantities in some states, they could not be expected to overtake or subsume the indigenous marketing set up present in all the other states. The government policy must recognize that sole reliance cannot be placed on regulated markets.

The results of Dharam Narain's study (1961) which showed that small farmer's contribution to marketed surplus was sizeable, attracted the attention of economists regarding the relationship between market supply and price level. The supply theory in traditional economics postulates a positive and direct relationship between market price and quantity of supply. In their controversial study, Mathur and Ezekiel (1961) put forth the hypothesis that market prices and the quantity of marketed surplus of foodgrains are inversely related. The hypothesis they tested was, "Farmers sell that amount of the output which will give them the amount of money needed to satisfy their cash requirements and retain the balance of their output for their own consumption ..., if prices rise, the sale of a smaller amount of foodgrains provides the necessary cash and *vice versa*. Thus prices and marketed surplus tend to move in opposite directions".

Their study was based on certain assumptions, namely (i) the presence of a non-monetised economy; (ii) that the cash needs of the farmers are fixed, and (iii) that own; consumption retentions of farmers are only the residuals. It was further assumed that farmers generally save in kind rather than in cash and that the foodgrain output in the short run remains fixed. These assumptions were severely criticized by Dandekar (1964) who pointed out that small farmers sold little of their foodgrains and depended on other sources to meet their cash needs such as wages of labour, sale of other crops and remittances received. Even the large farmers, according to Dandekar accounted for the larger part of the area and responded normally to economic stimuli rather than price stimuli. Thus, the Mathur Ezekiel proposition had little applicability in their case.

Krishnan (1965) made an empirical attempt to test the hypothesis of inverse relationship between marketed surplus and price of foodgrains. He estimated the price elasticity of marketed surplus by using the coefficients of price elasticity, income elasticity and the proportion of sale of farm produce by the following expression,

$$M = \sum_{1-r}^{r} - [\beta - \alpha],$$

where β and α are the income and price elasticities of the farmer's demand function and r is the proportion of output consumed by them. Krishnan found an inverse relationship between the proportions of marketed surplus and price changes without involving the assumptions of fixed cash requirements and saving habits. He observed the elasticity of marketable surplus with respect to price equal to –0.30. Just against Mathur and Ezekiel's contention that the quantity of foodgrains set aside for family consumption by subsistence farmers was a residual factor, Krishnan argued that for the same category of farmers, the retention set aside for household consumption were fixed and the quantity of marketed surplus was only a residual factor. However, both the studies concluded the existence of an inverse relationship.

Most of the empirical studies that propounded the theory relating to the behaviour of the farmer with regard to the market supply of foodgrains assumed one homogeneous community of agricultural producers. Dandekar (1964) and Chakraborthy (1968) disputed the validity of such aggregative assumption with regard to the market supply of foodgrains. They pointed out that the results of the disaggregate study would be different from that of an aggregative one. On the whole, the big farmers would dominate the market supply and their behaviour regarding market supply of foodgrains in response to price changes would not be defined as inverse.

By improving upon Raj Krishna (1965), Behrman (1966) estimated the price elasticity of output. He concluded that at the lower levels of sales-output ratio, the price elasticity of marketed surplus was negative and at the higher levels of the sales-output ratio, the price elasticity of marketed surplus was positive for wheat in Punjab. Bardhan and Bardhan (1969 and their revised version of 1971) analysed the national level data on consumption and output of the farm sector to derive the time series of marketed surplus of cereals. The purpose of their study was to observe the long-term responsiveness of prices to the output level. The main findings of their study were as follows: (i) The responsiveness of marketed surplus with respect to the ratio of cereal prices to the prices of other food products was positive; (ii) The responsiveness of marketed surplus with respect to the ratio of commercial crop prices to the prices of cereals was negative; and (iii) Ratio of cereal prices to non-cereal prices influenced the marketed surplus of cereals due to substitution in consumption at source.

In another attempt, Hassel (1975) used Kalpana Bardhan's data and developed a model to study the relationship between consumption decision and foodgrains price and farmer's income, while treating the marketing as residual. He observed from his analysis that short run price elasticity of marketed surplus was positive and its value ranged from 2.7 for the entire sample to more than 3 for large farmers. Further, the elasticity of marketed surplus with respect to output was observed to be much greater than unity. He concluded from his findings that farmers were price and income responsive as consumers and higher prices would result in larger quantities being marketed.

It is generally considered that small and marginal farmers are victims of exploitation and they receive lower prices for their produce when compared to their large farmer counterparts. This is because of differences in place of sale, time of sale, indebtedness, etc. Hence, this area of market equity has attracted many researchers who have attempted to identify the factors determining the prices received by the farmers. Some of these important studies are discussed below:

Jasdanwalla (1966) identified that factors such as location, place of sale, time of sale and financial obligations to private agencies were responsible for the price variations among the farmers. Rao and Rao (1976) threw light on inter-village and intra-village differences in prices received by farmers. They found that infrastructural under development which was common to all classes of farmers was the most important source of price difference. Small farmers received little lower prices on the whole, but it was the spatial differences that were more conspicuous. Such differences may be greater still in less developed millet tracts, where density of population was lower than in paddy areas, where infrastructural facilities were more concentrated spatially. Mukherjee (1983) in his study found that a rise or fall in cereal production leads to variation in the prices of cereals. He found that whenever the production of cereals declined, the prices of cereals increased. The increase in prices were reflected comparatively more in rice. However, this often led to a rise in the price of wheat also, even though its production did not decline when compared to the previous year's production.

Ninan (1988) in his study on market participation of small farmers, used farm level data for four villages in Kerala. The study made an attempt to find out whether there was a price bias in favour of any particular class of farmers and whether these price advantages were specific to a particular crop or to a choice of market outlets. It was observed by Ninan that the small farmers tried to concentrate on commercial crops while they grew food crops mostly for self-consumption. Big farmers, on the other hand, grew food crops not only for subsistence purposes, but also for the market. Further, he observed that there was no conclusive evidence to support the view that small farmers were paid less for their produce than what was offered to big farmers. Further, the price differentials across size classes were smaller when the market outlet was a co-operative as against an agent.

Market Structure, Price Spread and Margins, Market Integration and Marketing Efficiency

A pioneering research study on the structure of market organization for an important commercial crop namely, cotton was undertaken by Dantwala (1937, 1952). Incidentally, this can be considered as the foremost scientific research inquiry on market structure for any crop in India. Besides describing the functioning of the cotton market, he examined the competitive character and efficiency of marketing operations. He did not notice any exploitative character in the cotton market organization. The organization seemed to function efficiently by minimizing the cost of marketing. Information flowed quickly from one stage to the other. Thus, although the market operated efficiently, he also recorded certain malpractices leading to the conclusion that market forces did operate, but with constraints.

In addition to the studies conducted by the Directorate of Marketing and Inspection of the Government of India, individual attempts have been made to study the market structure for individual commodities confined to a particular state or *mandis*. Mathur and Kulkarni (1965) analysed the working of the Ghoti regulated market in Maharashtra. They found that there was a close understanding and personal relationship among traders, which enabled them to circumvent the market regulations. Mirchandani and Hirachandani (1965) studied the impact of market regulation in different states for the period of 1950-51 to 1965-66. They observed that regulation exercised a wholesome influence on the market structure and though, it generally raised the marketing efficiency by reducing the market charges, it could not eliminate the prevailing intermediaries. However, the highly increased amount of arrivals in the regulated markets was a clear indication of reduced sale at the village level.

Deen (1977) used the Lorenz Curve and Markov Chain Analysis to examine the structure and structural changes of four selected potato markets in the Farrukhabad district of Uttar Pradesh. He observed that the market structure showed a high degree of concentration in market share amongst both buyers and sellers. The study concluded that the potato market in this district was oligopolistic in structure and was far from perfect competition. Subbarao (1978) studied the efficacy of the existing market structure in the case of paddy/rice. He studied the existing marketing organization, reasons for different prices in different villages, the spatial integration of prices, government intervention, etc. He concluded that government intervention in the paddy marketing system in the form of compulsory levy both from the farmers as well as traders influenced the free market supply and paddy prices.

Bhide *et al.* (1981) studied structural changes of the arecanut market in Karnataka. They used the Lorenz Curve and the Markov Chain Analysis to analyse the degree of concentration. The study concluded that the degree of competitiveness was increasing over time in the arecanut market. Aulakh (1983) in his study on the foodgrain market structure in Punjab found that a few large buyers purchased the major share of arrivals from the farmers. The study concluded that foodgrain markets in Punjab were competitive as there was no indication of any collusion between the traders.

Some studies relating to the structure of markets also examined the problem of cost of marketing and price spread.

Krishnaswamy (1971) in his study on wheat markets in Rajasthan concluded that the marketing cost was not fixed and it varied between neighbouring markets. Distance between the primary and secondary wholesale markets contributed the highest percentage of cost of marketing the foodgrains. It was further observed that out of the total margins in marketing the product, the commission agents earned a major share. The wholesalers, due to the unusual trend of selling prices, earned a comparatively lower margin. He also observed that the wholesale prices and consequently margins were more elastic than retailer's margins, which were more or less constant due to the inelasticity of consumer's preferences prevalent in the retail trade.

Singh and Sidhu (1974) in their study on the Khanna market of Punjab found that 95 per cent of the total arrival of the groundnut in the Khanna market was purchased by the oil millers while the rest of the produce was purchased by retailers and consumers directly. They also studied the costs and returns of crushing by small, medium and large mills and found that the net return was directly related to size of the mill as the net profit for crushing one quintal of pod by large, medium and small sized mills was Rs. 30.92, Rs. 24.85 and Rs. 23.15, respectively.

Analysing the profitability of different marketing channels, Thakur (1974) pointed out that the most profitable channel from the producer's point of view was in the following order: consumer, retailer, wholesaler, commission agents, co-operatives and village itinerant merchants, respectively. Suryaprakash *et al.* (1979) analysed the price spread of arecanut, coconut, copra, cotton and groundnut in several regulated markets in Karnataka. They identified four different channels of distribution. It was observed that price spread was smaller in groundnut marketing than in other crops, *viz.* copra, coconut and cotton. They concluded that the differences in producer's share in different channels was due to the difference in commission charged by commission agents.

Singh *et al.* (1979) in their study on Punjab reported that in foodgrains marketing, the major change was that of government intervention. They concluded that it had brought about noticeable changes in the costs and margins by reducing the market middlemen. However, despite an increase in marketing efficiency, unfortunately the operating cost of the government agencies was relatively higher as compared to the private traders. Sinha *et al.* (1979) analysing the foodgrain price spread in Bihar also concluded that the two markets under study showed high marketing costs and a large price spread. This was due to handling and storage losses, high transport charges, higher costs of weighing, loading and unloading and high commission charges by intermediaries.

Talukdar (1985) concluded in his study on Assam that there was an indirect relationship between marketing cost and size of holdings and direct relationship between marketing cost and length of channel. It was observed that farmers received different prices due to differences in market arrival and channels of sale. Reddy *et al.* (1985) observed in their study that the producer's share in the consumer's rupee was quite low and price spread accounted for quite a big chunk of the consumer's rupee. It was further observed that there is considerable scope for improvement by creating co-operative infrastructure such as co-operative finance, processing, storage and marketing facilities. Gangwar and Pandey (1985) did a study on Haryana. Their research work pointed out that the efforts of the government ensuring a higher share for the producer in the price paid by the consumer through market intervention and price policies have not yielded the desired results. However, in the absence of government intervention and price policies, the producer's interest would have been still more adversely affected.

Rajagopal (1986) in his study of paddy marketing in the Chhattisgarh region of Madhya Pradesh took six performance indicators, *viz*. producer's share, marketing costs, middlemen's margins, price deviation and peak and lean seasonal price variability to calculate the marketing efficiency of different channels. He found that the most efficient channel was co-operatives, followed by agents/brokers to the rice millers; regulated markets; agents/brokers to the traders in village market in that order, respectively. It was observed that the farmer's response to the marketing channels was found significant in the co-operative sector, compared to other channels of paddy marketing.

Tripathi *et al*. (1995) pointed out that the high cost of packing material and the sizable amount of middlemen's margin reduced the benefits of apple growers. To increase the share of the producer in consumer's price, cheap and easily available packing material, low cost transportation and storage facilities need to be evolved. They concluded that there was a need to reduce the marketing channels up to the minimum possible extent. Patnaik (1995) concluded that the buyer's willingness to transact at the market yard was one of the pre-requisites for augmenting the share of the market yard as buyer's age old relationship was a major factor determining the place of disposal. To increase the share of market yards in groundnut arrivals, the government must enforce the market regulations in all markets. The study concluded that a single window system to undertake the activities of procurement, credit, storage and grading could be done by establishing Commodity Corporations relevant to a particular market.

Harriss Barbara's study (1996) examined several inside facts and figures with respect to agricultural commodity markets in Avanashi and Palladam *talukas* in the Coimbatore district of Tamil Nadu. She studied the marketing system of coarse grains (millets and pearl millets), paddy-rice, groundnut, tobacco, cotton and their by products. The study for the period 1979-80 was based on a primary sample of 149 firms and 506 sample farmers. Her study dealt with diverse issues like exchange relations and the marketed surplus, marketing activity, economic power and spatial pattern, capital and money in the market systems, labour, merchant's land and control over production and finally, state regulation, economic crime and bureaucratic corruption.

She observed that agricultural trade was urbanized with highly specialized market places. The top 20 per cent of the firms controlled 54 per cent of all commodity flows while the bottom 20 per cent controlled only 4 per cent. She observed that the paddy-rice trade was characterized by long distance origins and distances. Highlighting the higher concentration in the agricultural trade she concluded that those who controlled the marketing of agricultural produce obtained on an average some 15 times more income than those who directly controlled agricultural production.

Jha and Nagarajan (1998) made an attempt to study the wholesaler stock and hoarding in rice markets in India. They highlighted the inherent instability in the Indian grain markets, which aggravated basic tendency to hoard. The wholesalers were permanently holding non-optimal inventories. There was thus a persistent order imbalance in the wholesale market of India due to the dual nature of the grain markets. In a subsequent study on the structure of grain markets in India Jha *et al.* (1999) presented some interesting results. They observed that the price spread (margin) appears because of information asymmetry. Further the spread components showed a tendency to accumulate. They state that government intervention and the presence of a parallel controlled market is responsible for information asymmetry and that is responsible for spreads constantly adjusting upwards over time.

Pointing out a need for institutional reforms in the Indian agricultural marketing system Jairath's study (2002) indicated that there existed a system of multiple fees, cesses and taxes. The study observed that the multiplicity of the market fee system and its existence in a wide variation on the buyers/ sellers in different states, variation in rate of *mandi* commission on different crops, imposition of development fund/cess, substantial market charges and entry tax/octroi inflate the cost of production and widen the gap between the consumer and producer price. Further their complexity puts an additional burden on the food prices leading to creation of barriers on the movement of agricultural commodities within and across the states. This leads to inefficiency and unnecessary harassment of the producer-seller. The study made a policy suggestion that the government should review the Agricultural Produce Markets Acts of the states and unify them as one legislation to be governed by an independent and self-sufficient organization under the preview of a Ministry like that of FDA in the US.

Thus, in the above analysis, attempts were made to chalk out the marketing efficiency on the basis of market structure, price differentials, costs and margins. However, marketing efficiency has been investigated more directly through the study of relationship of prices in different market places. Such studies inquire whether movements of prices in different markets for the same commodity are synchronized or divergent. Synchronizing movements would imply an efficient relaying of price signals from the consumer's level to that of producers. It would also imply that there prevail conditions of perfect competition in the market.

Marketing efficiency is calculated by measuring the market integration between agricultural markets in these studies by correlating the time series of price data for different market places and products. This procedure builds on the rationale that if markets are perfectly competitive and spatially well integrated, differences in prices between markets will reflect transport and processing cost only. The bivariate correlation coefficient between a pair of such time series of prices will be equal to one. According to this reasoning, a lower correlation will reflect bottlenecks arising, for example, from lack of market information, lack of product homogeneity or presence of monopoly power. The studies undertaken with this method have yielded ambiguous results. Some of these important studies are discussed as follows:

Jasdanwalla (1966) studied the marketing and pricing efficiency in the Rajkot district of Saurashtra (Gujarat) during 1956-57 for two important cash crops, namely groundnut and cotton. She concluded that there was a significant degree of coordination in price movements between the upcountry and terminal markets. A significant degree of coordination was observed between the prices of the raw product (groundnut) and final product (groundnut oil). It was found that market perfection increased further through a significant reduction in seasonal variation in groundnut. Cummings (1967) examined the wholesale wheat trade to evaluate the role of prices and private trade in the functioning of the Indian wheat market. Time series data pertaining to wheat prices arrivals, stocks, etc., in the Khanna market in Punjab were analysed. Utilizing the technique of correlation among the wholesale prices in different markets, Cummings presented model correlation coefficients of price series between 27 North Indian wheat markets from 1956 to 1974 equal to 0.85 during times of free trade and 0.65 during government intervention. According to him, real world coefficients being less than one given that temporal and spatial frictions occur as a result of transport costs, lack of product homogeneity and uncertainty regarding the direction of movement of future prices.

Lele (1968,1971) investigated the problem of costs in detail in her study of the performance of the private marketing system with respect to wheat, rice and jowar in selected markets in India. She covered four states, the Punjab, West Bengal, Tamil Nadu and Maharashtra. Lele observed that the temporal and spatial price differences were largely explained by storage and transportation costs. Prices in different markets moved in unison, implying thereby a perfect system of signals in different markets. Further, the inter-year variations in prices were such that it would not pay the traders to carry over stocks from one year to the next continuously and earn out of this activity. She observed that a rigging up of the prices or exploitation of the producer in any other respect through explicit or implicit collusion among dealers at different stages was not observed. The higher price differentials (as in case of paddy-rice in West Bengal) were not due to the differences in milling equipment, but rather due to the governmental policies, which resulted into higher incidental costs. The observed marketing inefficiency was thus attributed mainly to the effect of governmental controls and not due to any inherent weaknesses of the marketing system as such. Lele found all price correlations between Delhi and five Punjab wholesale wheat markets from 1955 to 1965 exceeding 0.90. From her correlation analysis of Tamil Nadu paddy and rice wholesale prices, she found that only in 3 cases out of 507, correlation coefficients exceeded 0.8. Lele concluded that as the patterns of market flow were so diverse that the correlations in Tamil Nadu were slightly lower than those obtained in the Punjab or West Bengal. Harriss (1979) pointed out that the obvious reason for the diverse results obtained by Lele were the data used in the study.

Gupta (1973) made an attempt to study the pricing pattern in the selected markets of Madhya Pradesh. Looking into the supply response to prices, Gupta concluded that in Madhya Pradesh, farmers while allocating land, did not consider prices as an important variable. Cultivators generally marketed 50 to 70 per cent of their total surplus during the first three months of harvesting, and so the price during this period was recorded to be the lowest. Looking into the market integration, he observed that competitive market conditions prevailed among the various markets in the state during 1961-62 to 1965-66. He found the prices in these various markets were fairly associated with each other. The average correlation coefficients among different markets were recorded as, rice = 0.79, wheat = 0.71, jowar = 0.85 and groundnut = 0.91, during the above-said period.

Kainth's study (1982) showed that wheat markets were highly integrated with a price correlation coefficient varying from 0.83 to 0.93. The regional price differences in the case of wheat normally did not exceed the cost of transportation. According to Kainth, the high integration of these markets could be attributed to the development of roads, infrastructure, market intelligence and a better spread network of markets and purchase centres in the state. In the case of paddy, the markets were found to be less integrated as compared to wheat, the reason seemed to be the lesser mobility of paddy from one market to the other. Similarly, Thakur (1974) found that 71 per cent of correlation coefficients between seven Gujarat wheat markets during 1965-71 exceeded 0.75. However, he observed that on the whole, the existing foodgrains marketing system was not efficient, as was clear from the high profit margins of the intermediaries.

Muniyandi (1985) studied groundnut marketing in the North Arcot district of Tamil Nadu by taking data from three regulated *mandis* of Vellore, Arni and Tiruvannamalai. Correlation coefficients between the selected markets, i.e. Vellore, Arni, Tiruvannamalai and Chennai for the period 1977 to 1984 were calculated. The value of these coefficients was very high and significant ranging between 0.94 to 0.98. This led to the conclusion that the groundnut prices moved in unison and that the markets in the region were integrated. Furthermore, the spatial, temporal and form pricing efficiency was assessed by comparing the inter-market price differences with transport costs; seasonal price differences with storage cost, and finally, differences in oil and oilseed prices with the processing cost (by oil millers). It was observed that there were no excessive profits earned in any form and price differences in all these cases were normally less than their respective costs. Thus, the study concluded that the marketing system for groundnut in the North Arcot district was functioning efficiently. There was no evidence of price manipulations by traders either through collusive or exploitative activities.

Naik and Arora (1986) made an attempt to study the pricing efficiency of the arecanut market. They used primary data of a random sample of 50 producers from the Sisri market in Karnataka and wholesale price data of other secondary markets from all over the country to calculate the price integration of arecanut. From the analysis of correlation it was observed that correlation coefficients were mostly significant with very high values. It was found that all the primary markets were well integrated. In addition, the distant secondary markets like Delhi, Cochin and Mumbai were well integrated in terms of price movements. Regarding the integration between the wholesale and retail markets, it was observed that retail price at Nagpur were highly correlated with the wholesale prices at Sisri and Mangalore markets. However, retail prices in Kanpur were not found integrated with wholesale prices of the primary markets because of the long distance between the markets.

Jayaraj (1992) began his paper with a detailed discussion on the adequacy and non-adequacy of the correlation coefficient technique and finally applied this technique on both the raw data as well as the residuals. In addition, he applied a regression analysis to the residual price data. He used the monthly wholesale price data of groundnut kernels for the period 1975-76 to 1983-84 for 10 centres in Tamil Nadu. Jayaraj concluded from his analysis that price integration was efficient and instantaneous for a majority of the markets. The results of the correlation coefficients of the residual price series were lower than those obtained for absolute prices. As the residual prices were correlated significantly, that indicated real integration between different market centres. Moreover, Jayaraj explained that due to shortage of the production period, instantaneous price adjustment was given preference to short run and long run market integration as considered by Ravallion (1986).

In addition to these studies in India, there are many studies completed in West Africa that have used the correlation technique to calculate the degree of market integration. West African studies generally present much lower figures in comparison to Indian studies. These studies include Jones (1968), *Thodey* (1968), Hays (1975), Kohlers (1977), Berg (1977) and Southworth *et al.* (1979).

Correlation coefficients when calculated in this manner by using raw price data is however not free from shortcomings. Rudra (1982) pointed out that two price series can indeed differ by a large margin and yet they move together in the same direction and yield a unit correlation coefficient. In fact, in some of the studies discussed above, the correlation was found to be quite high between markets that had no physical contact, or during periods when one should expect contacts to be less intense. Hence, the technique has been criticized by a number of scholars and efforts have been made to search out new methods to look into the problem of market integration.

Blyn (1973) criticized the correlation technique by pointing out that there may be common, underlying trends in the series, which provide an upward bias to the results. Inflation or population growth, for example, may give rise to linear trends causing a perfect correlation between the two price series even if the markets in question are not even remotely integrated. Moreover, seasonal variations may be synchronized, for example, due to a common climatic pattern with planting and harvesting taking place at the same time, near all the markets included in the sample. This would lead to spurious correlation, even when there is no or little contact between the markets. Heytens (1986) pointed out that two functionally isolated markets might appear to be synchronized if prices in each are influenced by a third market or by a common factor.

To solve this problem, Blyn suggested that instead of correlating raw data; trend and season free data should be used to find out the market integration. He also calculated monthly coefficients from Cummings data after making it trend free and showed that this produced a correlation of 0.68, which was much below the Cummings figure (0.85).

Following a similar approach Subbarao (1978) in his study of rice in Andhra Pradesh calculated the correlation coefficient between de-trended and de-seasonalized wholesale monthly price data between the six selected markets during April 1968 to December 1971. The results of the study revealed that only four out of fifteen correlation coefficients exceeded the value of 0.80. Thus, he concluded that wholesale assembly markets were reasonably integrated, the ideal perfectly competitive environment as indicated by correlation coefficients close to unity was not prevalent. Further, the correlation coefficients of the study were lower than those obtained by others, *i.e.* without de-trending the data. Thus, the validity of the technique is weakened by the presence of auto-correlation in time and in space. Similarly, the results of Jayaraj's (1992) study showed that the correlation coefficients of the residual series (which are trend free) were lower than those obtained for absolute prices and so supported Blyn's results.

A spatially integrated market indicated by a high correlation coefficient, however, does not necessarily have to be competitive. Thus, this concept of correlation-based integration itself appears hazy from the viewpoint of assessing the degree of competition. This is because, as pointed by Timmer (1974) in his study of rice marketing margins in Indonesia, the integration methodology in time and space is based on the unidirectional model of price formation. Timmer suggested a two way model of price formation between the rural producer market and the urban consumer market. In this two way model, during the lean season, rural hinterland prices may rise above the urban prices. If the rural demand is significant, it becomes possible to reverse flow from urban, back to rural areas. According to Timmer, the marketing margin between rural and urban trade under the circumstances, could be positive, zero or negative. Thus, if a unidirectional model is replaced by Timmer's two way model of price formation; high, low or negative spatial price correlations are possible. So, exercise of great care is necessary before drawing inferences about the nature of competition from indices of market integration. If one allows for a two-way trade, the correlation coefficient appears to be an unsatisfactory tool, and may tell nothing about either market integration or the degree of competition.

Finally, the correlation method has been criticized by Harriss (1979) on the ground that a high correlation between two markets does not necessarily mean that these two markets are well integrated in the sense that a competitive network of traders exists which ensures that agricultural goods move between market places in swift response to price differences that exceed transport costs. High correlation could just as easily indicate stable margins and monopolistic imperfections in the marketing system as competitive conditions and efficiency. Similarly, a low correlation does not have to be an indication that markets are not well integrated.

Attempts have been made to search for new techniques of market integration, which are free from the above shortcomings. One such attempt was made by Monke and Petzel (1984). Their study was concerned with vertical integration between qualities of cotton, and the technique used was simply to regress one price on the other. Bi-variate regression of the form $P_i = \alpha + \beta P_j + e$ between time series of prices for different qualities was used to get an indication of constancy of discounts and premia for the prices of differentiated products. In addition, hedonic index estimation of the form $P = a + b_1D_1 + b_2D_2 + b_3D_3 + \ldots$ was used, where P is price and D_1, D_2, D_3... are Dummy variables, signifying different quality characteristics. However, while calculating market integration by the above regression method, no attention was paid to the error term e, which is generally auto-correlated in time series data and renders the whole analysis inconsistent.

Ravallion (1986) made an improvement in the simple bivariate model to extend this static method into a dynamic model of spatial price differentials. His model assumes a radical market configuration where regional markets are linked to a main central market. In his model, Ravallion devised tests to examine segmentation, long run and short run integration. Thus the stochastic difference equation model used by Ravallion had an advantage over the previous bivariate regression model as it used a sufficient number of lags to make the disturbance term white noise. However, OLS estimates of the coefficients of the radial model would be imprecise if the lags were of a relatively high order. The reason being multicolinearity between lagged values of the explanatory variables. If two non-stationary variables such as P_{it} and P_{jt} share common patterns, then since P_{it} and P_{jt} are related to their lags P_{it-k} and $P_{jt-k,}$ respectively, from transitivity, the presence of multicolinearity is inevitable. Furthermore, the specification of his equation raised the problem of spurious regression of trending variables, as pointed out by Granger and Newbold (1974).

Similarly, Heytens (1986) also based his index of market connectedness on OLS estimates of the following equation:

$$\Delta P_{it} = (a_i - 1)(P_{it-1} - R_{t-1}) + b_{io}\Delta R_t + (a_i + b_{io} + b_{i1} - 1) R_{t-1} + C_i X_{it} + e_{it-}$$

The index being a_{i1} $(b_{io} + b_{i1})$. However, OLS will yield biased and inconsistent estimates of the equation, since the ΔR_t term is endogeneous.

Following the shortcomings of the aforesaid techniques of market integration, a parallel line of research introduced the cointegration technique to study a long run relationship between different price series. A procedure has been developed for evaluating spatial market linkages within the framework of cointegration tests by Granger (1986), Engle and Granger (1987) and Engle and Yoo (1987). The general cointegration procedure is based on the fact that if two price series have a long run equilibrium relationship, though they have significant short run divergences, then these markets can be considered to be cointegrated in the long run. This is equivalent to stating that, if the two price series are cointegrated, there must be a long run equilibrium relationship between them, indicating that the markets are integrated. Recent applications of cointegration testing to spatial price relationships can be found in Ardeni, Goodwin and Schroeder, Palaskas and Harriss, etc. A brief review of these studies is given below.

Goodwin and Schroeder (1991) used the cointegration approach for an analysis of the integration of 11 regional cattle markets in the US, using weekly price series over the period 1980-87. They used seven empirical tests of Engle and Granger (1987) for cointegration analysis. The study concluded that several markets were not cointegrated over the 1980 through the 1987 period. Markets separated by long distances had a lower degree of cointegration than markets in close proximity. However, this divergence of price over long distance might be warranted by market conditions, but was not large enough to permit profitable trade through regional movements of cattle. A formal analysis of market characteristics revealed that distance between markets, industry concentration ratio, market volumes and market types exercised significant influences on cointegration relationship between markets.

Perhaps the first ever study conducted on Indian data using the latest technique of time series of cointegration was by Palaskas and Harriss (1993). To examine the dynamic relationship of market commodity prices in West Bengal, they analysed the weekly spot prices for the period of 1988 to 1990 for three commodities: rice, potato and mustard. Cointegration tests suggested that the markets were integrated, but a lower degree of integration of rice and mustard was identified. The hypothesis of full market integration was rejected. Thus, the study negated some of the results of the previous study done by Lele (1968). In addition, the study tried to locate the structural and institutional factors affecting the marketing performance. The factors found most important were the institutional set-up of marketing system, the availability of market information and the state regulatory policy.

In their study Carol and Wyeth (1994) observed that the procedure suggested by Ravallion was still widely used and they proved that the Ravallion model was a special case within the more general framework of cointegration. They used the reduced form of the error-correction mechanism, which made it possible to test for exogeneity as well as indicate the direction and strength of causality in price formation between markets. The method was illustrated with monthly data on rice prices in different parts of the Indonesian market. Out of the seven markets studied, cointegration was found in five markets. The results confirmed among other things that supply sources were more important than demand sources in driving prices.

Goletti and Babu (1994) undertook a study to see how market integration has been affected by market liberalization in Malawi. Several measures of integration such as cointegration, dynamic adjustments and price asymmetry were introduced to analyse both the co-movement of prices and the price adjustment over time. It was observed from the study that almost all markets exhibited cointegration, thereby suggesting a causal relationship among them. The number of markets that were cointegrated increased after liberalization took place in July 1987. However, the degree of integration was not perfect as adjustment of price changes to stock originating elsewhere was not 100 per cent and for most of the markets it was below 50 per cent. Contrary to the general belief that price increases are transmitted to consumers, whereas traders are the main beneficiaries of price decreases, it was observed; however, that supply (and demand) shocks were transmitted equally, both when they tend to increase prices and when they put a downward pressure on prices.

Diakosevvas (1995) examined market integration between the Australian and US beef prices at the farm gate level. Cointegration analysis and a time varying parameter estimation procedure based on the Kalman filter model was applied. The study used monthly beef price data over the period 1972 to 1993. The results of the study indicated that there was cointegration between the Australian and US beef prices, albeit not full. Further, the degree of convergence between the various price pairs had not substantially increased over time. Diakosevvas concluded that Australian prices could not unequivocally be adopted as world prices in empirical analysis. Sinharoy and Nair (1994) concluded in their study of pepper price variations in the international trade that the international prices of pepper for Indonesia and India had moved synchronously in the long run. This movement was despite the short run drifts and so indicated the integration of these world pepper markets. The study pointed out that there might be a kind of tacit collusion among exporters on market sharing and price parity. However, the results were not likely to vary even if stock adjustment and forward trading in pepper was considered. Jha *et al*. (1997) investigated rice and wheat market integration in India involving binary and multivariate cointegration. The period of study was January 1980 to December 1990. They observed that all pairs of I(1) prices of rice and wheat were cointegrated. They concluded that the markets of these two crops were highly integrated all over India.

The studies discussed so far on cointegration used the Augmented Dickey-Fuller procedure to test the null hypothesis of no cointegration of prices. Although this OLS approach is relatively simple and intuitive, it suffers from a number of shortcomings. One disadvantage is that the distribution of the test statistics is not invariant with respect to the nuisance parameter and therefore, the critical values given in Engle and Granger (1987) can be taken only as a rough guide. Second, the procedure of considering pairs of markets ignores any linkages, which might operate through a third market. Third, there may exist more than one long run relationship, but this cannot be captured by the Dickey-Fuller procedure. Fourth, the tests for identifying the driving forces in the two markets ignore the possible existence of multiple 'common trends' that would imply multiple dominant markets. Finally, given *a priori* belief that markets are in fact integrated, it is preferable to test the null hypothesis that prices are cointegrated.

A better and more powerful test for cointegration presented by Johansen (1988) is the Maximum Likelihood Procedure, 'multiple cointegration test', which can overcome many of the above problems. This technique is particularly important when testing for cointegration between more than two variables. Most of the recent studies have preferred Johansen to Engle-Granger. Asche *et al.* (1999) provides an excellent exposition of Johansen's procedure. The authors opine that the Johansen test provides the critical link in empirical work when prices are non-stationary, because it allows testing the hypotheses on the cointegration parameters in the framework of Composite Commodity Theorem in contrast to what is possible with the Engle-Granger test. The Composite Commodity Theorem and Law of One Price (LOP) imply that when markets are well integrated, a single aggregate quantity and price for the goods in question can be constructed. Applying these tests on time series data of five species of Atlantic salmon, and four Pacific species, the analysis observed that these species competed in the same market as evidenced by their cointegrated prices. They concluded that the law of one price held and the generalized Composite Commodity Theorem was proved.

Owen *et al*. (1997) examined the relationship between vegetable and tropical oil prices in the world market using Johansen's Maximum Likelihood Procedure and the Vector Autoregressive Approach. The study observed that despite the apparent similarities between these oil prices in terms of their general pattern of movement over time, the relationships were not found to be strong enough to label them as cointegrated. The VAR analysis indicated that substitution relationships appeared to drive price movements in the short run, while market based structural factors for each of the oils were important elements in the price formation process in the long run. Janaki *et al*. (1997) used Johansen procedure to study the effects of the Canada-United States exchange rate, the US pulp price and the domestic use of pulp on the Canadian pulp price. The study observed one long run relationship among the above-mentioned four variables. The relationship was considered as a long run inverse demand function for Canadian wood pulp. The short run analysis suggested that the US pulp price was more important than other variables in determining the price of pulp in Canada.

Ghosh (2000) used the maximum likelihood method of cointegration to examine integration in the intra and inter-state regional rice markets in four states, namely Bihar, Orissa, Uttar Pradesh and West Bengal in India. The period of study was March 1984 to April 1997. The cointegration results for Uttar Pradesh indicated that regional markets were integrated to an extent that the Law of One Price (LOP) held for 75 per cent of the ARWA variety of rice. However, no evidence was found in favour of LOP for the coarse/common rice in Bihar, Orissa and West Bengal even though regional markets were found to be integrated. The author argued that since markets were integrated there should not be any unnecessary restrictions on inter-regional movement of foodgrains.

Goodwin and Piggott (2001) evaluated spatial price linkages and dialy price dynamics among regional corn and soyabean markets in North Carolina utilizing asymmetric, threshold, auto-regression and error-correction models. Their results confirmed that such markets were tightly integrated. The results confirmed the significance of threshold effects and suggested that their presence might significantly influence spatial price linkages. They recognized the fact that the models that explicitly recognized threshold behaviour imply much faster adjustments to deviations from equilibrium than is the case when thresholds were ignored. Wilson (2001) used full information Maximum Likelihood and Johansen's VAR procedure to derive cross-price, own-price, non-price and short run equilibrium elasticities for Indian wheat, jowar, paddy-rice, groundnut, rapeseed and mustard seed using monthly wholesale prices for important markets. The test results indicated an increasing degree of market integration for wheat, paddy-rice, rape and mustard seed, which contrasted with the findings of jowar and groundnut in the post liberalization period of the 1990s.

Barrett and Li (2002) attempted to bridge price based and quantity based approaches to the study of spatial market integration. They introduced a new methodology using ML estimation of a mixture distribution model incorporating price, transfer cost and trade flow data. The study showed the distinction between market integration and competitive market equilibrium. The study also derived intuitive measures of inter-market tradability, competitive market equilibrium, perfect integration, segmented equilibrium and segmented disequilibrium. They used those estimates to derive semi-parametric measures of time varying regime probabilities to track changing market conditions. Unlike widely used price analysis techniques such as cointegration, their method was well suited to market linkages exhibiting time varying, non-stationary or non-additive transfer costs and discontinuous or bi-directional trade. They observed that competitive equilibrium and tradability prevailed for the vast majority of the time in pacific soyabean meal markets, even though trade flows were intermittent at monthly frequency on most international routes.

Baffes and Gardner (2003) examined the degree of transmission between the world prices and domestic prices for eight countries and ten commodities. The main characteristic of these countries was that they all undertook policy reforms during mid-1980s to early 1990s. The paper investigated the effect of reforms on the speed at which signals were transmitted to domestic markets and on the extent of price transmission. The study observed that Chile, Mexico and Argentina were the only countries whose domestic commodity markets were integrated with world markets. For other countries, namely Ghana, Madagascar, Indonesia, Egypt and Colombia, in the case of only a few country/commodity pairs was found having some pass through of world price changes. In terms of the effect of reforms, in the majority of the cases, the hypothesis of a structural break following the reform year was rejected.

Finally, Rapsomanikis *et al*. (2004) discuss time series applications to market integration. The paper examines a number of issues related to the definition of market integration and price transmission, the usefulness and limitations of time series econometrics and the interpretation of the estimated parameters. The extent of price transmission is defined in terms of notional components such as completeness, dynamics and asymmetry of adjustment and a testing framework is applied with each component being tested individually. The authors argue that collectively these tests can be utilized to assess market integration and the extent to which policies and other distortions affect price transmission.

Following the above discussion, this study uses Johansen's procedure for testing price integration for different commodities. As has been discussed in the above studies, cointegration tests represent a necessary, rather than sufficient condition and must be supplemented by information on market structure. With these caveats in mind, the empirical analysis in this study should be considered as an attempt to examine the market integration in Haryana.

3

Agricultural Production and Marketing System

State and the Districts Surveyed

Physiographic Setting

The two districts under study, namely Kaithal and Sirsa are a very important constituent of the agricultural economy of Haryana. The present Kaithal district was part of Kurukshetra till 1989-90 and after its seclusion Kurukshetra remains one of the smallest districts of the state. Kaithal district is situated in the north of Haryana. To its north-east is Kurukshetra district. Karnal and Panipat make boundaries from the east and south-east and Jind covers this district from the south and south-west. The district makes state boundaries with Punjab in the north and north-west. It has a population of 9,45,631 as per the 2001 census constituting 4.49 per cent of the total population of the state. It has an area of 2,317 square kilometres constituting 5.24 per cent of the total area of the state and thus ranks eight in the state. Having 408 persons per square kilometre, the district is less densely populated as compared to the state average of 477 persons per square kilometre according to the 2001 census.

Kaithal district has a sub-tropical continental monsoon climate. The rainfall distribution is comparatively satisfactory in relation to the western parts of Haryana. The southern and western parts of the district receive lesser rainfall than its northern and eastern parts. The district receives rainfall from the monsoon and a few showers from cyclones. According to the Census Atlas series of Haryana, the average annual rainfall for Kurukshetra (Kaithal) district on a 5 to 80 years average basis is 706 mm. On the whole, the district is remarkably flat. Saraswati and Ghaggar are the important rivers of the district. A good network of canals provides irrigational facilities in addition to tubewell irrigation, which is common in the district. It is one of the more prosperous districts from the agricultural point of view.

Sirsa district lies along the western boundary of the state. It is surrounded by Punjab state in the north and north-east, by Hisar district in the east and by Rajasthan state in the south and south-west. With an area of 4277 square kilometres, Sirsa is the largest district after Bhiwani, though population wise, it stands eighth in the state. The topography of the district is that of a level plain and it is comparatively hot and dry. Ghaggar is the only river associated with this district. The average annual rainfall in the district is 378.8 mm. The rainfall is very uncertain and transpires mainly during the monsoon season. Because of a low water table and other problems, the tubewell is not as popular a means of cultivation/irrigation as it is in the Kaithal district. Sirsa district is still more thinly populated than Kaithal as the density of population in Sirsa is 260 persons per square kilometre. Agriculture is the mainstay of the people and it plays a predominant role in the economy of the district.

Growth Performance of Agriculture

In the mid-sixties, high yielding variety (HYV) seeds were introduced in India. Haryana became one of the pioneers in adopting the new technology. This led to a phenomenal increase in production in the agricultural sector. Wheat and rice have been the two most successful crops of the new technology. This HYV technology led to a rapid increase in productivity and of the area under these two crops. As a result, the output of wheat in Haryana increased from 1059 thousand tonnes in 1966-67 to 7108 thousand tonnes in 1992-93 and further to 9437 thousand tonnes in 2001-02. The output of rice increased from 223 thousand tonnes to 1880 thousand tonnes and further to 2726 thousand tonnes during the same time period. Table 3.1 presents the area, pròduction and yield of selected crops in Haryana and for both Kaithal and Sirsa districts during 2001-02. The table shows that productivity of wheat was 41.5 quintals per hectare in Sirsa and 45 quintals per hectare in Kaithal. Both the districts exceeded the state average of 41 quintals per hectare. In the case of rice, the productivity of Sirsa district exceeded the figure both for

Table 3.1: Area, Production and Yield of Major Crops (2001-02).

	Haryana			*Sirsa*			*Kaithal*		
	Output	*Area*	*Yield*	*Output*	*Area*	*Yield*	*Output*	*Area*	*Yield*
Rice	2726	1028	2652	118	37	3201	402	161	2494
Jowar	22	104	209	—	—	—	—	0.1	—
Bajra	832	586	1422	5	3.4	1208	—	—	—
Maize	47	18	2584	—	—	—	—	0.4	—
Wheat	9437	2300	4103	1005	242	4152	769	169	4548
Barley	86	30	2880	16	6	2590	—	0.1	—
Gram	122	143	853	14	16	866	—	0.5	—
Total Pulses	148	189	786	15	19	774	0.4	0.8	500
Total Foodgrains	13298	4253	3127	1159	307	3777	1180	337	3504
Rapeseed mustard	800	536	1490	76	51	1499	3.0	1.6	1490
Total Oilseeds	805	545	1479	77	52	1477	3.4	1.9	1489
Cotton	722	629	195	232	215	183	1.0	1.1	181
Sugarcane	927	161	5758	11	2	5741	29	5.2	5753

Note: Area in '000 hectares; production in '000 tonnes, except cotton which is in '000 bales of 170 kgs., each and yield in kilograms per hectare.

Source: Statistical Abstracts of Haryana.

Kaithal as well as for the state as a whole, although the area under rice in Sirsa was very meagre.

Table 3.2 presents the compound growth rates of area, production and yield of major crops in the post green revolution period in Haryana. Analogous to the case of All India, the post-green revolution period in the present case is also divided into three phases, *i.e.* 1966-67 to 1979-80, 1980-81 to 1989-90 and 1990-91 to 2001-02. The growth rates for the whole period, *i.e.* 1966-67 to 2001-02 are also presented in the table. It is clearly evident from the table that in the first phase, the growth rate of yield was impressive only for rice (5.3%) and wheat (2.1%) among the food crops. Among the cash crops, only cotton-lint experienced a significant positive growth rate in yield (1.4%). Incidentally, these crops also experienced a significant expansion in the area. Almost all other crops, *viz*. all coarse cereals and pulses and most of the oilseeds had a negative trend growth in area during the first phase of the green revolution.

During the second phase, only wheat was able to maintain its momentum of above five per cent trend growth in output among the foodgrains. However, unlike the first phase during which expansion in area of wheat contributed mainly to higher output, in the second phase the major increase in output came from enhancement in yield rate. The production of rice increased at a rate of 11.5 per cent per annum in the first phase as a result of 6.2 per cent per annum increase in area and 5.3 per cent per annum increase in the yield rate. The trend growth in production of rice in the second phase, however, declined to 2.2 per cent due to fall in growth rate of area and complete stagnation of yield rate.

The noteworthy transformation that took place in the state's cropping pattern during the second phase of green revolution was that of shift from foodgrains towards oilseeds.

It is clearly evident from the results of trend growth rates in the table that a major shift in area took place from coarse cereals and pulses towards oilseeds and to some extent towards fibres. Area under rape-seed mustard observed 7.4 per cent trend growth rate leading to 7.2 per cent trend growth in the area of total oilseeds during the 1980s. Significant expansion in area under oilseeds might have been induced by an impressive increase in the yield rate (6.1%) of these crops. Thus, as an outcome, the state experienced an all time high (13%) increase in total production of oilseeds during this period. Cotton lint also observed a 4.6 per cent per annum increase in output as a result of a significant increase in area during the second phase of green revolution. Thus, a significant increase in the output of oilseeds in Haryana in the 1980s played a leading role in the country's achievement of self-sufficiency in edible oils.

The third phase of the green revolution coincides with the advent of liberalization in the Indian economy. The Government of India initiated a process of economic reforms in 1991, which involved deregulation, reduced government participation in economic activities and liberalization. Though the reforms were not initiated to directly affect the agriculture sector, the sector was affected indirectly by a devaluation of the exchange rate, liberalization of external trade and disprotection to industry (Chand 2004). The agriculture sector was further exposed to the world trade with the signing of the AOA under the WTO trade regime, requiring an opening up of the domestic market. All these changes on the domestic front had implications for the cropping pattern as well. The output growth, which was concentrated in very narrow pockets of irrigated areas became broad based and gained momentum. Indian agriculture which was till the early eighties centred around foodgrain crops started witnessing a process of diversification which resulted into fast growth in non-foodgrain output like milk, fishery, poultry, fruits and vegetables which appeared to be largely market driven.

The trends in growth of area and output in the state in the 1990s largely followed the trends discussed in the Indian agriculture sector. The trend growth rate of foodgrains output was observed as 4.2 per cent in the 1970s, while it came down to 4.1 per cent in 1980s and further to 3.4 per cent in the 1990s. However, area expansion in wheat and rice continued to be positive in the state and probably was the outcome of a significant fall in area under oilseeds. While during the 1980s there was a significant increase in the yield rate of oil seeds leading to a shift in area from coarse cereals and pulses towards oilseeds, in the 1990s on the other hand, the stimulus growth in yield was completely absent. Further, the influx of cheap imported edible oils as a result of the opening up of the Indian economy (reduction in custom duty on edible oils) led the price of oilseeds to touch the bottom level. As a consequence, farmers in the state once again shifted from oil seeds partly to wheat and rice and partly to high value cash crops like fruits and vegetables.

The rapid increase in output of foodgrains and oilseeds in the post-green revolution period was made possible by the intensive use of available land area, shifts in cropping patterns, increased use of HYV seeds, fertilizers and tractors. The following section is devoted to a discussion of these factors.

Land Utilization

The broad land use in both the districts as well as in the state is shown in Table 3.3. It is evident from the table that cultivable area as a proportion of total geographical area was as high as 87 per cent in the state and 95 per cent in Sirsa district. The net area sown as a proportion of total geographical area in the

Table 3.2: Trend growth rate of production, area and yield of the principal crops in Haryana (%).

Name of the crop		*1966-67 to 1979-80*	*1980-81 to 1989-90*	*1990-91 to 2001-02*	*1966-67 to 2001-02*
Rice	P	11.51*	2.22	4.10*	6.57*
	A	6.19*	2.37***	5.11*	4.70*
	Y	5.33*	-0.14	-1.01	1.87*
Jowar	P	-5.12**	-3.16	-6.65*	-1.73*
	A	-4.88*	0.27	0.01	-2.25*
	Y	-0.24	-3.43	-6.66*	0.52
Bajra	P	-2.21	-3.55	4.61***	0.88
	A	0.01	-4.03**	0.22	-1.76*
	Y	-2.22	0.47	4.40***	2.64*
Maize	P	-2.45	-6.66**	-0.94	-3.73*
	A	-0.55	-7.19*	-6.30*	-6.05*
	Y	-1.90	0.53	5.36*	2.32*
Wheat	P	6.73*	5.77*	3.83*	5.62*
	A	4.63*	1.92*	2.29*	2.70*
	Y	2.10**	3.85*	1.54*	2.92*
Total coarse cereals	P	-2.81	-3.04	2.77	-0.19
	A	-1.33**	-3.74**	-0.30	-2.33*
	Y	-1.49	0.71	3.08***	2.14*
Gram	P	-1.83	1.56	-12.77**	-4.72*
	A	-1.66	-8.67***	-12.34*	-5.33*
	Y	-0.16	10.23***	-0.44	0.62
Total pulses	P	-1.70	-0.27	-12.48**	-4.22*
	A	-1.88	-5.58	-11.37*	-4.82*
	Y	0.18	5.30	-1.11	0.60
Total food-grains	P	4.23*	4.05*	3.43*	4.13*
	A	0.95**	-0.75	1.25*	0.28**
	Y	3.28*	4.80*	2.17*	3.85*
Rapeseed mustard	P	0.18	13.73*	-0.57	8.50*
	A	-1.17	7.42**	-1.83	4.98*
	Y	1.35	6.31*	1.26	3.53*
Total oilseeds	P	0.07	13.25*	-1.30	8.22*
	A	-1.35	7.15**	-2.31***	4.82*
	Y	1.42	6.10*	1.01	3.40*
Cotton lint	P	4.48*	4.63**	-2.53	4.18*
	A	3.05*	3.50**	1.02	3.68*
	Y	1.44*	1.13	-3.56***	0.50***
Sugarcane	P	0.83	3.28**	0.90	0.97*
	A	1.32	0.33	0.35	-0.24
	Y	-0.50	2.95***	0.55	1.21*

Notes: *Significant at 1%, **significant at 5%, ***significant at 10%.
Source: Statistical Abstracts of Haryana.

two districts was higher than the state as a whole. As irrigation facilities like canals and tubewells were higher in Kaithal district in comparison to Sirsa district, its cropping intensity was higher than for Sirsa district. It is clearly evident from the table that almost all the cultivable area of the state was under plough. Only 5 per cent of the land was noted as fallow land, which could be brought in for cultivation in the future. Thereby, any rise in output in the state in the near future could come only through a further increase in yield rate through enhanced irrigation facilities, multiple cropping, application of latest farm technologies and by diversification towards more market oriented high value crops like fruits and vegetables, oilseeds, fibres, etc.

Table 3.3: Pattern of land utilization (2001-02) ('000 Hectares).

Nature of land use	*Haryana*	*Sirsa*	*Kaithal*
Total area according to village papers	4372 (100.0)	427 (100.0)	228 (100.0)
Forests	45 (1.03)	2 (0.47)	3 (1.32)
Land not available for cultivation	526 (12.03)	21 (4.92)	28 (12.28)
Fallow and other uncultivated land	235 (5.38)	35 (8.20)	0 (0.00)
Net sown area	3566 (81.56)	370 (86.65)	197 (86.40)
Cultivable area	3801 (86.94)	405 (94.85)	197 (86.40)
Area sown more than once	2752 (62.95)	284 (66.51)	180 (78.95)
Total cropped area	6318	664	377
Cropping intensity	1.77	1.79	1.91

Note: Figures in Parentheses are percentage to total area according to village papers.

Source: Statistical Handbook of Haryana, 2002-03.

Size of Land Holdings

With the rise in population, the average size of holdings has been on the decline. This is true both in the case of districts as well as for the state under study. According to the Agricultural

Census 1980, the average size of holdings in Sirsa district was 6.07 hectares against the 3.52 hectare size of the state average. In 1995-96, the average size of the holdings fell to 3.15 and 2.13 hectares in the district and state, respectively. The percentage of holdings and area of different sizes for both the districts and the state is given in Table 3.4.

Table 3.4: Percentage of holdings and area under different farm size categories.

Size group (hect.)	*Haryana*				*Sirsa*				*Kaithal*			
	% of holdings		*% of area*		*% of holdings*		*% of area*		*% of holdings*		*% of area*	
	1980-81	*1995-96*	*1980-81*	*1995-96*	*1980-81*	*1995-96*	*1980-81*	*1995-96*	*1990-91*	*1995-96*	*1990-91*	*1995-96*
0.00-1.00	32.18	47.14	4.65	11.00	17.44	32.66	1.86	5.58	37.45	49.96	6.45	11.77
1.01-2.00	19.19	19.59	8.70	12.87	16.75	19.73	4.53	9.07	20.13	19.21	11.22	13.62
2.01-4.00	20.84	19.01	17.43	24.91	23.23	24.52	12.72	22.44	22.77	16.96	23.75	22.63
4.01-10.0	21.37	11.94	37.88	33.26	30.41	19.11	36.31	36.81	16.10	11.20	36.49	30.83
> 10.00	6.42	2.32	31.34	17.97	12.17	3.98	44.58	26.11	3.56	2.67	22.09	21.16
All size	100	100	100	100	100	100	100	100	100	100	100	100
Avg*	—	—	3.52	2.13	—	—	6.07	3.15	—	—	2.69	2.18

Note: *Average size of holdings in hectares.
Source: Statistical Abstracts of Haryana.

It is clear from the table that in 1995-96 the average size of holdings in Sirsa was higher than Kaithal and the state as a whole. The distribution of holdings as well as area in Kaithal district was not very different from that of Haryana as a whole. However, the distribution of holdings was more equitable in Sirsa district as the percentage of marginal holdings was less while the percentage of large holdings was more than that in the state as well as for Kaithal district. The above table shows that marginal holdings are the highest for both the districts and the state. The highly unequal distribution of holdings is evident from the fact that in the state in 1995-96, the bottom 66.7 per cent households were small and marginal farmers operated only 23.8 per cent of area, while 14.2 per cent of the households at the top belonged to the medium and large categories, who operated 51 per cent of the total operated area.

Irrigation

Tubewells and canals are the main sources of irrigation in Kaithal district as the rainfall in this district is seasonal, inadequate and subject to frequent variations. Its erratic nature may harm crops in the absence of artificial irrigation. In the southern part of the district where the water table is very low, well or tubewell irrigation is not profitable. This problem has been solved to some extent by the construction of canals. In other parts, the depth of the water table is on an average 150 feet below the soil surface and rises as we move towards the east and north. Tubewell irrigation is becoming very popular especially in areas where the water table is not very low. During 2002-03 there were 25,654 diesel and 28,038 electric pump sets in Kaithal district with a ratio of one pump set to 3.7 hectares of net sown area.

At the time of Haryana's formation as a separate state, irrigation facilities were completely lacking in Sirsa district. Underground water in most parts of the district had a high level of carbonates and bicarbonates and was not suitable for irrigation. Before the commissioning of the Bhakra Nangal Project, canal irrigation was not sufficient and there was a single crop system in the district. But later on with exploration deep boring was done at various places in the district. A ground water testing laboratory was established in 1974 and the exploration revealed that fresh water was available along the

Ghaggar, popularly known as the *Nali* area. On both sides of the *Nali* area the ground water was suitable and could be used by blending it with canal water or with a specific doze of gypsum.

As a result of these efforts and with the commencement of irrigation from Bhakra Nangal Project, there has been a significant improvement in the irrigational facilities in Sirsa district. The extension of canal irrigation, installation of tubewells and other minor irrigation schemes have led to a manifold increase in the irrigated area of the district. As the average depth of water varies from two metres in the south-western parts to 27 metres in the north-western parts of the district, the number of tubewells increase as we move from north-west to south-west. There is continuous encouragement by the government to install tubewells to supplement the canal water. In recent years, sprinkler irrigation is becoming popular in the district. Although, there was a fall in area irrigated by tubewells in the nineties, there was a continuous rise in the number of pumping sets from13,546 in 1980-81 to 24,703 in 1991-92 and further to 37,745 in 2002-03. As against the 3.7 hectares to one pump set ratio of Kaithal, Sirsa accounted for a 9.8 hectares to one pump set in 2002-03.

In 2001-02, the net irrigated area as a percentage of net sown area in Kaithal and Sirsa districts was respectively, 99.5 and 84.6 per cent against the state average of 82.4 per cent. Similarly, the gross irrigated area as a percentage of gross cropped area in the two districts was 99.7 and 91.4 per cent, respectively against 86.9 per cent of the state average. Table 3.5 shows the area irrigated through different sources in both the districts. It is clear from the table that a substantial portion of the total area of Kaithal and Sirsa districts was irrigated by canals. There was a consistent rise in irrigated area in proportion to net sown area in Sirsa district over the years. In this district the total area irrigated by tubewells and other sources was 64,000 hectares in 1980-81, which fell to 33,000 hectares in 1992-93 and increased slightly to 37,745 hectares in 2002-03. This rapid fall in irrigated area by tubewells during late eighties and nineties was an outcome of the falling water table.

Table 3.5: Net irrigated area by source (% of total irrigated area).

	Year	*Govt. Canals*	*Tubewell and other sources*	*Total*	*NIA as % of NSA*
Haryana	1975-76	59.1	40.9	100.0	48.4
	1980-81	54.4	45.6	100.0	59.2
	1990-91	51.4	48.6	100.0	72.7
	2001-02	48.4	51.6	100.0	82.4
Sirsa	1975-76	86.1	13.9	100.0	41.7
	1980-81	77.8	22.2	100.0	72.6
	1990-91	88.0	12.0	100.0	71.3
	2001-02	81.8	18.2	100.0	84.6
Kaithal	1990-91	46.7	53.3	100.0	98.4
	2001-02	50.5	49.5	100.0	99.5

Source: Statistical abstracts of Haryana.

However, this problem of a falling water table is taking a turn for the worse in Kaithal district in recent years. This is also apparent from the table that percentage of area irrigated by tubewells in this district has come down from 53 per cent to 49 per cent in the 1990s. The previous system of simple centrifugal boring workable by 5 horsepower boosting pump is now failing. The system of submersible boring which is workable only by 10 or 15 horsepower though successful is however very expensive and not economical for small and marginal farmers. As a consequence, they are leasing out their land to the large farmers. In addition, this new system may cause a major havoc to the water table resource in the future. Therefore, it becomes necessary to shift the cropping pattern towards those crops, which need less water and are more eco-friendly.

Cropping Pattern

The crops grown in Haryana are divided into two main categories, namely kharif and rabi locally known as *sawani* and *asadhi*. The main kharif crops are rice, bajra and cotton while the main rabi crops are wheat, gram and other pulses and oilseeds. Some particulars about the crops grown in the state and both the districts are given in Table 3.6.

Table 3.6: Cropping pattern (area sown as a percentage of gross cropped area).

	Haryana			*Sirsa*			*Kaithal*	
	1980-81	1992-93	2001-02	1980-81	1992-93	2001-02	1992-93	2001-02
Rice	8.86	12.09	16.26	3.82	4.25	5.60	32.82	42.68
Bajra	15.93	10.87	9.27	3.54	1.20	0.51	2.60	1.62
Wheat	27.08	33.55	36.40	18.60	31.65	36.40	45.85	44.75
Total cereals	57.99	60.00	64.33	27.34	38.73	43.34	81.98	89.15
Gram	13.22	6.63	2.26	29.81	10.65	2.39	0.28	0.13
Total pulses	14.55	7.89	2.99	30.11	10.76	2.86	1.10	0.21
Total food-grains	72.56	67.85	67.31	57.46	49.50	46.20	83.08	89.36
Rapeseed mustard	5.49	9.61	8.49	8.76	7.65	7.65	1.75	0.42
Total oilseeds	5.70	10.07	8.62	8.80	7.87	7.80	1.92	0.50
Cotton lint	5.79	9.10	9.96	18.76	30.43	32.44	2.29	0.29
Sugarcane	2.07	2.36	2.55	0.06	0.02	0.24	2.29	1.38
Fodder and others	13.88	10.62	11.55	14.92	12.18	13.31	10.42	8.46

Source: Statistical Abstracts of Haryana.

As the soil of Kaithal district is mostly alluvial loamy and the district has abundant irrigation facilities, the region is very conducive for rice cultivation. Table 3.6 shows that 87 per cent of the total cultivable area of the district was devoted to rice and wheat alone in 2001-02, up from 79 per cent in 1992-93. Coarse cereals and pulses occupied only 2 per cent of gross cropped area. Cash crops namely, oilseeds, cotton and sugarcane shared only 2.2 per cent of gross cropped area in 2001-02, a decline from 6.5 per cent in 1992-93. In the southern area of the district, cotton and rapeseed mustard substitute for rice because of a lack of water in that area.

Sirsa district may be divided into two tracts, namely the Ghaggar belt and the Rohi belt or the semi-arid zone. The Ghaggar belt extends to an area of 3 to 5 kilometres (at some places to 7 kilometres) on both sides of the river (known as the *Nali* area), which passes through Sirsa, Rania and a part of Bada-Gudha blocks. The soils around this belt are loamy to clay loam in texture. This soil is very fertile and paddy, cotton and wheat are the most important crops of this tract (see Table 3.6). The soils of the remaining tract are sandy to sandy loam in texture which is not very conducive for agriculture. There are also sand dunes lying on the north-western border of the district adjoining Rajasthan and these cause great damage to the crops in the summer season.

A clear shift in cropping pattern in Sirsa district is evident from the above table. During 1980-81, gram occupied the maximum area followed by cotton and wheat. However, the second phase of the green revolution saw a major shift from gram and other pulses towards cotton and wheat. In the absence of any technological breakthrough in productivity of pulses, the shift continued in the third phase as well leaving the pulses as a marginal crop in the district as well as in the state (see Table 3.6). Thus in the 1990s, wheat and cotton, respectively became the major rabi and kharif crops of the district. This shift from gram to wheat and cotton was basically due to better economy and climatic suitability of these two crops.

Finally, looking at the cropping pattern of the state, a brief glimpse at Table 3.6 indicates that wheat and rice were the two main rabi and kharif crops in the state. Rapeseed mustard was the other major rabi crop which was grown in the southern parts of the state where irrigation intensity was less and the crops were more dependent on rainfall. Among kharif crops, bajra and cotton lint occupied the largest area after rice as is evident from the table. Thus rice, wheat and cotton occupied 63 per cent of total cultivable area in the state. Adding the area under bajra and rapeseed mustard, these five crops together accounted for more than 80 per cent of the total cropped area in the state during 2001-02.

Area under HYV Seeds

The green revolution that was an outcome of the quantum jump in the yield of rice and wheat was by and large heralded by higher use of HYV seeds of these crops. It is seen from Table 3.7 that in the state as well as in both the districts, around 70 to 80 per cent of rice area and almost the whole area for wheat was covered by HYV seeds during the 1990s. It was mentioned elsewhere that as there was little possibility of an increase in the area under plough, an attempt should be made to cover more crops by means of HYV seeds to raise the production and productivity of these crops.

Table 3.7: Use of HYV seeds of foodgrains (%).

		Rice	*Maize*	*Bajra*	*Wheat*
Haryana	1990-91	72.5	45.7	67.3	98.9
	2001-02	64.9	50.3	80.3	98.1
Sirsa	1990-91	80.8	—	62.5	98.9
	2001-02	69.9	—	—	99.0
Kaithal	1990-91	70.6	100.0	75.0	99.4
	2001-02	71.5	—	88.2	98.9

Source: Statistical Abstracts of Haryana

Thus, with the advent of the green revolution, agricultural production in the state has increased at a rapid rate. The development of market yards coupled with a regulated marketing system has further added to the prosperity of the farmers in the state by regulating the sale and eliminating unauthorised market charges. A brief description of the regulated marketing system in Haryana follows.

Regulated Marketing System in Haryana

In the traditional subsistence economy, the marketing system was unregulated and the farmers sold their produce in the village to the shopkeeper, trader, itinerant merchants or to the big landlords. This unregulated marketing system suffered from various ills and exploited the farmers. This system was characterized by sharp trading practices such as sale under cover, over-weighing of farmer's produce and social and religious charges on the producer seller. It became necessary to reform and regulate the marketing system. Thus, with a view to providing a better regulation of buying and selling of agricultural produce in the wholesale market and safeguarding the interests of the cultivators, 'The Punjab Agricultural

Produce Markets Act' was enacted in 1939. The scope of the Act was enlarged in 1961. As a result of these regulations, opportunities for sharp trading practices have been eliminated or narrowed down considerably in the regulated wholesale markets. With the growth of these markets the farmers of Haryana bring their produce in the market and the practice of sale at village has been completely marginalised. The progress in the establishment of these regulated markets in Haryana is given below in Table 3.8.

Table 3.8: Number of regulated markets in Haryana

		Regulated Markets	*Sub-yards*	*Average number of villages served per market*	*Average area served per market (square kms.)*
Haryana	1980-81	88	92	—	—
	1990-91	97	165	69	456
	2002-03	106	177	64	417
Sirsa	1980-81	5	7	—	—
	1990-91	6	18	53	713
	2002-03	6	18	54	713
Kaithal	1990-91	8	15	31	350
	2002-03	7	16	39	331

Source: Statistical Abstracts of Haryana.

These regulated markets work on democratic principles. With a view to exercising effective supervision and control, each market has a market committee, which is a corporate body having representatives of growers, traders and local bodies. At least half the members of the committee are grower's representatives, either elected or nominated by the government. The remaining members are trader's representatives duly elected by the traders licensed by the market committees, representatives of municipal committees and some government nominees. The chairman is elected by the market committee[1].

Functions of the Market Committee

The main functions of the market committee are the following: To frame bye-laws defining the local market practices and fixing the market charges payable to the various market functionaries; The provision of facilities for arranging prompt payment of sale proceeds to producer-sellers; Supervision of the weighment of produce for ensuring the standard weights and measures used; and The fair settlement of disputes between buyers and sellers and dissemination of reliable and up-to-date market intelligence. This regulated marketing system works through *mandis* or market yards.

Market Yard

After harvest, the product is carried from the countryside to the *mandis* through various transport modes like cart, tractor-trolley, tempo and trucks. There is no separate allocation of space in the market yard for different kinds of produce. So, in the absence of specialized commodity markets all kinds of farm products are brought and sold in the same market yard.

Most of the markets in Haryana are very old and the shops are scattered. With the breakthrough in agricultural production, the problem of inadequate existing market yards to accommodate the increased marketed surplus especially of wheat and paddy has arisen. In many cities, numerous products have to be accommodated in the narrow tracts of old style built *mandis* which has become problematic so that a development of new market yards with all the modern facilities has occurred. But even these new yards are not sufficiently spacious and are far from satisfactory solutions to the problems of the farmers. In addition, along with the new yards, the old markets with inadequate facilities and other problems are still in operation.

There is no provision for covered platforms in the *mandis*. During the harvest time of wheat and paddy, all the markets old as well as new suffer from overflow and congestion. The situation is further aggravated by the absence of separate cart and cattle sheds in the market yards. After unloading the produce the farmers park their carts or tractors in a haphazard manner. Though, the Marketing Board in the state is attempting to provide adequate marketing infrastructure facilities and other amenities, the present situation does not lead to complacency[2].

Market Functionaries

In market yards, there are a number of functionaries operating, for example:

(i) Public Agencies—procuring wheat on behalf of the government,
(ii) Wholesale Traders,
(iii) *Arhatias* or Commission Agents,
(iv) Weighmen, and
(v) *Palladars*.

Public Agencies

The State Government, FCI and the Haryana State Cooperative Marketing Federation (HAFED) procure wheat in the Haryana markets. Some of these agencies appoint private traders as their agents who arrange for the payment to the farmers, weighment and transportation of the produce to godowns, while others operate directly.

Wholesale Traders

In earlier years, these agencies used to play a key role in marketing, especially for that of wheat. But with the stepping in of the Public Agencies, the numbers of these traders have been reduced almost to non-existence in the markets of the state.

Arhatias or Commission Agents

In Haryana's *mandis*, most of the *arhatias* perform the functions of both *kachha* and *pucca arhatias*. *Kachha arhatias*, *i.e.*, the commission agents are traditional money-lenders for the farmers. They provide loans not only for agricultural purposes but advance money to meet all the manner of needs like day-to-day activities and social functions-marriages, etc. These loans are generally realized from the sale proceeds of the farmers. Under the circumstances, the farmers are obliged to sell their produce through such *kachha arhatias*. Otherwise also, the producers have to bring their produce to *kachha arhatias* as sale/purchase of all agricultural commodities in the state is permitted through regulated markets only. Apart from strong financial links with the farmers, the *kachha arhatias* help the farmers in getting a better price for their produce by rendering the services of assembling, grading, cleaning, etc. Sometimes, *arhatias* also provide transportation facilities and other implements like bags, cultivators, etc. to the farmers.

Almost all the sellers sell their produce through a commission agent. Big buyers also prefer to buy through an agent because the agent brings with him several sellers at a time thereby making dealing easier. It is also more convenient for the buyer to make a single payment to the commission agent rather than making several payments to individual sellers. The *kachha arhatias* generally pay the farmers on the same day or within a few days on behalf of the buyer and reimburse the money later from the buyer[3].

The state agencies also engage *pucca arhatias* who perform the job of bidding, weighing, filling, loading, keeping watch on the stock purchased, arranging labour when the labour contracts fail and ensuring delivery at godowns. Sometimes *pucca arhatias* also advance money to *kachha arhatias* on behalf of the state agencies.

After receiving the produce in the market, it is displayed in bulk in different lots belonging to various cultivators on the auction platform in front of the commission agents' shops. The commission agents arrange the unloading, cleaning and dressing of all the lots displayed on the auction platform by employing the *palladars* and other unskilled labourers in the market. Payments to these labourers are made for their operations by the commission agents on behalf of the farmers.

After the lots are cleaned and dressed, the auction is arranged by the commission agent, *i.e.*, *kachha arhatia*, calling the bids offered by the prospective buyers in the market. The sale price is thus finalized in the open auctioning. If the producer (seller) is ready to sell at the price determined by open bidding, the commission agent arranges for filling of the produce in the bags supplied by the buyers, weighing, stitching and final delivery of the lot to the buyer. On weighment of the lot, the *kachha arhatia* arranges the payment to the producer-seller after subtracting charges of unloading, dressing, cleaning, etc. This payment is recovered later on from the buyer along with the other expenses incurred on behalf of the buyer, *i.e.* filling, weighing and stitching and commission of the commission agent for carrying out all these operations[4]. In case the buyer is not a licensee of the market committee, the commission agent also recovers the market fee at the rate of two per cent from such buyers and deposit the same to the market committee, otherwise the liability to deposit market fee remains with the licensed buyers.

Weighmen

Weighmen are the persons engaged for weighing operations of agricultural commodities in the market. They may be employees of commission agents or traders or they may work independently. They charge from the commission agent if being his employees or from buyer or on whose behalf weighment is done. Their charge is called *tulai*.

Palladars

Palladars are the labourers in the market who perform all sorts of job connected with sale of produce in the market, *e.g.*, loading, unloading, filling, stitching, cleaning, dressing and assisting in weighment, etc. Charges are paid to them by anyone they are employed by. Their charges are called *palladari, majdoori* or *hamali*. In the market, all functionaries are licensees of the market. However, this rule is not followed so strictly in case of *palladars*.

Transportation

Means of transportation are highly developed in Haryana. About 98.99 per cent of villages in Haryana are linked with *pucca* roads (Table 3.10). Table 3.9 shows the length of existing *pucca* and *kachha* roads over the years in Haryana.

Table 3.9: Construction of roads in Haryana*.

	Progressive length of roads in Haryana (Kms)		
Year	*Metalled*	*Unmetalled*	*Total*
1966-67	5321	816	6137
1970-71	9107	2409	11516
1975-76	15280	1059	16339
1980-81	18260	2256	20516
1985-86	20285	2056	22341
1990-91	21797	1220	23017
1995-96	22568	918	23486
2000-01	22960	746	23706
2002-03	23050	446	23496

Note : *Maintained by Public Works Department, (B&R Branch), Haryana
Source: Statistical Abstracts of Haryana.

Table 3.10: Percentage of villages connected with metalled road.

	Percentage of villages		
	Haryana	*Sirsa*	*Kaithal*
1980-81	97.31	97.79	-
1985-86	98.00	98.74	-
1990-91	98.99	98.74	99.31
1995-96	98.99	98.74	99.31
2000-01	98.99	98.74	99.31
2002-03	99.62	100.0	100.0

Source: Statistical Abstract of Haryana.

Market Arrivals

The increased production of wheat and rice in the post-green revolution period has resulted in a rapid increase in arrivals of these commodities in the *mandis*. Market arrivals in the state and the districts under study are presented in Table 3.11. It is clear from the table that paddy, wheat, cotton and oil-seeds were the main crops in terms of arrivals in Haryana. However, due to inter-state and inter-district sale by the

Table 3.11: Market arrivals in Haryana and the selected districts ('000 Quintals).

	Haryana		*Sirsa*		*Kaithal*	
	1992-93	2002-03	1992-93	2002-03	1992-93	2002-03
Paddy	24094 (79.46)	35207	906 (75.88)	2474	4396 (90.86)	4889
Bajra/jowar	289 (3.89)	438	14 (18.04)	6	4 (3.41)	29
Maize	96 (17.53)	110	4 (-)	3	2 (11.35)	1
Wheat	19006 (26.74)	59048	2546 (31.85)	7571	3791 (62.24)	5644
Barley	883 (71.77)	272	96 (41.57)	33	1 (4.25)	0
Gram	255 (9.80)	141	78 (16.99)	20	0.4 (4.00)	0
Pulses	162 (4.98)	110	4 (82.20)	10	4 (12.18)	4
Oilseeds	2205 (39.45)	2609	165 (33.52)	346	45 (82.24)	1
Cotton	7105 (29.62)	2028	2544 (29.99)	943	35 (18.56)	0

Note: Figures in parentheses are market arrivals as per cent of total output produced.

Source: Statistical Abstracts of Haryana.

farmers, the percentage of output marketed does not show the real picture. Whereas, in the case of paddy and barley above 70 per cent of the produce was marketed while only 34 per cent of oilseeds and 50 per cent of cotton were marketed. This is despite the fact that these two crops are cash crops and are grown only for the market.

In 1992-93 there were six regulated markets each in both the districts surveyed namely, Kaithal and Sirsa. Arrivals of different crops in those markets are given in Tables 3.12 and 3.13. These tables reveal that the farmers in Haryana produce for the market. 62 per cent of wheat and 91 per cent of rice arrivals in Kaithal district is ample proof of this fact.

Table 3.12: Market Arrivals in Kaithal (1992-93) (Quintals).

Name of the Market	*Paddy*	*Bajra/ Jowar*	*Maize*	*Wheat*	*Barley*	*Gram*	*Pulses*	*Oilseeds*	*Cotton*
Cheeka	1865127 (42.4)	59 (1.3)	29 (1.3)	903868 (23.8)	16 (1.9)	32 (7.9)	1463 (36.4)	2511 (5.6)	0
Dand	288710 (6.6)	1 (0.02)	0	353459 (9.3)	13 (1.5)	10 (2.5)	50 (1.2)	193 (0.4)	0
Fatehpur Pundri	206269 (4.7)	7 (0.2)	4 (0.2)	422718 (11.2)	8 (0.9)	0	121 (3.0)	2286 (5.1)	0
Kaithal	1784448 (40.6)	2725 (61.5)	2236 (98.5)	1597429 (42.1)	443 (52.1)	348 (86.4)	2217 (55.1)	38412 (84.9)	15453 (44.5)
Kalyat	156003 (3.5)	1638 (37.0)	0	415526 (11.0)	370 (43.5)	13 (3.2)	169 (4.2)	1828 (4.0)	19254 (55.5)
Siwan	75649 (1.7)	0	0	97707 (2.6)	0	0	0	0	0
Total (District)	4396206 (100)	4430 (100)	2269 (100)	3790707 (100)	850 (100)	403 (100)	4020 (100)	45230 (100)	34707 (100)
Output	4838300	130000	20000	6090000	20000	10000	43000	55000	110000
Arrival as % of output	90.90	3.40	11.34	62.24	4.25	4.03	9.35	82.24	31.55

Note : *Figure is converted from rice to paddy using conversion factor of 100 kg. paddy = 62 kg. rice (see Chattopadhyay and Sen, 1988).

Figures in parentheses are percentages of total district arrivals.

Source: Production Statistical Abstracts of Haryana; Arrival: Haryana Agri. Mktg.Bd. Panchkula.

Table 3.13: Market Arrivals in Sirsa (1992-93) (Quintals).

Name of the Market	*Paddy*	*Bajra/ Jowar*	*Maize*	*Wheat*	*Barley*	*Gram*	*Pulses*	*Oilseeds*	*Cotton*
Dabwali	0	1176 (8.2)	112 (2.8)	401616 (15.8)	33415 (35.0)	2278 (2.9)	143 (3.5)	29858 (18.1)	409866 (16.1)
Ding	0	30 (0.2)	0	58931 (12.3)	966 (1.0)	287 (0.4)	19 (0.5)	2909 (1.8)	50590 (2.0)
Ellanabad	100441 (11.1)	682 (4.7)	32 (0.8)	229353 (9.0)	8067 (8.4)	22262 (28.5)	138 (3.4)	15059 (9.1)	512050 (20.1)
Kalanwali	0	168 (1.2)	159 (4.0)	361681 (14.2)	16005 (16.7)	9906 (12.7)	186 (4.5)	51512 (31.2)	468152 (18.4)
Rania	355904 (39.3)	3 (0.02)	9 (0.2)	290820 (11.4)	0	0	92 (2.2)	0	17854 (0.7)
Sirsa	449327 (49.6)	12.369 (85.7)	3632 (92.1)	1203364 (47.3)	37145 (38.9)	43402 (55.5)	3534 (85.9)	65913 (39.9)	1085509 (42.7)
Total (District)	905672 (100)	14428 (100)	3944 (100)	2545765 (100)	95598 (100)	78135 (100)	4112 (100)	165251 (100)	2544021 (100)
Output	1193500	80000	-	7680000	230000	460000	463000	493000	4990000
Arrival as % of output	75.88	18.00	-	33.14	41.56	17.00	0.9	33.5	51.00

Note : *Figure is converted from rice to paddy using conversion factor of 100 kg. paddy = 62 kg. rice (see Chattopadhyay and Sen, 1988).

Figures in parentheses are percentages of total district arrivals.

Source: Production Statistical Abstracts of Haryana; Arrival: Haryana Agri. Mktg. Bd. Panchkula.

To sum up the chapter, Haryana has remained in the forefront in adopting the new technology in agriculture. The agricultural production after the green revolution has grown at a rapid rate. The first phase of the green revolution in the seventies saw a transformation in the state economy through an over hovering production of wheat and rice. The second phase in the eighties brought self-sufficiency in the edibles with rapid increase in the production of oilseeds in the state. By the 1990s it appears that the state's agriculture is moving towards maturity with diversification towards high value cash crops like fruits, vegetables, milk and dairying, etc. The two districts under study, namely Sirsa and Kaithal are prosperous in agriculture with a suitable climate and sufficient irrigation facilities like tubewells and canals. Finally, the agricultural commodity markets in the state are regulated and the farmers appear to produce for the market.

NOTES

1. Rice Economy of India, Economic and Statistical Advisor to the Government of India, January 1961, p. 203.
2. Marketing of Wheat in Punjab and Haryana, Directorate of Marketing and Inspection, Ministry of Rural Reconstruction, Government of India, Faridabad, 1981, p.23.
3. In most of the cases, the farmer is heavily indebted to the *arhatia* and after making previous payments, the former is not interested to take back whatever balance is left, but to get his day-to-day needs financed by the *arhatia* till the next crop is harvested.
4. According to the market committee rules, the commission agents charge their commission only from the buyers. Sellers do not have to pay any commission for their sale.

4

Market Integration and Efficiency in the Pre and Post-Liberalization Periods

The Background

In recent years, the efficiency of agricultural marketing for different regions and commodities has become the subject-matter of considerable empirical research. Economic efficiency, which is our greater concern, is different from technical efficiency, which reflects efficiency in the physical handling of the product. An 'economically efficient' marketing system will ensure that the benefits realized by a proper handling of the product and elimination of waste, are transmitted to producers in the form of a higher price of their product and to the consumer in the form of a reduction in their money cost (Subbarao 1989).

To measure the marketing efficiency, different methods have been adopted in the literature of agricultural economics. These methods can be grouped in two broad categories, namely:

(a) Price spread and marketing margins techniques; and
(b) The technique of working of markets, their structure and their extent of integration.

A brief description of these two techniques is given as follows:

Price Spreads and Marketing Margins Techniques

The price spread, sometimes also termed as marketing margin, is the difference between the price received by the producer and price paid by the consumer for a given commodity in a market at a point of time. The studies on price spread determine whether the existing marketing margins are excessive in relation to the services rendered by the market. Generally, the markets with fewer amounts of margins are considered to be more efficient markets. Comparisons are made with the same product at different points of time or in different regions of a country or with the same commodity in different countries in order to give a general insight into the relative positions on a scale of allocative efficiency.

However, in the spread and margin studies, while evaluating whether or not marketing margins are excessive in relation to the services rendered, a considerable amount of subjective judgment would be involved. Moreover, the demand and supply for marketing services is not reflected by the static margin studies as the former is determined by consumer income and the latter by factor prices and technological change. So, the degree of competitiveness or efficiency of the marketing system cannot be inferred from such studies.

Such margin studies can be made dynamic in time and space by using the following hypotheses:

(i) Prices should differ between geographic areas of a country only by the transportation costs from one point to another.

(ii) The price of a storable commodity at one point of time should not exceed the price in the previous period by more than the cost of storage plus normal profits.

(iii) The price of a processed product should exceed the price of the same unprocessed product only by the processing cost plus normal profits.

However, the main objection to the margin methodology incorporating space, time and form dimensions is that it suffers from a subjective value judgement regarding what is an acceptable rate of return for the marketing services. The very high or very low margins cannot be regarded as indicators of marketing efficiency without going into the causal mechanisms underlying the observed high or low margins.

The Technique of Working of Markets, their Structure and their Extent of Integration

The second technique, *i.e.*, the working of the market structure and market integration technique examines the marketing efficiency by directly comparing the present market system with the requirement of a perfectly competitive market. This approach examines the organizational structure of the market. It looks into such matters which influence the nature of competition as the number and types of agents/buyers operating in the trade; the ease or difficulty of entry into the trade; modes of disposal and sale alternatives available; handling, grading and storage followed by different agencies; temporal and spatial pricing efficiency among the markets and the ability of the system to adapt to new and changing situations, etc.

Assessing the economic efficiency of the markets under the latter methodology, a wide range of literature is available wherein the time series price data have been used very extensively to throw light on the degree of competitiveness among the markets. By this method, bivariate correlation coefficients are estimated between the time series of spot prices for identical goods or a bundle of goods at different market places to evaluate the degree of market integration. It is assumed that in spatially separated markets, in the absence of any external disturbances, the prices of identical goods should move in unison in response to the forces of demand and supply. The accuracy and speed by which prices adjust in the market is taken as an index of interdependence among the markets, which is an indicator of efficiency. Thus, according to this methodology, which has remained the most common measure of market integration and although, has been severely criticized, a statistically significant correlation coefficient between the time series of prices prevailing at different wholesale markets can be expected to be close to unity if the markets are integrated[1].

However, there are a number of inferential dangers in bivariate modeling of this sort[2]. The basic problem is that two functionally isolated markets can appear to be synchronized if prices in each are influenced by a third market or by a common factor (Heytens 1986). Two price series that pose significant upward trends due to general inflationary pressure, common seasonality or any other synchronous common factor will yield a relatively high positive correlation. Such trends must be removed before performing an analysis for the purpose of inferences (Blyn 1973). Any measurement errors or omitted variables would yield imprecision in a test equation based on the static bivariate model. Under such conditions, this method fails hopelessly as a test for market integration. Lastly, the dynamic properties of the series are overlooked by the simple correlation analysis. Consequently, the fact that two commodities, for example, may be distinct at a given point of time, yet are becoming unified over time would be missed.

The study of market integration received a renewed interest with the application of regression analysis. However, the conventional approach of market integration with the help of regression may misrepresent or twist the true results as they have failed to explore the time series properties. Such properties may have important implications for the spatial linkages of a market, for example, the stationarity of the variables analysed by Nelson and Plosser (1982). Furthermore, an analysis making use of price differences may suffer because such transformations are *ad-hoc* in nature and may be inappropriate for a given price series (Goodwin and Shroeder 1991).

Alternative procedures for evaluating spatial market linkages have been developed within the framework of cointegration tests by Granger (1986), Engle and Granger (1987) and Engle and Yoo (1987). The general cointegration procedure appeals to the fact that deviations from equilibrium conditions for two economic variables, which are non-stationary when taken by themselves, should be stationary. The logic is that economic forces should prohibit persistent long run deviations from equilibrium conditions, although significant short run deviations may be observed. An important implication is that while individual economic variables such as prices may move at a wider scale, certain pairs of such variables should not diverge from one another in the long run. Cointegration of a pair of prices is a necessary condition for them to share a common long run component. To test the hypothesis of market integration in this study, an attempt is made using these recent developments in the theory of time series. The details of the theoretical background of cointegration techniques and the related tests of market integration are given in Annex 4.1A. A brief outline of the

Johansen procedure is presented in the next section followed by the application of these tests on price series of four crops, namely wheat, paddy, mustard seed and gram in Haryana.

Cointegration—Johansen's Procedure

Cointegration among the price series is tested using Johansen's (1988) maximum likelihood procedure based on the error-correction representation[3]:

$$\Delta z_t = \varphi_k \ \Delta z_{t-k} + \prod z_{t-1} + \mu + \varepsilon_t$$

where z_t is vector of I(1) processes. The rank of $\prod$ equals the number of cointegrating vectors, which is tested by maximum eigenvalue and likelihood ratio test statistics. In estimation of the Johansen procedure, a constant term has been used to capture the left out variables. The number of lags used in the model has been decided on the basis of the Akaike information criterion (Akaike 1969).

Data Description

The integration tests elaborated above were carried out on log monthly prices of wholesale *mandis* in Haryana for four crops, namely, wheat, paddy PR, mustard seeds and gram. In order to make a comparison, the study is divided into pre and post-liberalization periods. The pre-liberalization period comprises of 1978-79 to 1989-90 while the post-liberalization period includes 1990-91 to 2002-03. These tests are applied on nine wheat markets, six mustard seed markets and four paddy (PR) and gram markets each. The data were collected from Economic and Statistical Organization Haryana (ESO), Chandigarh. These markets are well-dispersed markets all over Haryana and belong to general wholesale commodity markets in agriculture.

Several of the price series had a small number of missing observations. These gaps in price series were filled up by the previous months price of the same market as due to the fact that price missing was because of non-availability of market arrivals during that month in the respective *mandis*. It is considered that the previous month's price prevails in the *mandis* until the new arrivals and so the new price is determined[4]. Above all, only those markets and crops have been chosen for the analysis of integration which had either no or a very few gaps. Markets and crops with large gaps were dropped from the analysis.

Tests for the Unit Root

The empirical tests of cointegration must be preceded by a test of non-stationarity for the individual economic variables under consideration. In all cases, calculations are carried out on logs of the prices[5]. A potential problem and source of error when applying the ADF test is that it is sensitive to the presence of drift and time trends in the regression. So, while testing for the stationarity, the regression is run without including any trend factor and with including time trend as in the equation below and the F test is applied to check whether β and γ both are equal to zero or not.

$$\Delta P_{it} = \alpha + \beta P_{it-1} + \gamma t + \sum_{k=1}^{M} \delta k \, \Delta P_{it-k} + e_{it}$$

The observed value of F statistics are calculated by imposing the restriction β = γ = 0 in the above equation. These observed F values are compared with tabulated F (D-F) values which are available in Davidson and Mackinnon (1993: 565). In determining the order of the lag, the following Akaike's

'Final Prediction Error' (FPE) criterion is followed (Akaike 1969),

$$FPE(M) = \left[1 + \frac{M+1}{N}\right]\left[\frac{N}{N-1-M}\right]\left[\frac{RSS}{N}\right],$$

where RSS = Residual sum of squares
N = Number of observations
M = Number of lags used.

The ADF test results for wheat, rice, gram and mustard are presented in Tables 4.1.1, 4.2.1, 4.3.1 and 4.4.1, respectively for the pre and post-liberalization periods. It is evidently clear from the results of Table 4.1.1 that in the case of wheat prices in levels, the ADF test does not reject the unit root hypothesis at the 5 per cent level during both the periods. In case of the first difference of the series, the hypothesis was however rejected in both the periods mostly at the one per cent level. Similarly, it is apparent from the table that the F test does not reject the trend unit root in prices in levels, while it clearly rules out any unit root in the first difference in almost all of the cases. Thus all the nine price series of wheat were integrated of order one. In the case of paddy and gram, the unit root hypothesis was not rejected for prices in levels during both the periods (Tables 4.2.1 and 4.3.1). In case of the first difference of price series of both these crops, the hypothesis was rejected during both the periods mostly at the one per cent significance level indicating that all the four series of rice and that of gram were stationary of order one. The F test results were in consonance with those of ADF results and further confirmed that all the four price series of both these crops were stationary of the first order.

The results of unit root, however, were different in the case of mustard seed. During the pre-liberalization period, all the six price series had unit root in levels, while all the series were found stationary at first difference. In the post-liberalization period surprisingly all the six series were stationary in levels. The ADF test as well as the F test rejected the hypothesis of unit root in all the cases either at the one per cent or five per cent level. The implication is that long run association between the markets was ruled out for mustard seed crop and thereby there could not be any possibility of the existence of a cointegration relation between these markets in the post-liberalization period.

Application for Cointegration

Wheat

After having established that all the nine price series of wheat have the same long run characteristics, the next step is to examine the rank of Π or the number of cointegrating vectors present among these series. In a system of nine non-stationary variables, we can have nine different stochastic trends, one for each variable, while there is a possibility for at the most, eight cointegrating vectors, because the system must contain at least one stochastic trend for the variables to be non-stationary by themselves. According to Dickey *et al*. (1991), "Cointegrating vectors could be thought of as representing constraints that an economic system imposes on the movement of the variables in the system in the long run. Hence, the more cointegrating vectors there are, the more stable the system is."

According to Gonzalez and Helfand (2001) any commodity complexes to be integrated in the true sense must share a common trend and so have a common integrating factor. They further stated that if there was more than one common trend, for example two, some prices could be generated by the first common trend, some by the second and some by a combination of the first and second trends. Such markets cannot be characterized as integrated because the long run movements in prices would be governed by different components. For the existence of a common integrating factor for all prices, all the price series must be cointegrated and the rank of Π must be (n-1) cointegrating vectors (Kumar and Sharma 2003). In other words, in a system of nine price series, there must exist eight cointegrating vectors if these markets are to be integrated and have a common information-sharing path.

The results of the Johansen-Juselius method of multivariate cointegration tests for nine wheat price series are presented in Table 4.1.2. Both the maximum eigenvalue test and the trace test results indicate the presence of eight cointegrating vectors at the five per cent significance level for both pre and post-liberalization periods. This implies that all the nine markets were in fact cointegrated and had a common sharing of information on price changes in the long run.

As the cointegration tests are not based on a structural model, it is difficult to interpret the long run elasticities in terms of signs and magnitudes given by the cointegration relationship. However, by exactly identifying the multivariate system with (n-1) cointegrating relations we can find out the relative magnitude of the bivariate relationship between all the cointegrating variables (for detailed illustration see Annex 4A). In a bivariate vector of the sort (α–β), the value of α=1 and the value of β should be equal to –1 if the two markets are integrated and share a common path. Table 4.1.3 presents the magnitude of bivariate relationships for these nine price series for both pre and post-liberalization periods.

It is seen from the table that there were 36 possible combinations of bivariate markets for the above nine wheat prices series. The β coefficient was significant in all the cases during both the periods without any exception. The value of the β coefficient hovered around –1 with a range between –0.91 to –1.09 during the pre-liberalization period and between –0.95 to –1.05 during the post-liberalization period. The average value of the β coefficient was measured at –1.00 in the pre-liberalization period and slightly less than –0.99 during the post-liberalization period. The above empirical evidence suggests that all the wheat markets in Haryana exhibited a long run relationship during both the periods. The farmers transferred their produce form one market to the other according to the price changes as the markets were linked together and arbitrage through trade tied their prices together. Inter-market linkages ware perfect during both the periods without any significant change.

Paddy

The results of multivariate cointegration for four paddy markets are presented in Table 4.2.2. It is evidently clear from the results that all the four markets were integrated as both the maximum eigenvalue test and the trace test confirmed the presence of three cointegrating vectors during both the periods. Table 4.2.3 presents the magnitude of the bivariate relationship between different combinations of these four paddy markets. There could be six possible combinations of bivariate relations of the four price series. It is seen from the table that the values of the β coefficients were significant during both the periods without any exception. The range of β coefficients was measured as –0.92 to –1.11 in the pre-liberalization period, which widened to –0.83 to –1.27 in the post-liberalization period. The average value of the β coefficient, however, did not change significantly during these two periods as it was measured at –1.01 and –1.04 in the pre and post-liberalization periods, respectively. Thus, the cointegration results of paddy indicate that all the four markets were cointegrated with having a common long run path. Inter-market linkages were observed during both the periods albeit a little less than that of wheat in the post-liberalization period.

Gram

In a similar case to that of paddy, gram also observed three cointegraing vectors in a system of four price series (see Table 4.3.2) indicating an integration of all the four markets with a common sharing path during both the periods. All the six bivariate coefficients during both the periods were statistically significant (see Table 4.3.3). The value of the β coefficients in the case of gram, however, was much distant to the unit value as compared to the case of wheat and paddy discussed previously. The average value of the β coefficient was measured as –0.91 in the pre-liberalization period, which further went down to –0.85 in the post-liberalization period. The range of coefficients also widened from –0.80 to –1.05 in the pre-liberalization to –0.71 to –1.04 in the post-liberalization period. Thus the analysis of cointegration in pulses (gram) reveals that although markets were integrated during both the periods, inter-market linkages were less efficient in pulses as compared to wheat and rice, especially after the implementation of reforms in the 1990s.

Mustard-seed

As pointed out earlier, all the six price series in mustard-seed were integrated of order one in the pre-liberalization period while these series were stationary in the post-liberalization period. Therefore, cointegration relationship is developed only for the pre-liberalisation period. The results are presented in Table 4.4.2. In a set of six price series, there can be at the most five possible cointegraing vectors. It can be seen from the results of the table that the trace test rejected the hypothesis of four cointegrating vectors at a ten per cent significant level thus accepting the hypothesis of the existence of five cointegrating vectors in a set of six price series. The maximum eigenvalue test on the other hand could not reject the hypothesis of the existence of four cointegrating vectors at the 10 per cent significance level, thus accepting that there were in fact four cointegrating relations in the system. Thus, the two tests were not uniform in their results in the case of mustard-seeds. After trying various combinations we observed that it was the Hodal market, which was not found integrated by the maximum eigenvalue test (see Table 4.4.2). There were 15 combinations of bivariate relationships as displayed in Table 4.4.3. It is seen from the table that all the coefficients were significant without exception. The range of bivariate coefficients lay between –0.85 to –1.13. The average value of the β coefficient was measured as–0.99.

Thus, in the case of oilseeds (mustard-seed), it was observed that no long run integration existed in the post-liberalization period. In the pre-liberalization period, all the six markets were observed as being cointegrated with a common sharing path. The inter-market linkages among these six price series were found perfect and comparable with that of wheat and rice during the corresponding period.

The Error-Correction Model

The cointegration tests whether there is any long run association among a group of variables. An explanation for the long run interdependence among the variables lies in the short run dynamics. One would like to know the intertwined relationship in the short run giving way to a long run association. The error-correction model enables us to analyse the short run dynamics present in the time series variables (Engle and Granger 1987). The advantage of the error-correction model is that it allows for the short run dynamics as well as an assessment of the degree of convergence towards the long run relation as shown by the cointegration. The model is formulated by including the respective variables in their first differences, their lagged values and the lagged residuals from the cointegration equations.

Wheat

The error-correction results for wheat are presented in Table 4.1.4 for the pre-liberalization period and in Table 4.1.5 for the post-liberalization period. The results show that the estimates of the error-correction coefficients were highly significant and their signs were negative. This implies that the short run price movements along the long run equilibrium path were stable. The coefficients of the error-correction terms indicate the speed of convergence to the long run growth path as a result of a shock in their own prices. The range of error-correction coefficients was observed between –0.44 to –0.85 with an average value of –0.65 in the pre-liberalization period. In the post-liberalization period, the range widened slightly between –0.34 to –0.87 and the average value of error-correction coefficients was measured as –0.60. Thus, the magnitude of error-correction for these nine markets indicate a lag of 1-2 weeks period in the transmission of information from one market centre to the other. Figure 4.1 displays the long run path of price adjustments during pre and post-liberalization periods based on normalized cointegration relations as estimated above. It is clearly evident from the plots that diversions across the long run path were stable during both the periods. With few exceptions, the amplitudes of deviations were not very different in the pre and post-liberalization periods.

Fig. 4.1: Long-term price adjustment path during the pre and post-liberalization periods—Wheat.

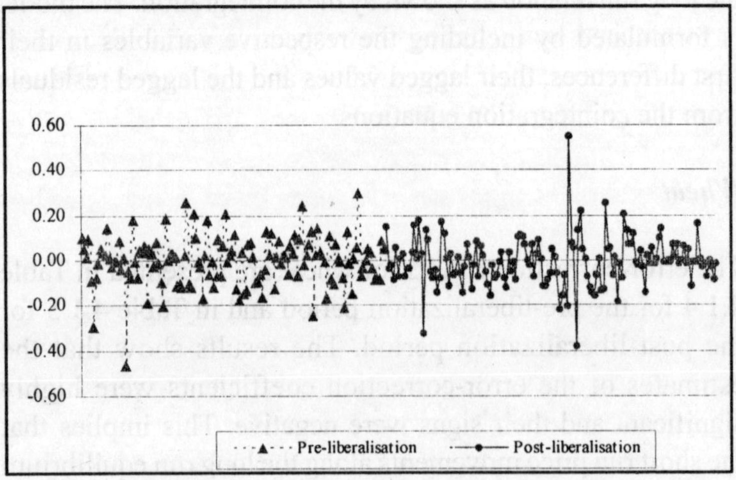

The cointegration results observed a strong long run relationship between all the nine markets. However, the results of error-correction reveal a weak association between these markets in the short run. It is seen from the table that significant short run associations were missing in most of the cases. Finally, given the fact that the error-correction equations are estimated in difference form the value of R^{-2} was reasonably low ranging between 0.08 to 0.39 in the pre-liberalization period and 0.13 to 0.40 in the post-liberalization period. Thus, the above analysis of wholesale wheat prices indicates that the markets were integrated in the long run. Price adjustment among the markets took a time period of around 1-2 weeks. While prices were tied together in the long run, they drifted apart in the short run because of paucity of available information and lack of quicker dissemination of available information.

Paddy

Tables 4.2.4 and 4.2.5 present the results of the ECM equations for the pre and post-liberalization periods. It is seen from the tables that the coefficients of the error-correction term were highly significant with a desired negative sign. The speed of adjustment was 33 per cent for the Kaithal market during the pre-liberalization period, which increased to 38 per cent in the post-liberalization period. For Karnal the speed of adjustment increased from 36 to 43 per cent and for Sirsa from 31 to 36 per cent from pre to the post-liberalization period. However, the value of the coefficient decreased from 43 to 36 per cent in case of Ambala during the same time period. The magnitude of error correction for these four markets averaged at around 0.36 for the pre-liberalization and

Fig. 4.2: Long-term price adjustment path during the pre and post-liberalization periods—Paddy.

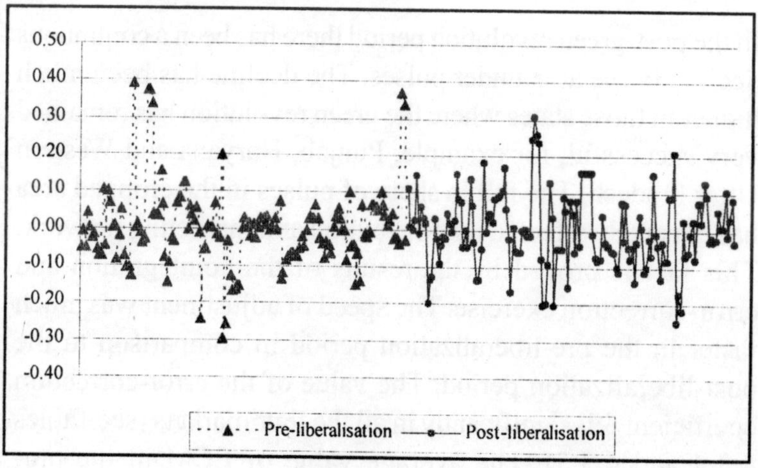

0.39 for the post-liberalization period indicating a lag of 2-3 weeks in the transmission of information from one market centre to the other.

The extent of a stable long run relationship between these four markets is also evident from Fig. 4.2. The fluctuations around the long run path were slightly less in the post-liberalization period compared to pre-liberalization period. Regarding the short run associations between the four market centres, the results of the error-correction reveal a very weak association between them. It is seen form the table that a significant short run association was observed only among Karnal-Kaithal and Sirsa-Kaithal during both the periods.

Thus, the above analysis of the wholesale paddy prices indicates that markets were integrated in the long run although price transmission was found to be lacking in the short run. Price adjustment among the markets was taking a time period of around 2-3 weeks and the adjustment process was found to be quicker in the post-liberalization period compared to the pre-liberalization period.

Gram

In the post-green revolution period there has been a continuous decline in the area under pulses. The decline has been much higher in those states where the green revolution has remained very successful, for example, Punjab, Haryana and Western Uttar Pradesh. The fall in share of pulses in the cropped area has adversely affected its distribution and marketing network. This fact is proved by the results of the cointegration and error-correction exercise. The speed of adjustment was much faster in the pre-liberalization period in comparison to the post-liberalization period. The value of the error-correction coefficient fell significantly in all the four markets (see Tables 4.3.4 and 4.3.5). The average value of ECM in the pre-liberalization period was measured at –0.60, which fell down to –0.29 in the post-liberalization period. Thus, the process of shock absorption and price adjustment was much faster, from 1-2 weeks in the pre-liberalization, which widened into 3-4 weeks in the post-liberalization period.

A worsening of the marketing network in gram is also evident from the long run cointegration relation. It is visible from Fig. 4.3 that the magnitude of price fluctuations was much higher in the post-liberalization as compared to pre-liberalization period. The short run associations between the four market centres were weakest as compared to the case of wheat and paddy. It is seen form the table that no significant short run association was observed in the pre-liberalization period. In the post-liberalization period, however, Sirsa-Ambala, Sirsa-Rohtak, Sirsa-Rewari and Rohtak-Rewari were seen as having a significant association between themselves. Thus we can conclude that the markets were found to be strongly integrated in the pre-liberalization period, which saw a dilution in the post-liberalization period. The time period of shock absorption and error-correction got extended from 1-2 weeks to 3-4 weeks in a months time.

Fig. 4.3: Long-term price adjustment path during the pre and post-liberalization periods—Gram.

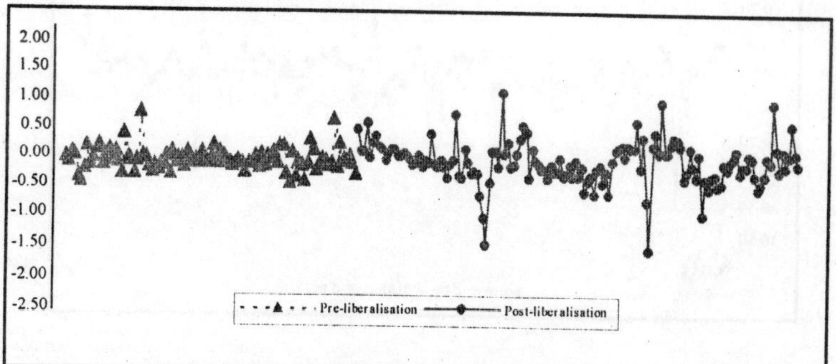

Mustard-seed

Table 4.4.4 presents the results of the ECM equation for the pre-liberalization period as no long run relationship was found for the post-liberalization period in the case of mustard-seeds. It is seen from the table that the coefficients of the error-correction term for all the six markets were significant and had a negative sign. The speed of adjustment was observed between -0.18 to -0.70. The average value of error-correction for these six markets was measured as -0.42 which was approximately as high as that of paddy indicating a lag of 2-3 weeks in the transmission of information from one market centre to the other. The short run associations between the six market centres were almost non-existent (see Table 4.4.4). Thus, the above analysis of the wholesale mustard-seed prices indicates that markets were integrated in the long run although price transmission was found to be lacking in the short run. Price adjustment among the markets took a time period of around 2-3 weeks.

Fig. 4.4: Long-term price adjustment path during the pre-liberalization period—Mustard-seed.

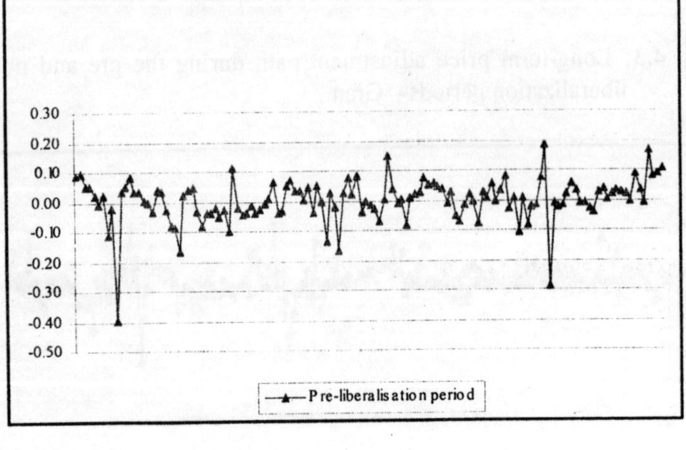

To sum up the chapter, the empirical evidences suggest that all wheat markets in Haryana exhibited a long run relationship during both the periods. The farmers transferred their produce from one market to the other according to the price changes as the markets were linked together and arbitrage through trade tied their prices together. Inter-market linkages were perfect during both the periods without any significant change. Price adjustment among the markets was taking a time period of around 1-2 weeks. While prices were tied together in the long run, they drifted apart in the short run. In the case of paddy, all the four markets were cointegrated and had a common long run path. Inter-market linkages were observed during both the periods albeit a little less than that of wheat in the pre-liberalization period. Price adjustment among the markets was taking around a 2-3 week time period and the adjustment process was found to be quicker in the post-liberalization period compared to the pre-liberalization period.

The analysis of cointegration in pulses (gram) revealed that although markets were integrated during both the periods, inter-market linkages were less efficient in pulses as compared to wheat and rice, especially after the implementation of the reforms in the 1990s. In other words, the markets were found strongly integrated in the pre-liberalization period, which saw a dilution in the post-liberalization period. The time period of shock absorption and error-correction got extended from 1-2 weeks in the pre-liberalization period to 3-4 weeks in the post-liberalization period. In the case of oilseeds (mustard-seed), it was observed that no long run integration existed in the post-liberalization period. In the pre-liberalization period, all markets except one were observed as cointegrated with a common sharing path. The inter-market linkages among these six price series were found perfect and comparable with that of wheat and rice during the corresponding period. Price transmission, however, was found to be lacking in the short run. Price adjustment among the markets was taking around a 2-3 week time period.

Thus we can conclude that agricultural *mandis* in Haryana were well integrated with each other in the long run. In the short run, however, price transmission was found to be lacking, because of scarce availability of information and lack of a quicker dissemination of the available information.

Table 4.1.1: Augmented Dickey Fuller (ADF) Test for Unit Root: Wheat.

Series	*Levels*				*First Difference*			
	Constant only	*Constant and Time Trend*	*F Test β-0 γ- 0*	*No. of Lags*	*Constant only*	*Constant and Time Trend*	*F Test β-0 γ- 0*	*No. of Lags*
Sample: 1979-04 to 1990-03								
Log Ambala	–1.35	–1.65	1.72	10	–6.91*	–6.95*	24.20	9
Log Kaithal	–1.17	–1.45	1.34	10	–6.76*	–6.79*	23.05	9
Log Karnal	–1.20	–1.94	2.06	8	–6.89*	–6.89*	23.81	7
Log Jind	–1.02	–2.27	2.64	9	–6.88*	–6.87*	23.60	8
Log Sonepat	–1.26	–2.69	3.69	6	–7.41*	–7.39*	27.32	5
Log Narwana	–1.28	–2.25	2.67	12	–3.30**	–3.28	5.54	11
Log Sirsa	–1.29	–1.65	1.68	9	–7.57*	–7.58*	28.86	8
Log Hodal	–1.16	–1.53	1.40	10	–7.05*	–7.05*	24.96	9
Log Narnaul	–1.34	–2.13	2.67	10	–7.79*	–7.80*	30.40	8
Sample: 1990-04 to 2002-03								
Log Ambala	–2.23	–3.20	5.96	3	–8.66*	–8.77*	38.46	2
Log Kaithal	–2.34	–3.70**	7.36	1	–8.04*	–8.13*	33.08	2
Log Karnal	–2.40	–2.11	4.05	11	–5.35*	–5.71*	16.39	10
Log Jind	–1.84	–2.77	4.42	3	–9.32*	–9.38*	43.99	2
Log Sonepat	–2.32	–2.50	4.56	9	–5.23*	–5.50*	15.23	12
Log Narwana	–2.20	–2.85	4.91	3	–9.73*	–9.82*	48.30	2
Log Sirsa	–2.40	–1.61	3.39	12	–6.93*	–7.23*	26.20	8
Log Hodal	–2.14	–2.91	5.30	12	–3.86*	–4.11*	8.52	11
Log Narnaul	–1.66	–2.64	3.78	3	–9.72*	–9.74*	47.41	2

Notes:

(1) * Significant at the 1% Level, ** Significant at the 5% Level.

(2) Critical Values of ADF statistics are –3.73 (1%) and 3.17 (5%) (Engle and Yoo, 1987), critical Value of F test is 6.49 (5%) (Davidson and Mackinnon, 1993, p. 565).

(3) The optimum lag length was determined by Akaike Information Criterion (AIC).

Table 4.1.2: Johansen's Maximum Eigenvalue and Trace Test for the Number of Cointegrating Vectors in Wheat.

Series tested for cointegration	*Null Hypothesis*	*Alternative Hypothesis*	*Eigen-value*	*Maximum Eigen (ξ_r)*	*Trace (η_r)*	*Order of VAR©*
(Sample: 1979-84 to 1990-93)						
Log Ambala,	r = 0	r = 1	0.58	115.7*	535.6*	1
Log Kaithal,	r ≤ 1	r = 2	0.51	93.8*	419.9*	
Log Karnal,	r ≤ 2	r = 3	0.47	83.5*	326.1*	
Log Jind,	r ≤ 3	r = 4	0.38	63.6*	242.6*	
Log Sonepat,	r ≤ 4	r = 5	0.35	56.8*	179.0*	
Log Narwana,	r ≤ 5	r = 6	0.33	52.3*	122.2*	
Log Sirsa,	r ≤ 6	r = 7	0.26	38.9*	69.9*	
Log Hodal,	r ≤ 7	r = 8	0.19	27.1*	31.0*	
Log Narnaul, Intercept	r ≤ 8	r = 9	0.03	3.9	3.9	
(Sample: 1990-94 to 2002-03)						
Log Ambala,	r = 0	r = 1	0.59	126.9*	570.0*	1
Log Kaithal,	r ≤ 1	r = 2	0.53	107.8*	443.1*	
Log Karnal,	r ≤ 2	r = 3	0.45	86.0*	335.2*	
Log Jind,	r ≤ 3	r = 4	0.41	76.9*	249.2*	
Log Sonepat,	r ≤ 4	r = 5	0.38	67.8*	172.3*	
Log Narwana,	r ≤ 5	r = 6	0.25	41.2*	104.5*	
Log Sirsa,	r ≤ 6	r = 7	0.24	39.4*	63.3*	
Log Hodal,	r ≤ 7	r = 8	0.11	16.9*.	23.9*	
Log Narnaul, Intercept	r ≤ 8	r = 9	0.05	7.0	7.0	

Note:

*(**) denotes rejection of the hypothesis at 5%(10%) significance level.

© Order of VAR is determined by the AIC, SBC and adjusted LR Test.

Table 4.1.3: The Bivariate Coefficients based on Exactly Indentified Cointegrating Vectors between the Selected Wheat Markets.

	Ambala	*Kaithal*	*Karnal*	*Jind*	*Sonepat*	*Narwana*	*Sirsa*	*Hodal*	*Narnaul*
(Sample: 1979-84 to 1990-93)									
Ambala	1.00								
Kaithal	-0.95 (29.4)	1.00							
Karnal	-0.96 (-21.4)	-1.01 (-26.1)	1.00						
Jind	-.97 (-21.8)	-1.02 (-29.0)	-1.01 (-24.5)	1.00					
Sonepat	-0.99 (-22.5)	-1.04 (-29.9)	-1.03 (-21.1)	-1.02 (-23.5)	1.00				
Narwana	-0.91 (-20.1)	-0.96 (-26.2)	-0.95 (-29.5)	-0.94 (-24.9)	-0.92 (-21.4)	1.00			
Sirsa	-1.00 (-24.9)	-1.05 (-36.8)	-1.04 (-27.8)	-1.03 (-25.0)	-1.01 (-21.5)	-1.10 (-23.3)	1.00		
Hodal	-0.99 (-25.0)	-1.05 (-32.0)	-1.04 (-26.2)	-1.02 (-24.7)	-1.00 (-27.1)	-1.09 (-25.5)	-1.00 (-22.9)	1.00	
Narnaul	-0.96 (-12.4)	-1.01 (-13.9)	-1.00 (-11.7)	-0.99 (-13.4)	-0.97 (-12.3)	-1.05 (-10.8)	-0.96 (-13.8)	-0.96 (-11.4)	1.00
(Sample: 1990-94 to 2002-03)									
Ambala	1.00								
Kaithal	-1.05 (-30.1)	1.00							
Karnal	-1.05 (-67.7)	-1.00 (-31.9)	1.00						
Jind	-1.02 (-42.4)	-0.97 (-21.5)	-0.97 (-40.6)	1.00					
Sonepat	-1.05 (-46.2)	-1.01 (-28.5)	-1.00 (-43.7)	-1.03 (-38.6)	1.00				
Narwana	-1.01 (-61.2)	-0.97 (-29.6)	-0.97 (-68.9)	-0.99 (-41.3)	-0.96 (-46.4)	1.00			
Sirsa	-1.03 (-18.9)	-0.98 (-13.2)	-0.98 (-19.0)	-1.01 (-24.4)	-0.97 (-16.6)	-1.01 (-20.3)	1.00		
Hodal	-1.00 (-40.7)	-0.95 (-33.1)	-0.95 (-39.0)	-0.98 (-31.6)	-0.95 (-51.8)	-0.98 (-42.7)	-0.97 (-15.6)	1.00	
Narnaul	-1.00 (-20.4)	-0.96 (-21.8)	-0.96 (-20.8)	-0.98 (-18.5)	-0.95 (-21.6)	-0.99 (-22.6)	-0.98 (-13.3)	-1.00 (-24.0)	1.00

Note: Figures in parentheses are respective 't' values

Table: 4.1.4: Reduced Form VECM for Wheat (Period 1979-84 to 1990-93).

	ΔLog Ambala	*ΔLog Kaithal*	*ΔLog Karnal*	*ΔLog Jind*	*ΔLog Sonepat*	*ΔLog Narwana*	*ΔLog Sirsa*	*ΔLog Hodal*	*ΔLog Narnaul*
ECM	-0.72	-0.55	-0.44	-0.81	-0.72	-0.63	-0.64	-0.85	-0.45
	(-5.4)	(-3.3)	(-2.9)	(-4.9)	(-5.3)	(-4.3)	(-3.9)	(-5.0)	(-4.6)
ΔLog Ambala $_{-1}$	0.22	0.19	0.23	0.01	0.25	0.09	0.10	0.07	-0.20
	(1.8)	(2.1)	(1.9)	(0.1)	(1.8)	(0.6)	(0.8)	(0.6)	(-1.2)
ΔLog Kaithal $_{-1}$	-0.11	-0.16	-0.17	-0.12	-0.13	-0.28	-0.23	-0.07	0.01
	(-0.7)	(-1.3)	(-1.1)	(-0.6)	(-0.7)	(-1.6)	(-1.5)	(-0.4)	(0.1)
ΔLog Karnal $_{-1}$	0.00	0.02	0.02	-0.05	-0.24	0.03	0.09	-0.08	-0.28
	(0.0)	(0.1)	(0.1)	(-0.3)	(-1.5)	(0.2)	(0.6)	(-0.6)	(-1.5)
ΔLog Jind $_{-1}$	0.15	0.04	0.08	0.01	0.13	0.16	0.09	0.06	0.06
	(1.5)	(0.5)	(0.8)	(0.1)	(1.1)	(1.4)	(0.9)	(0.6)	(0.4)
ΔLog Sonepat $_{-1}$	-0.06	-0.01	-0.07	0.03	-0.08	-0.04	0.06	-0.03	0.19
	(-0.7)	(-0.1)	(-0.8)	(0.3)	(-0.8)	(-0.4)	(0.7)	(-0.3)	(1.7)
ΔLog Narwana $_{-1}$	-0.06	-0.06	-0.06	0.05	-0.07	-0.07	-0.12	-0.01	0.13
	(-0.6)	(-0.8)	(-0.6)	(0.4)	(-0.6)	(-0.6)	(-1.1)	(-0.1)	(1.0)
ΔLog Sirsa $_{-1}$	0.13	0.13	0.10	0.36	0.22	0.19	0.14	0.20	0.11
	(1.0)	(1.3)	(0.7)	(2.1)	(1.4)	(1.2)	(1.1)	(1.4)	(0.6)
ΔLog Hodal $_{-1}$	0.22	0.23	0.18	0.28	0.30	0.23	0.24	0.37	0.45
	(1.6)	(2.2)	(1.4)	(1.6)	(1.9)	(1.5)	(1.8)	(2.6)	(2.6)
ΔLog Narnaul $_{-1}$	-0.09	-0.06	-0.06	-0.03	-0.01	0.03	0.02	-0.05	-0.04
	(-1.1)	(-0.9)	(-0.8)	(-0.3)	(-0.1)	(0.3)	(0.2)	(-0.6)	(-0.4)
Constant	0.00	0.00	0.00	0.00	0.00	0.00	0.00	0.00	0.00
	(0.5)	(0.5)	(0.8)	(0.3)	(0.3)	(0.5)	(0.6)	(0.5)	(0.2)
R^2	0.35	0.44	0.20	0.36	0.47	0.35	0.24	0.28	0.33
$\bar{R}^2$	0.25	0.35	0.08	0.27	0.39	0.25	0.12	0.17	0.24
Log Likelihood	196.3	232.9	201.5	167.6	179.0	180.3	198.6	190.88	162.6
D-W	1.99	2.01	2.02	2.00	2.06	2.04	1.98	1.99	1.99
AIC	-2.70	-3.26	-2.78	-2.27	-2.44	-2.46	-2.74	-2.62	-2.19
SBC	-2.31	-2.86	-2.39	-1.87	-2.05	-2.07	-2.34	-2.23	-1.80
LM(12)	1.54	2.17**	1.97**	1.40	0.34	1.39	2.13**	1.77	1.08
ARCH(12)	1.32	2.99*	0.75	0.07	0.09	0.17	2.03**	0.21	3.21*
Heteroskedasticity	0.71	1.29	1.38	0.33	0.65	0.30	0.94	0.63	1.34
Reset (Ramsay) (1)	5.13**	0.59	7.47*	5.43**	3.49	1.73	0.78	0.06	10.7*

Table: 4.1.5: Reduced Form VECM for Wheat (Period 1990-94 to 2002-03)

	ΔLog Ambala	*ΔLog Kaithal*	*ΔLog Karnal*	*ΔLog Jind*	*ΔLog Sonepat*	*ΔLog Narwana*	*ΔLog Sirsa*	*ΔLog Hodal*	*ΔLog Narnaul*
ECM	-0.65	-0.48	-0.70	-0.52	-0.63	-0.71	-0.47	-0.87	-0.34
	(-3.8)	(-4.7)	(-3.8)	(-3.7)	(-4.3)	(-3.3)	(-4.5)	(-5.8)	(-4.5)
ΔLog Ambala $_{-1}$	-0.13	-0.29	-0.27	-0.27	0.14	0.06	-0.20	-0.06	-0.17
	(-0.9)	(-2.3)	(-2.0)	(-2.2)	(1.1)	(0.4)	(-1.4)	(-0.5)	(-1.2)
ΔLog Kaithal $_{-1}$	0.05	0.05	0.12	0.24	-0.07	0.04	0.00	-0.06	0.15
	(0.4)	(0.5)	(1.1)	(2.3)	(-0.6)	(0.3)	(0.0)	(-0.5)	(1.2)
ΔLog Karnal $_{-1}$	-0.06	0.12	0.04	0.00	-0.06	-0.02	0.01	0.10	0.03
	(-0.4)	(0.9)	(0.3)	(0.0)	(-0.5)	(-0.2)	(0.0)	(0.7)	(0.2)
ΔLog Jind $_{-1}$	-0.16	0.00	-0.23	-0.03	-0.05	-0.10	-0.08	-0.09	-0.21
	(-1.1)	(0.0)	(-1.7)	(-0.2)	(-0.4)	(-0.7)	(-0.5)	(-0.7)	(-1.4)
ΔLog Sonepat $_{-1}$	-0.24	-0.26	-0.22	-0.19	-0.25	-0.30	-0.23	-0.39	-0.23
	(-2.0)	(-2.4)	(-2.0)	(-1.8)	(-2.2)	(-2.4)	(-2.0)	(-3.3)	(-1.8)
ΔLog Narwana $_{-1}$	0.50	0.70	0.45	0.64	0.30	0.40	0.26	0.31	0.28
	(3.1)	(4.8)	(2.8)	(4.4)	(1.9)	(2.3)	(1.6)	(1.9)	(1.6)
ΔLog Sirsa $_{-1}$	0.09	-0.02	0.00	-0.11	0.13	0.04	0.23	0.27	0.03
	(0.6)	(-0.1)	(0.0)	(-0.9)	(1.0)	(0.3)	(1.7)	(1.9)	(0.2)
ΔLog Hodal $_{-1}$	0.13	0.03	0.26	0.09	0.06	0.29	0.21	0.15	0.28
	(1.1)	(0.2)	(2.1)	(0.8)	(0.5)	(2.2)	(1.6)	(1.2)	(2.0)
ΔLog Narnaul $_{-1}$	0.03	0.03	0.05	-0.01	0.01	-0.01	0.07	0.05	-0.04
	(0.4)	(0.5)	(0.7)	(-0.2)	(0.1)	(-0.1)	(0.9)	(0.6)	(0.4)
Constant	0.01	0.00	0.01	0.01	0.00	0.01	0.00	0.00	0.00
	(1.0)	(0.9)	(1.1)	(1.2)	(0.7)	(1.2)	(0.6)	(0.8)	(0.4)
R^2	0.39	0.47	0.36	0.35	0.45	0.23	0.27	0.37	0.36
R^{-2}	0.31	0.40	0.28	0.26	0.37	0.13	0.17	0.29	0.27
Log Likelihood	215.4	230.7	218.9	230.6	220.3	204.5	214.1	215.9	203.8
D-W	1.89	2.00	2.05	1.90	1.90	1.95	1.92	2.05	1.96
AIC	-2.74	-2.95	-2.79	-2.95	-2.81	-2.59	-2.72	-2.75	-2.58
SBC	-2.37	-2.58	-2.42	-2.58	-2.44	-2.22	-2.35	-2.38	-2.21
LM(12)	1.45	0.91	3.88*	1.18	1.82	1.37	0.84	2.07**	1.03
ARCH(12)	1.68	1.23	1.28	1.40	1.21	1.54	0.91	3.41*	1.83**
Heteroskedcity	1.78**	1.27	1.91*	2.71*	2.99*	1.62**	4.01*	2.19*	1.15
Reset (Ramsay) (1)	4.17**	1.28	2.31	0.13	6.23**	4.95**	3.69	4.65**	2.99

Table 4.2.1: Augmented Dickey Fuller (ADF) Test for Unit Root: Paddy (PR).

Series	*Levels*				*First Difference*			
	Constant only	*Constant and Time Trend*	*F Test* $\beta=0$ $\gamma=0$	*No of Lags*	*Constant only*	*Constant and Time Trend*	*F Test* $\beta=0$ $\gamma=0$	*No of Lags*
Sample: 1978-10 to 1990-09								
Log Ambala	-1.10	-1.83	1.83	12	-5.66*	-5.68*	16.11	11
Log Kiathal	-1.78	-1.52	2.21	12	-3.95*	-4.22*	8.90	11
Log Karnal	-1.51	-3.84**	7.43	3	-9.91*	-9.88*	48.81	2
Log Sirsa	-1.68	-1.55	1.94	9	-7.21*	-7.32*	26.82	8
Sample: 1990-10 to 2002-09								
Log Ambala	-2.11	-1.73	2.73	10	-6.87*	-7.08*	25.04	9
Log Kiathal	-2.13	-3.44	6.28	3	-10.60*	-10.62*	56.38	2
Log Karnal	-2.22	-2.31	3.52	5	-7.92*	-8.04*	32.33	4
Log Sirsa	-2.36	-1.85	3.55	12	-4.96*	-5.36*	14.35	11

Notes:

(1) * Significant at the 1% Level, ** Significant at the 5% Level.

(2) Critical Values of ADF statistics are—3.73 (1%) and 3.17 (5%) (Engle and Yoo, 1987), critical Value of F test is 6.49 (5%) (Davidson and Mackinnon, 1993, p. 565).

(3) The optimum lag length was determined by Akaike Information Criterion (AIC).

Table 4.2.2: Johansen's Maximum Eigenvalue and Trace Test for the Number of Cointegrating Vectors in Paddy (PR).

Series tested for cointegration	*Null Hypothesis*	*Alternative Hypothesis*	*Eigen-value*	*Maximum Eigen* (ξ_r)	*Trace* (η_r)	*Order of VAR©*
(Sample: 1978-10 to 1990-09)						
Log Ambala, Log Kaithal Log Karnal Log Sirsa, Intercept	r = 0	r = 1	0.32	54.6*	132.1*	1
	r ≤ 1	r = 2	0.26	42.6*	77.5*	
	r ≤ 2	r = 3	0.17	27.7*	34.9*	
	r ≤ 3	r = 4	0.05	7.3	7.3	
(Sample: 1990-10 to 2002-09)						
Log Ambala, Log Kaithal Log Karnal Log Sirsa, Intercept	R = 0	r = 1	0.31	53.3*	144.6*	1
	r ≤ 1	r = 2	0.27	46.0*	91.2*	
	r ≤ 2	r = 3	0.23	38.1*	45.2*	
	r ≤ 3	r = 4	0.05	7.1	7.1	

Note:

*(**) denotes rejection of the hypothesis at 5%(10%) significance level.

© Order of VAR is determined by the AIC, SBC and adjusted LR Test.

Table 4.2.3: The Bivariate Coefficients based on Exactly Indentified Cointegrating Vectors between the Selected Paddy (PR) Markets.

	Ambala	*Kaithal*	*Karnal*	*Sirsa*
(Sample: 1978-84 to 1990-99)				
Ambala	1.00			
Kaithal	0.93 (-14.7)	1.00		
Karnal	-0.92 (-12.2)	-0.99 (-14.6)	1.00	
Sirsa	-1.02 (-16.6)	-1.09 (-12.9)	-1.11 (-11.8)	1.00
(Sample: 1990-10 to 2002-09)				
Ambala	1.00			
Kaithal	-1.27 (-15.1)	1.00		
Karnal	-1.25 (-13.7)	-0.98 (-11.3)	1.00	
Sirsa	-1.06 (16.4)	-0.83 (-13.7)	-0.84 (-13.1)	1.00

Note: the figures in parentheses are respective 't' values.

Table: 4.2.4: Reduced Form VECM for Paddy (PR) (Period 1978-10 to 1990-09).

	ΔLog Ambala	*ΔLog Kaithal*	*ΔLog Karnal*	*ΔLog Sirsa*
ECM	-0.43 (-5.1)	-0.33 (-4.9)	-0.36 (-4.4)	-0.31 (-4.7)
ΔLog Ambala $_{-1}$	-0.02 (-0.2)	-0.02 (-0.2)	0.00 (0.0)	-0.06 (-0.9)
ΔLog Kaithal $_{-1}$	0.04 (0.4)	0.06 (0.8)	-0.22 (-1.9)	-0.17 (-2.2)
ΔLog Karnal $_{-1}$	0.02 (0.3)	0.04 (0.6)	0.00 (0.1)	0.01 (0.2)
ΔLog Sirsa$_1$	0.00 (0.0)	-0.06 (-0.7)	-0.17 (-1.3)	-0.06 (-0.7)
Constant	0.01 (1.1)	0.01 (0.9)	0.01 (1.5)	0.01 (1.6)
R^2	0.24	0.18	0.21	0.21
R^{-2}	0.20	0.14	0.17	0.17
Log Likelihood	154.0	185.8	133.3	194.4
D-W	1.96	1.95	2.03	1.99
AIC	-2.03	-2.47	-1.74	-2.59
SBC	-1.86	-2.30	-1.58	-2.42
LM(12)	1.32	0.96	0.32	2.57*
ARCH(12)	1.91**	2.16**	1.80	1.68
Heteroskedasticity	0.67	2.58*	2.57*	1.61
Reset (Ramsay)(1)	0.68	17.23*	23.70*	0.44

Table: 4.2.5: Reduced Form VECM for Paddy (PR) (Period 1990-10 to 2002-09).

	ΔLog Ambala	*ΔLog Kaithal*	*ΔLog Karnal*	*ΔLog Sirsa*
ECM	-0.37 (-4.8)	-0.38 (-4.8)	-0.43 (-5.5)	-0.36 (-4.3)
ΔLog Ambala $_{-1}$	0.02 (0.2)	0.05 (0.6)	-0.13 (-1.5)	0.03 (0.4)
ΔLog Kaithal $_{-1}$	-0.06 (-0.6)	-0.04 (-0.5)	-0.17 (-1.8)	-0.19 (-1.9)
ΔLog Karnal $_{-1}$	0.06 (0.8)	-0.03 (-0.4)	-0.01 (-0.1)	0.09 (1.1)
ΔLog Sirsa$_1$	-0.03 (-0.3)	0.10 (1.2)	-0.06 (-0.6)	0.02 (0.2)
Constant	0.01 (1.2)	0.00 (0.7)	0.01 (1.2)	0.01 (1.1)
R^2	0.18	0.23	0.26	0.21
R^{-2}	0.14	0.19	0.23	0.17
Log Likelihood	170.1	182.1	163.0	161.0
D-W	1.98	1.97	2.07	1.98
AIC	-2.25	-2.42	-2.15	-2.13
SBC	-2.09	-2.25	-1.99	-1.96
LM(12)	1.62	1.43	0.94	3.89*
ARCH(12)	0.25	1.23	0.62	0.79
Heteroskedasticity	1.70	2.42*	0.38	1.97**
Reset (Ramsay) (1)	0.24	2.81	0.40	4.16**

Table 4.3.1: Augmented Dickey Fuller (ADF) Test for Unit Root: Gram.

Series	*Levels*				*First Difference*			
	Constant only	*Constant and Time Trend*	*F Test* $\beta=0$ $\gamma=0$	*No of Lags*	*Constant only*	*Constant and Time Trend*	*F Test* $\beta=0$ $\gamma=0$	*No. of Lags*
Sample: 1982-84 to 1990-93								
Log Ambala	-1.23	-2.10	2.21	3	-6.73*	-6.68*	22.42	2
Log Rohtak	-1.29	-2.25	2.53	1	-6.63*	-6.59*	21.72	1
Log Sirsa	-1.16	-2.00	2.00	1	-6.35*	-6.31*	19.92	1
Log Rewari	-1.29	-2.33	2.72	1	-7.11*	-7.07*	25.02	1
Sample: 1990-94 to 2002-03								
Log Ambala	-2.58	-3.24	5.45	1	-9.48*	-9.48*	44.91	1
Log Rohtak	-1.23	-2.62	3.43	4	-8.04*	-8.01*	32.12	3
Log Sirsa	-1.58	-2.60	3.40	1	-8.28*	-8.25*	34.07	1
Log Rewari	-1.44	-2.88	4.15	3	-7.32*	-7.28*	26.58	3

Notes:

(1) * Significant at the 1% Level, ** Significant at the 5% Level.

(2) Critical Values of ADF statistics are—3.73 (1%) and 3.17 (5%) (Engle and Yoo, 1987), critical Value of F test is 6.49 (5%) (Davidson and Mackinnon, 1993, p. 565).

(3) The optimum lag length was determined by Akaike Information Criterion (AIC).

Table 4.3.2: Johansen's Maximum Eigenvalue and Trace Test for the Number of Cointegrating Vectors in Gram.

Series tested for cointe-gration	*Null Hypoth-esis*	*Alternative Hypothesis*	*Eigen-value*	*Maximum Eigen* (ξ_r)	*Trace* (η_r)	*Order of VAR©*
(Sample: 1982-84 to 1990-93)						
Log Ambala, Log Rohtak Log Sirsa, Log Rewari, Intercept	r = 0	R = 1	0.52	70.9*	170.6*	1
	r ≤ 1	r = 2	0.44	56.0*	100.0*	
	r ≤ 2	r = 3	0.35	41.2*	43.7*	
	r ≤ 3	r = 4	0.03	2.5	2.5	
(Sample: 1990-94 to 2002-03)						
Log Ambala, Log Rohtak Log Sirsa, Log Rewari, Intercept	r = 0	r = 1	0.27	45.6*	98.8*	2
	r ≤ 1	r = 2	0.19	31.2*	53.2*	
	r ≤ 2	r = 3	0.12	18.1*	22.1*	
	r ≤ 3	r = 4	0.03	3.7	3.7	

Note:

*(**) denotes rejection of the hypothesis at 5%(10%) significance level.

© Order of VAR is determined by the AIC, SBC and adjusted LR Test.

Table 4.3.3: The Bivariate Coefficients based on Exactly Indentified Cointegrating Vectors between the Selected Gram Markets.

	Ambala	*Rohtak*	*Sirsa*	*Rewari*
(Sample: 1982.84 to 1990.93)				
Ambala	1.00			
Rohtak	-0.80 (-25.3)	1.00		
Sirsa	-0.85 (-30.0)	-1.05 (-39.2)	1.00	
Rewari	-0.81 (-26.4)	-1.01 (-50.2)	-0.96 (-45.1)	1.00
(Sample: 1990.94 to 2002.03)				
Ambala	1.00			
Rohtak	-0.73 (-6.0)	1.00		
Sirsa	-0.69 (-6.9)	-0.93 (-18.1)	1.00	
Rewari	-0.71 (-5.5)	-0.97 (-30.6)	-1.04 (-16.9)	1.00

Note: Figures in parentheses are respective 't' values.

Table: 4.3.4: Reduced Form VECM for Gram (Period 1982.84 to 1990.93).

	ΔLog Ambala	*ΔLog Rohtak*	*ΔLog Sirsa*	*ΔLog Rewari*
ECM	-0.63 (-5.0)	-0.62 (-2.9)	-0.23 (-1.1)	-0.92 (-4.1)
ΔLog Ambala $_{-1}$	-0.07 (-0.6)	0.09 (0.7)	0.09 (0.7)	0.05 (0.4)
ΔLog Rohtak $_{-1}$	0.14 (1.0)	0.06 (0.3)	-0.11 (-0.7)	-0.02 (-0.1)
ΔLog Sirsa $_{-1}$	0.09 (0.5)	-0.14 (-0.7)	-0.01 (0.0)	0.04 (0.2)
ΔLog Rewari$_1$	-0.05 (-0.3)	0.11 (0.6)	0.02 (0.1)	0.09 (0.6)
Constant	0.00 (0.4)	0.01 (0.9)	0.01 (1.0)	0.01 (0.8)
R^2	0.40	0.17	0.04	0.26
R^{-2}	0.35	0.10	-0.03	0.20
Log Likelihood	116.9	101.3	108.3	104.4
D-W	1.86	2.00	2.00	2.04
AIC	-2.27	-1.94	-2.09	-2.01
SBC	-2.06	-1.73	-1.88	-1.79
LM(12)	0.96	0.76	0.53	0.54
ARCH(12)	0.93	0.26	0.46	0.33
Heteroskedasticity	0.39	0.15	0.63	0.42
Reset (Ramsay) (1)	0.94	0.24	0.26	3.78

Table: 4.3.5: Reduced Form VECM for Gram (Period 1990.04 to 2002.03).

	ΔLog Ambala	*ΔLog Rohtak*	*ΔLog Sirsa*	*ΔLog Rewari*
ECM	-0.28 (-4.6)	-0.35 (-2.9)	-0.03 (-0.4)	-0.50 (-4.6)
ΔLog Ambala $_{-1}$	0.00 (0.0)	0.06 (0.9)	0.12 (2.1)	0.04 (0.7)
ΔLog Ambala $_{-2}$	-0.02 (-0.2)	-0.06 (-0.9)	0.07 (1.5)	-0.03 (-0.5)
ΔLog Rohtak $_{-1}$	0.11 (0.7)	-0.09 (-0.8)	-0.21 (-2.2)	0.02 (0.2)
ΔLog Rohtak $_{-2}$	0.17 (1.5)	-0.10 (-1.0)	-0.06 (-0.8)	0.03 (0.3)
ΔLog Sirsa $_{-1}$	0.15 (0.9)	0.09 (0.7)	0.04 (0.4)	0.03 (0.2)
ΔLog Sirsa $_{-2}$	-0.25 (-1.6)	-0.17 (-1.3)	-0.22 (-2.1)	-0.41 (-3.7)
ΔLog Rewari$_1$	0.22 (1.3)	0.41 (3.1)	0.33 (3.0)	0.36 (3.1)
ΔLog Rewari$_2$	-0.14 (-0.9)	0.08 (0.7)	0.02 (0.1)	0.15 (1.4)
Constant	0.00 (-0.3)	0.00 (0.7)	0.00 (0.6)	0.00 (0.5)
R^2	0.31	0.32	0.18	0.31
R^{-2}	0.26	0.27	0.11	0.25
Log Likelihood	137.6	167.8	196.7	188.1
D-W	2.05	2.02	1.94	1.92
AIC	-1.74	-2.16	-2.57	-2.45
SBC	-1.50	-1.92	-2.32	-2.20
LM(12)	1.36	0.73	1.69	1.06
ARCH(12)	0.84	0.36	0.81	1.07
Heteroskedasticity	1.28	8.61*	1.71**	15.02*
Reset (Ramsay) (1)	1.22	10.4*	3.26	0.09

Table 4.4.1: Augmented Dickey Fuller (ADF) Test for Unit Root: Mustard-seed.

Series	*Levels*				*First Differece*			
	Constant only	*Constant and Time Trend*	*F Test* $\beta=0$ $\gamma=0$	*No. of Lags*	*Constant only*	*Constant and Time Trend*	*F Test* $\beta=0$ $\gamma=0$	*No. of Lags*
Sample: 1979-84 to 1990-93								
Log Ambala	-2.77	-3.56**	6.48	1	-7.54*	-7.54*	28.42	2
Log Jind	-2.21	-2.73	3.91	1	-8.08*	-8.08*	32.68	1
Log Sonepat	-2.56	-2.63	4.00	1	-8.86*	-8.93*	39.92	1
Log Sirsa	-2.05	-2.49	3.22	1	-6.26*	-6.24*	19.54	2
Log Hodal	-1.62	-2.43	3.05	8	-5.83*	-5.82*	16.97	7
Log Narnaul	-2.41	-2.95	4.46	3	-6.05*	-6.04*	18.26	2
Sample: 1990-94 to 2002-03								
Log Ambala	-3.82*	-4.42*	10.30	1				
Log Jind	-3.46**	-4.16*	9.19	1				
Log Sonepat	-3.85*	-4.61*	11.27	1				
Log Sirsa	-3.80*	-4.48*	10.35	1				
Log Hodal	-4.05*	-4.44*	10.67	1				
Log Narnaul	-3.20**	-3.87**	8.00	12				

Notes:

(1) * Significant at the 1% Level, ** Significant at the 5% Level.

(2) Critical Values of ADF statistics are—3.73 (1%) and 3.17 (5%) (Engle and Yoo, 1987), critical Value of F test is 6.49 (5%) (Davidson and Mackinnon, 1993, p. 565).

(3) The optimum lag length was determined by Akaike Information Criterion (AIC).

Table 4.4.2: Johansen's Maximum Eigenvalue and Trace Test for the Number of Cointegrating Vectors in Mustard-seed.

Series tested for cointegration	*Null Hypothesis*	*Alternative Hypothesis*	*Eigenvalue*	*Maximum Eigen* (ξ_r)	*Trace* (η_r)	*Order of VAR©*
(Sample: 1979-84 to 1990-93)						
Log Ambala, Log Jind, Intercept	r = 0	r = 1	0.28	42.5*	48.9*	2
	r ≤ 1	r = 2	0.05	6.4	6.4	
Log Ambala, Log Jind, Log Sonepat, Intercept	r = 0	r = 1	0.31	49.9*	95.7*	1
	r ≤ 1	r = 2	0.26	39.3*	45.8*	
	r ≤ 2	r = 3	0.05	6.6	6.6	
Log Ambala, Log Jind, Log Sonepat, Log Sirsa, Intercept	r = 0	r = 1	0.41	69.8*	165.7*	1
	r ≤ 1	r = 2	0.30	46.2*	95.9*	
	r ≤ 2	r = 3	0.28	43.4*	49.7*	
	r ≤ 3	r = 4	0.05	6.4	6.4	
Log Ambala, Log Jind, Log Sonepat, Log Sirsa, Log Narnaul, Intercept	r = 0	r = 1	0.48	87.4*	224.6*	1
	r ≤ 1	r = 2	0.30	47.6*	137.2*	
	r ≤ 2	r = 3	0.29	45.5*	89.6*	
	r ≤ 3	r = 4	0.25	37.9*	44.1*	
	r ≤ 4	r = 5	0.05	6.2	6.2	
Log Ambala, Log Jind, Log Sonepat, Log Sirsa, Log Narnaul, Log Hodal, Intercept	r = 0	r = 1	0.50	90.4*	247.0*	1
	r ≤ 1	r = 2	0.32	51.8*	156.5*	
	r ≤ 2	r = 3	0.30	46.2*	104.8*	
	r ≤ 3	r = 4	0.25	38.7*	58.6*	
	r = 4	r = 5	0.10	13.7	19.8**	
	r ≤ 5	r = 6	0.05	6.1	6.1	

Note:

*(**) denotes rejection of the hypothesis at 5% (10%) significance level.

© Order of VAR is determined by the AIC, SBC and adjusted LR Test.

Table 4.4.3: The Bivariate Coefficients based on Exactly Indentified Cointegrating Vectors between the Selected Mustard-seed Markets.

	Ambala	*Jind*	*Sonepat*	*Sirsa*	*Narnaul*	*Hodal*
	(Sample: 1979-84 to 1990-93)					
Ambala	1.00					
Jind	-0.85 (-16.4)	1.00				
Sonepat	-0.96 (-20.1)	-1.13 (-25.1)	1.00			
Sirsa	-0.93 (-18.3)	-1.10 (-24.7)	-0.97 (-27.3)	1.00		
Narnaul	-0.94 (-15.6)	-1.11 (-19.5)	-0.98 (-19.9)	-1.01 (-24.8)	1.00	
Hodal	-0.90 (-5.2)	-1.06 (-5.0)	-0.94 (-5.4)	-0.97 (-4.9)	-0.96 (-5.1)	1.00

Note: Figures in parentheses are respective 't' values.

Table: 4.4.4: Reduced Form VECM for Mustard-seed (Period 1979-04 to 1990-03).

	ΔLog Ambala	*ΔLog Jind*	*ΔLog Sonepat*	*ΔLog Sirsa*	*ΔLog Narnaul*	*ΔLog Hodal*
ECM	-0.35 (-3.1)	-0.41 (-3.6)	-0.70 (-4.3)	-0.44 (-2.9)	-0.41 (-3.6)	-0.18 (-2.7)
ΔLog Ambala $_{-1}$	0.20 (1.8)	0.01 (0.1)	-0.02 (-0.3)	0.10 (1.0)	-0.03 (-0.3)	-0.01 (-0.1)
ΔLog Jind$_{-1}$	-0.15 (-1.0)	0.05 (0.5)	0.07 (0.6)	-0.10 (-0.8)	0.11 (0.9)	-0.15 (-0.9)
ΔLog Sonepat$_{-1}$	0.22 (1.2)	0.15 (1.0)	0.08 (0.6)	0.20 (1.2)	-0.12 (-0.8)	0.18 (0.9)
ΔLog Sirsa $_{-1}$	-0.03 (-0.2)	-0.22 (-2.0)	-0.07 (-0.7)	-0.18 (-1.5)	0.01 (0.1)	0.01 (0.1)
ΔLog Narnaul $_{-1}$	-0.10 (-1.1)	0.06 (0.7)	0.01 (0.1)	-0.05 (-0.5)	0.13 (1.6)	0.07 (0.7)
ΔLog Hodal $_{-1}$	0.18 (1.4)	0.01 (0.1)	0.05 (0.5)	0.08 (0.7)	-0.09 (-0.8)	0.07 (0.5)
Constant	0.01 (0.9)	0.00 (0.6)	0.00 (0.6)	0.01 (0.7)	0.00 (0.6)	0.01 (0.6)
R^2	0.15	0.21	0.23	0.28	0.34	0.13
R^{-2}	0.07	0.14	0.16	0.21	0.28	0.05
Log Likelihood	138.6	164.2	167.8	149.4	156.7	119.3
D-W	2.03	2.00	1.96	2.03	2.03	1.95
AIC	-1.92	-2.31	-2.36	-2.08	-2.19	-1.63
SBC	-1.66	-2.04	-2.10	-1.82	-1.93	-1.36
LM(12)	1.10	1.04	0.67	1.22	0.91	1.89**
ARCH(12)	0.31	0.52	0.91	2.16**	0.74	0.92
Heteroskedasticity	1.49	2.44*	0.69	2.12*	3.06*	1.15
Reset (Ramsay) (1)	2.80	2.75	2.69	0.70	0.05	1.65

ANNEXURE—4A

MARKET INTEGRATION: THE METHODOLOGY OF COINTEGRATION

Market Integration

The basic rational for the measurement of market integration is to understand the interaction among prices in spatially separated markets. In the extreme case of two markets, A and B being completely segmented, the prices of the same commodity should not be related to each other. If the area where market A is located experiences a bad harvest, prices will suddenly increase. In market B, there is no reason to assume that a bad harvest has also occurred. In the absence of communication flows between the two markets, prices in B would not show any movement. On the other hand, if A and B were integrated, the price in B would also increase. This is because some product would flow from B to A, decreasing the available supply in B. At the same time, the price in A would be lower because of increased supply. Therefore, the co-movement of prices gives an indication of the degree of market integration. Thus integrated markets are defined as markets in which prices of homogeneous products do not behave independently. Independent markets can be studied in a disaggregate manner, while integrated markets may be amenable to aggregate analysis.

The hypothesis that markets are integrated has been traditionally tested using a static price regression as in the equation below:

$$P_{it} = a + b\,P_{jt} + e_t$$

where P_{it} and P_{jt} are the prices in i^{th} and j^{th} markets, respectively, a is the intercept and e_t is the random error term. In this specification, market integration requires the slope of the coefficient to be 1.0 and the constant term to be zero. Using this technique, researchers frequently accepted the hypothesis of market integration. No attention, however, was paid to the properties of the error term e_t, *e.g.*, to the problem of auto-correlation. Unbiasedness property of OLS requires that the error term has no discernible structure whatsoever, otherwise the price in P_j market cannot be said to be able to provide all the information about the price in P_i market. If for example, the error term in the above equation has first order auto-correlation $e_t = \rho e_{t-1} + v_t$ then by substituting it in the above equation, one notices that:

$$P_{it} = a + b\,P_{jt} + \rho e_{t-1} + v_t$$

So that P_{jt} does not incorporate all available information and therefore the two markets cannot be perfectly integrated. Furthermore, Granger and Newbold (1974) have demonstrated that under the presence of the auto-correlated disturbances in the regression analysis of non-stationary variables, the usual significance tests on the coefficients are invalid.

The Methodology of Cointegration[6]

The fundamental insight of the cointegration analysis is that although many economic time series may tend to trend upwards or downwards over time in a non-stationary fashion, groups of variables may drift together. If there is a tendency for some linear relationship to hold between a set of variables over a long period of time, then such relationships are identified with the help of cointegration techniques.

Cointegration tests begin with premise that for a long run equilibrium relationship to exist between two price or any other variables, it is necessary that they have the same inter-temporal characteristics. The first step, therefore, requires testing the stationarity of the variables. Integration tests are a prerequisite for cointegration. To determine the order of integration, one should note that a time series (P_t) is stationary if the joint distribution of P_t and P_{t+T} is independent of time (t), though it does not depend on the lag (the length of which is designated by 'T'). For example, a time series P_t given as:

$$P_t = \mu_t + e_t$$

where e_t is random variable with $E(e_t) = 0$, $E(e_t)^2 = \sigma^2$ and $E(e_t, e_s) = 0$, for $t \neq s$. Note that P_t has constant mean μ and variance σ^2 over time *i.e.*,

$$E(P_t) = \mu \text{ for all values of } t$$
$$V(P_t) = \sigma^2 \text{ for all values of } t.$$

A series, with constant mean and variance is said to be stationary. There is also a weaker definition of stationarity, which is usually sufficient for practical purposes. This exists in a time series when the first and second moments of the joint distribution are independent of time, *i.e.*,

$$E(P_t) = \mu \text{ for all values of } t$$
$$E[(P_t - \mu)(P_{t-T} - \mu)] = \tau(T),\ T = 0, 1, 2, 3, \ldots$$

More formally (P_t) is second order or 'weak' stationary, if the expectation of P_t is a finite constant; the variance is constant and finite; and the co-variance depends only on T.

Consequently, against time, it will fluctuate around a constant mean and the amplitude of fluctuations will not vary with time.

Stationarity is an important aspect of time series analysis. Without stationarity, serious errors can be committed in drawing inferences from the time series data. Note that this problem is one of testing and not of estimation. For illustrative purposes, consider a simple one variable regression model:

$$P_{it} = \alpha + \beta P_{jt} + e_t$$

The Gauss-Markov assumptions require that the error term e_t be white noise, which also implies that it is stationary. Suppose, instead, that e_t was not stationary and, in fact, was a random walk with a drift:

$$e_t = \mu + e_{t-1} + v_t$$

where $\mu > 0$, and v_t is white noise, with mean zero and variance σ^2. First observe that e_t is non-stationary as its mean is not invariant with time. Moreover, by recursive substitution the above equation can be written as:

$$e_t = \mu + [\mu + e_{t-2} + v_{t-1}] + v_t$$

$$= (\mu + \mu + \mu \ldots) + \sum_{i=0}^{\infty} v_{t-i}$$

Taking expectations, $E(e_t) = \infty$ and $var(e_t) = \infty$. Thus, e_t has both, infinite mean and infinite variance. In regression models,

$$\hat{\beta} = \frac{\Sigma (P_{jt}-\bar{P}_j)(P_{it}-\bar{P}_i)}{\Sigma (P_{jt}-\bar{P}_j)^2}$$

$$\hat{\beta} = \frac{\text{Var}(e_t)}{\text{Var } \beta = \quad S (P_{jt}-\bar{P}_j)^2},$$

where the bar over a variable represents its mean. Since e_t has infinite variance, so will the variance of estimated β. Thus, though the estimated β coefficient is highly consistent, the variance of the standard error is not and so making any inferences impossible from such time series regression analysis.

Any series, which grows over time is non-stationary, since its mean is growing over time, regardless of the behaviour of its variance. Most of the macro-economic variables are trended, and therefore, tend to be non-stationary, which can have profound implications. For example, if a structural variable, like real output, is truly mean and variance non-stationary, shock to that will have permanent real effects. One way of guaranteeing that (P_t) is stationary is to say that it is integrated of order zero [denoted $P_t \sim I(0)$]. More generally it can be said that P_t is integrated of order n [usually written: $P_t \sim I(n)$] if $\Delta^n P_t \sim I(0)$. The Box-Jenkins methodology repeatedly differences the series to get the series stationary. If the new series, constructed by first difference of the original series, does not look stationary, then the first difference series is differenced again. If the first difference of a series is stationary, the series is said to be integrated of order one *i.e.*, $P_t \sim I(1)$.

The scheduled procedure for determining the order of integration of a time series is the 'Augmented Dickey-Fuller (ADF) Test' (Dickey and Fuller, 1979). This test requires regressing ΔP_{it} on a constant, P_{it-1} and several lags of ΔP_{it} (enough to avoid auto-correlated disturbances), *i.e.*,

$$\Delta P_{it} = \alpha + \beta P_{it-1} + \sum_{k=1}^{M} \delta_k \Delta P_{it-k} + e_{it}$$

The t statistic of the estimated coefficient of P_{it-1} is used to test the following null and alternative hypotheses:

$$H_o: P_{it} \sim I(1) \text{ Vs. } H_1: P_{it} \sim I(0)$$

The critical values will be negative and larger than standard critical t values. So, they are called 'ADF Statistics' rather than t statistics and are available in Engle and Yoo (1987), Fuller (1976) and in Mackinnon (1990). If the null hypothesis set out above cannot be rejected then P_{it} cannot be stationary and it may be I(1) or I(2) or have an even higher order of integration. To find out the order of integration, the test is repeated with ΔP_{it} in place of P_{it}. Thus, regressing $\Delta^2 P_{it}$ on a constant, ΔP_{it-1} and several lags of $\Delta^2 P_{it}$ *i.e.*,

$$\Delta^2 P_{it} = \alpha + \beta \Delta P_{it-1} + \sum_{k=1}^{M} \delta_k \Delta^2 P_{it-k} + e_{it}$$

The ADF statistics therefore tests the following:

$$H_0: \Delta P_{it} \sim I(1) \text{ vs } H_1: \Delta P_{it} \sim I(0)$$

i.e., $H_0: P_{it} \sim I(2) \text{ vs } H_1: P_{it} \sim I(1)$

If the ADF statistic is not large and negative, H_0 cannot be rejected and P_{it} cannot be I(1). In that case, the test is repeated with $\Delta^3 P_{it}$ as the dependent variable and so on, until the order of integration is determined.

The lagged terms in P_{it} are included purely to avoid auto-correlated disturbances. Without these, the t statistic on P_{it-1} would be the 'ordinary' rather than the 'Augmented' Dickey-Fuller test, known as DF test. Consider the regression equation,

$$P_{it} = \rho P_{it-1} + e_t$$

where e_t is a classical error term. It is assumed without loss of generality that $\rho>0$. This is well known auto-regressive AR(1) Model, which is stationary if and only if $|\rho|<1$ and since,

$$V(P_{it}) = \frac{d^2}{(1-\rho)^2}$$

must be non-negative, the only other possibility is that $|\rho| = 1$. When at the extreme $\rho = 1$, P_{it} is a random walk, which is I(1) and contains a unit root. For this reason, the Dickey- Fuller Test procedure is also known as a test for a unit root[7]. Subtracting P_{it-1} from both sides and rearranging gives the following equation:

$$\Delta P_{it} = (\rho-1) P_{it-1} + e_t$$

which is Dickey Fuller regression, assuming $\rho>0$. The null hypothesis $P_{it} \sim I(1)$ is now equivalent to the coefficient on P_{it-1} in the D-F regression being zero and so for the I(0) process one can have a one-sided alternative that the coefficient on P_{it-1} is significantly less than zero for P_{it} to be stationary.

After identifying the time series properties (*i.e.* the order of integration) of individual price series, the next step is to test for cointegration between them. It is already pointed out that when the two series are cointegrated, they are tied together in some way even though they are trending. The theory of cointegration is based on the idea that although two-time series, say P_{it} and P_{jt} are integrated (non-stationary), their difference or some other linear combination of them is stationary. Price integration, therefore, means a long run relationship between the two price series after transient effects from all other factors, such as local characteristics, have disappeared.

To see whether two variables are cointegrated, the Engle-Granger 'two step' procedure is followed (Engle and Granger 1987). The first step involves cointegration of the two time series, say P_{it} and P_{jt} which are of the same order of integration, say I(1) and there is some linear combination of these which is I(0). This is called cointegration of order (1,1) and in this case, the cointegrating vector is the vector of coefficients of a linear combination of the series, which is stationary. The relationship between two price series can be expressed in terms of,

$$P_{it} = a + b\, P_{jt} + e_t$$

where e_t is the deviation from equilibrium and this equilibrium error in the long run tends to zero (*i.e.* its mean is zero with finite variance) and b is the cointegrating coefficient. This equilibrium error of the cointegration equation has to be stationary for cointegration between two integrated variables to hold good.

The second step involves the dynamic error-correction representation of the cointegrated variables. If two variables are integrated of the same order and thus can be cointegrated, then according to Engle and Granger two-step procedure, there exists an error-correction representation of the variables where the error corrects the long run equilibrium. This is also known as Granger Representation Theorem (Engle and Granger 1987; Banerjee *et al*. 1993). The dynamic model is obtained by introducing the residuals into the system of variables in levels. This is represented by,

$$\Delta P_{it} = \alpha_o + \alpha_1 \ \Delta P_{jt} + \beta(P_i - b\,P_j)_{t-1} + \sum_{k=1}^{M} (\delta_{1k} \ \Delta P_{it-k} + \delta_{2k} \ \Delta P_{jt-k}) + e_{it}$$

It is evident from the above equation that the disequilibrium in the previous period (t–1) is an explanatory variable. Here it can be said that if in period (t–1), P_{it} exceeds the equilibrium price, the change in P_{it} will lead the variable to approach the equilibrium value. Hence, the expected sign of β will be negative. The speed at which the price approaches equilibrium depends on the proximity of β to –1. The term $\alpha_1 \ \Delta P_{jt}$ expresses the variation in P_{it} associated with P_{jt} and is considered to be the immediate or short run effect.

However, the cointegration technique using the Augumented Dickey-Fuller procedure suggested by Engle and Granger to test the null hypothesis of no cointegration of prices is open to a number of criticisms. First, the distribution of the test statistics is not invariant with respect to the nuisance parameter and therefore the critical value given in Engle and Granger can be taken only as a rough guide. Second, the procedure of considering pairs of markets ignores any linkages, which might operate through a third market. Third, more than one long run relationships cannot be captured by the Dickey-Fuller procedure. Fourth, the tests for identifying the driving forces in the two markets ignore the possible existence of multiple common trends, which would imply multiple dominant markets. Finally, given a prior that markets are in fact integrated, it is preferable to test the null hypothesis that prices are cointegrated.

A better and powerful test for cointegration presented by Johansen (1988) is the maximum likelihood procedure 'multiple cointegration test' which overcomes the problems of Engle-Granger. This technique is particularly important when testing for cointegration between more than two variables. It also permits us for testing for the validity of any restriction on cointegrating relationships implied by economic theory[8]. The further advantage of this procedure is that when there are 'n' price series and (n–1) potential cointegrating relationships, it first tests the null of zero cointegrating relationships. If that is rejected, it then tests the null that there is only one cointegrating relationship, and if that is also rejected it goes for two, three ... up to (n–1) cointegrating relationships. Thus, in this method existence of the number of cointegraing relationships is decided within the procedure itself. Similarly, it also allows us to find out what are the variables which are endogenous and the ones which are exogenous in the system through the 'error-correction procedure.' Because of these reasons the Johansen procedure has been used to test for price integration in the present case.

APPENDIX—4.1A

ML estimates subject to exactly identifying restriction(s)
Estimates of Restricted Cointegrating Relations, Converged after 2 iterations
Cointegration with restricted intercepts and no trends in the VAR

132 observations from 1979M4 to 1990M3. Order of VAR=1, chosen r =8.

List of variables included in the cointegrating vector:

LAMBL	LKTL	LKNL	LJND	LSNPT
LNRWN	LSRS	LHDL	LNRNL	Intercept

List of imposed restriction(s) on cointegrating vectors:

a1=1; a2=0; a3=0; a4=0; a5=0; a6=0; a7=0; a8=0; b1=0; b2=1; b3=0; b4=0; b5=0; b6=0; b7=0; b 8=0; c1=0; c2=0; c3=1; c4=0; c5=0; c6=0; c7=0; c8=0; d1=0; d2=0; d3=0; d4=1; d5=0; d6=0; d7=0; d8=0; e1=0; e2=0; e3=0; e4=0; e5=1; e6=0; e7=0; e8=0; f1=0; f2=0; f3=0; f4=0; f5=0; f6=1; f7=0; f8=0; g1=0; g2=0; g3=0; g4=0; g5=0; g6=0; g7=1; g8=0; h1=0; h2=0; h3=0; h4= 0; h5=0; h6=0; h7=0; h8=1;

	Vector 1	Vector 2	Vector 3	Vector 4	Vector 5	Vector 6	Vector 7	Vector 8
LAMBL	1	0	0	0	0	0	0	0
LKTL	0	1	0	0	0	0	0	0
LKNL	0	0	1	0	0	0	0	0
LJND	0	0	0	1	0	0	0	0
LSNPT	0	0	0	0	1	0	0	0
LNRWN	0	0	0	0	0	1	0	0
LSRS	0	0	0	0	0	0	1	0
LHDL	0	0	0	0	0	0	0	1
LNRNL	-0.96	-1.01	-1.00	-0.99	-0.97	-1.05	-0.96	-0.96
Intercept	-0.19	0.11	0.05	-0.02	-0.16	0.35	-0.15	-0.14

LL subject to exactly identifying restrictions = 1919.9

NOTES

1. Price integration has been tested using the simple bivariate model, see, *e.g.*, Jasdanwalla (1966), Cummings (1967), Lele (1971), Jones (1968, 1972), Subbarao (1978), Southworth, Jones and Pearson (1979), Kainth (1982), Stigler and Sherwin (1985), Neal (1987).
2. This bivariate approach has been severely criticized, see *e.g.* Blyn (1973), Granger and Newbold (1974), Harriss (1979), Timmer (1974, 1984), Boyd and Brorsen (1986), Heytens (1986), Ravallion (1986), Dercon (1995), Barrett (1996).
3. For details of the Johansen procedure, see Asche, Bremnes and Wessels (1999 and 2001) and Goodwin and Piggott (2001).
4. The trend price is not used to fill the gap in order to avoid the imposed trend or non-stationarity into the data.
5. Ravallion (1986) suggested that unit prices better reflect the nature of transport and other costs. However, as pointed by Lloyd and Rayner (1993), the inclusion of relative prices in a linear regression requires regressing logs on logs. In fact, there should be little difference empirically whichever is used, except the way in which we interpret the coefficients.
6. For recent discussion of this issue, see Monke and Petzel (1984), Uri and Lin (1992), Alderman (1993), Ardeni (1989), Dries and Unnevehr (1990), Faminow and Benson (1990), Ravallion (1986), Sexton *et al.* (1991), Goodwin and Schroeder (1991), Palaskas and Harriss (1993), Alexander and Wyeth (1994), Sinharoy and Nair (1994), Goletti and Babu (1994), Diakosavvas (1995).
7. Nelson and Plosser (1982) showed that a lot of macro-economic variables, which seem to be trended, are actually better characterized as processes containing unit roots.
8. See Muscatelli and Hurn (1992) for a comparison of the Johansen procedure with the Engle and Granger approach.

5

Economic Profile and Production Structure of the Respondents

Market efficiency in agriculture to an extent depends on the attitude of farmers towards the market. As marketing starts right from the decision to produce a commodity, it is appropriate therefore to look into the economic profile of the farmers selected for the study before examining any related marketing aspects. Production on the farm constitutes the basis of the farmer's marketable or marketed surplus. Hence, an analysis of the production structure of the households surveyed would be of great help in an understanding of the marketed surplus and the marketing efficiency of households as analyzed in the next two chapters.

Household Characteristics

The four hundred households surveyed in the study were divided into five sub-categories on the basis of the net operated area as discussed in the first chapter. Table 5.1 shows that there was a direct relationship between farm size and family size. Family size rose from 5.0 members in case of marginal farmers to 11.2 members in case of large farmers, thus giving an average family size of 7.2 members. Due to the prevalence of the joint family system among the large farmers, their family size was generally higher. On the other hand, small farmers had a nuclear family system, resulting into a smaller family size.

Distribution of Land Holdings

Table 5.1 shows the inequality in the distribution of land holdings among the cultivators. Out of the operated area of the households surveyed, large farmers defined as those operating more than 25 acres of land, constituted only 10 per cent of the households in our sample, and accounted for as high as 38 per cent of the area. On the other hand, marginal farmers constituting 24 per cent of the holdings had only 4 per cent of the total operated area. Looking at the relative distribution of land among farmers, one finds that cultivators having above 10 acres, constituted 28 per cent of the holdings and had 68 per cent of operated area. Those having less than 10 acres at the bottom constituted the remaining 72 per cent of holdings and had only 32 per cent of the operated area. Table 5.2 shows the distribution of owned and operated area across different farm size classes. It is discernible from the

Table 5.1: Household Characteristics.

Farm Size	*Kaithal*			*Sirsa*			*Total*		
	No of households	*Household size*	*%age of area operated*	*No of households*	*Household size*	*%age of area operated*	*No of households*	*Household size*	*%age of area operated*
Marginal	48 (24.1)	5.3	4.0	48 (23.9)	4.7	3.7	96 (24.0)	5.0	3.9
Small	47 (23.6)	6.5	9.7	48 (23.9)	5.9	9.6	95 (23.8)	6.2	9.6
Semi-medium	48 (24.1)	7.5	19.7	48 (23.9)	6.7	17.8	96 (24.0)	7.1	18.7
Medium	38 (19.1)	10.1	30.5	36 (17.9)	8.1	29.7	74 (18.5)	9.1	30.1
Large	18 (9.0)	8.8	36.2	21 (10.4)	13.2	39.2	39 (9.7)	11.2	37.8
Total	199 (100)	7.4	100.0	201 (100)	7.0	100.0	400 (100)	7.2	100.0

Note: Figures in parentheses are percentage of total households.

table that for total households the net operated area exceeded owned cultivated area for all size classes of farmers. It indicates that the leased in land exceeded leased out land for all the categories. Table 5.2 also shows this, as net leased in land (*i.e.*, land leased in minus land leased out) for total households was positive for all the farmers. Looking at the net leased in area across the various farm sizes, it is observed that the net leased in area rose with the rise in farm size. On an average, the net area leased in was only 0.04 acres in the case of marginal farmers, while it was 5.36 acres in case of large farmers. It is probable that as large farmers had farm assets like tractor, trolley, harvester, etc., leasing in provided them with the optimal land size to utilize these existing implements to achieve economies of scale.

Irrigation

Table 5.2 shows irrigated and unirrigated area by farm size classes. It is evident from the table that the percentage of irrigated area to net operated area of marginal and small farmers was comparable with that of medium and large farmers, on account of the institutional loans for tubewells provided by banks and cooperative societies. In some cases where small farmers did not have this facility, they generally hired it from the neighbouring farmers. However, Kaithal being predominantly a tubewell irrigated area had 97 per cent of operated area irrigated, whereas Sirsa, which was predominantly canal irrigated, had 73 per cent operated area irrigated. The relative difference in the level of irrigation was reflected in the cropping pattern of these two regions. In the kharif season, Kaithal was dominated by the paddy crop, which needs assured irrigation, while cotton, which is less water prone when compared to paddy was grown in the Sirsa district in the kharif season.

Table 5.2: Land details per household (Acres).

Farm Size	*Owned area*	*Owned cultivated area**	*Net area leased in***	*Net operated area*	*Gross cropped area*	*Cropping intensity*	*Irrigated area*	*Unirri-gated area*
				Kaithal				
Marginal	1.71	1.71	-0.10	1.61	3.31	2.06	1.49 (92.9)	0.11
Small	4.04	4.04	-0.04	3.99	7.94	1.99	3.70 (92.8)	0.29
Semi-medium	5.44	4.81	2.55	7.93	15.90	2.00	7.66 (96.6)	0.27
Medium	12.79	12.79	2.71	15.50	30.17	1.95	15.16 (97.8)	0.34
Large	36.03	36.03	2.83	38.86	73.78	1.90	38.53 (99.1)	0.33
Total	8.38	8.36	1.34	9.72	18.94	1.95	9.46 (97.4)	0.26
				Sirsa				
Marginal	1.74	1.44	0.20	1.69	2.82	1.67	1.16 (68.5)	0.53
Small	4.46	3.96	0.46	4.33	7.60	1.75	3.30 (76.1)	1.04
Semi-medium	6.26	5.97	2.29	8.06	13.82	1.72	6.09 (75.6)	1.96
Medium	15.03	14.07	3.81	17.89	28.90	1.62	11.82 (66.1)	6.07
Large	37.14	32.93	7.52	40.45	66.68	1.65	31.50 (77.9)	8.95
Total	9.55	8.68	2.17	10.79	17.93	1.66	7.93 (73.4)	2.87
				Total				
Marginal	1.73	1.58	0.04	1.65	3.07	1.86	1.33 (80.4)	0.32
Small	4.25	4.00	0.21	4.16	7.77	1.87	3.50 (84.0)	0.67
Semi-medium	5.85	5.67	2.42	7.99	14.86	1.86	6.88 (86.0)	1.12
Medium	13.88	13.41	3.25	16.66	29.55	1.77	13.53 (81.2)	3.13
Large	36.63	34.36	5.36	39.72	69.96	1.76	34.74 (87.5)	4.97
Total	8.97	8.52	1.76	10.26	18.44	1.80	8.69 (84.7)	1.57

Notes: Figures in parentheses are percentage of net operated area.
*Own cultivated area = Owned area—uncultivated area.
**Net area leased in = Area leased in—Area leased out.

Cropping Pattern

The cropping pattern of the households surveyed is presented in Table 5.3. The point to be noted from the table is that the two districts did not differ much in case of rabi crops as wheat was the main rabi crop of both the regions. However, paddy was the main kharif crop of Kaithal district and cotton was the main kharif crop of Sirsa district. The table presents the cropping pattern of all the 400 households clubbed together.

Krishna Bharadwaj (1974) using farm management data for the mid-fifties concluded in her study, 'The very small farmers who are compulsively involved in markets tend to

Table 5.3: Cropping pattern of all the households (Percentage of gross cropped area).

Farm size	*Wheat*	*Paddy*	*Coarse grains*	*Pulses*	*Oilseeds*	*Cotton lint*	*Fodder and other crops*
Marginal	38.3	13.3	1.5	5.6	6.0	14.4	20.9
Small	38.1	12.6	2.9	3.0	4.2	16.8	22.4
Semi-medium	42.7	16.5	2.7	5.4	5.1	14.3	13.3
Medium	39.4	16.7	3.1	6.2	6.4	16.6	11.6
Large	34.3	21.3	3.8	7.1	5.5	14.9	13.1
Total	38.0	17.8	3.2	6.0	5.6	15.4	14.0

devote a higher proportion of their area to cash crops while the small farmers who can to some extent protect themselves from markets tend to produce predominantly subsistence crops. The middle cultivators, who can secure some surplus over subsistence, appear to produce a variety of crops including crops of high value requiring careful management (vegetables), while big farmers in the better irrigated areas like Punjab and Uttar Pradesh devote a considerable proportion of their area to high value cash crops'. The production and market conditions have undergone a complete change over the years leading to permanent changes in the cropping pattern too. From the table, it is implicit that the size-specific constraints of the types suggested by Bharadwaj are out of the question now. The 'distress cropping pattern' pursued by marginal farmers mentioned in her study was nowhere in sight. Marginal and small farmers participated in the market as equally as did large farmers.

The most important crop of the region was wheat, which alone occupied 38 per cent of the gross cropped area. Among the kharif crops, paddy and cotton were the main crops of the two regions, respectively, each covering around one-sixth of the gross cropped area. Other crops like oilseeds, pulses and coarse cereals were less important in terms of area devoted. In addition to these crops, a few cultivators also grew sugar-cane and some vegetables. However, their proportion being negligible, these are included in the other crops (along with fodder crops). Fodder crops (kharif and rabi) accounted for 14 per cent of gross cropped area and constituted another important crop of the region.

Table 5.3 reveals that barring paddy and fodder crops the percentage of all other crops remained more or less constant across different farm size classes. In the case of paddy and fodder, one finds that marginal and small farmers devoted a higher percentage of their area to fodder crops compared to other categories of farmers and a lesser percentage of area to paddy. The reason for low rice cultivation seems to be that rice cultivation requires the ownership of an assured means of irrigation like the pump set and tubewells in which case small and marginal farmers though as equally competent as large farmers did not own these resources unlike the large farmers. Both small as well as large farmers tried to supplement their income by dairying and livestock and therefore, a significant proportion of their area was devoted to fodder crops. However, small farmers were relatively more dependent on this source of income and so devoted a comparatively higher area to fodder crops than did the large farmers.

Borrowing

Liberal institutional finance, an important element for development, put to productive uses can strengthen the overall economic position of the borrowers. The vast literature available on rural development indicates not only the short supply of funds but also the irregular flow of liquidity to the target groups. There are also reports that suggest that the funds were usurped by the well to do, and this was also experienced by the author during the field survey as a common allegation or complaint by the small cultivators.

Table 5.4 puts forward the household borrowing position. It is evidently clear from the table that the loan needs of large farmers were much higher than that of small farmers. The loan per household by marginal farmers was calculated as only Rs. 5,171 compared to Rs. 80,659 by large farmers. However, analysing per acre loans by different farm size categories, one observes that an inverse relationship with farm size was discernible. The point to be highlighted from the table is that institutional loans were also accessible to marginal and small farmers, although its absolute amount was much lower compared to the large and medium farmers.

Table 5.4: Per household Borrowing (Rs.).

Farm Size	*Kaithal*			*Sirsa*			*Total*		
	Institutional loans	*Non-institutional loans*	*Total loans per acre*	*Institutional loans*	*Non-institutional loans*	*Total loans per acre*	*Institutional loans*	*Non-institutional loans*	*Total loans per acre*
Marginal	3848 (76.4)	1188	3129	3056 (57.6)	2250	3144	3452 (66.8)	1719	3137
Small	6574 (58.9)	4596	2800	3048 (20.6)	11729	3410	4793 (36.9)	8200	3121
Semi-medium	1698 (65.0)	5750	2075	9620 (33.5)	19125	3568	10159 (45.0)	12438	2827
Medium	21213 (56.5)	16342	2423	4764 (13.8)	29806	1932	13211 (36.6)	22892	2167
Large	46407 (68.9)	21111	1745	37619 (41.1)	54048	2266	41813 (51.8)	38846	2031
Total	13337 (63.1)	7789	2174	8539 (31.1)	18891	2542	10926 (45.0)	13368	2368

Note: Figures in parentheses are percentage of total loans per household.

Assets

Table 5.5 presents group wise data on assets other than land holdings which include—farm machinery and equipment, *viz.*, tractor, harvester, pump set, engine, bullock cart, trolley, etc., and buildings used for keeping livestock and grains. As expected, there seems to be a positive relationship between per household assets and farm size. A similar relationship was observed between the farm size and investment made for the storage purpose - which includes bins, *kachha kothas, pucca kothies*, steel drums, godowns, etc. Storage investment as a percentage of assets declined with the rise in farm size indicating that with the rise in farm size storage investment rises far less proportionately than the rise in farm assets. This is because in the regions surveyed, large farmers, *vis-à-vis* small farmers stored grains generally for the consumption purpose only (as will be seen in the next chapters). Therefore, large farmers did not spend a higher amount on storage investment.

Table 5.5: Storage investment and assets* other than land (Rs. per household).

Farm Size	*Kaithal*			*Sirsa*			*Total*		
	Storage investment	*Assets*	*SI as a percentage of assets*	*Storage investment*	*Assets*	*SI as a percentage of assets*	*Storage investment*	*Assets*	*SI as a percentage of assets me*
Marginal	5499	25029	22.0	4267	10731	39.8	4883	17880	27.3
Small	8045	50838	15.8	6288	21008	29.9	7157	35776	20.0
Semi-medium	11010	64927	17.0	7013	51217	13.7	9011	58072	15.5
Medium	16758	170232	9.8	11472	112208	10.2	14186	142004	10.0
Large	20611	370114	5.6	19374	256890	7.5	19945	309147	6.5
Total	10946	99689	11.0	8274	66747	12.4	9604	83136	11.5

Note: *Assets include buildings used for livestock and grain keeping, farm machines and equipments and livestock used for cultivation and transportation (carts etc.).

Inputs Use

Tables 5.6 and 5.7 present the composition of material and other costs of production by various farm size categories. Material cost comprises the cost of inputs other than leasing in land and labour cost. Economies of scale in farming are evident from the tables as per acre material cost fell with the rise in farm size in both the regions. These economies of scale were realized because some factors of production like bullocks, tractor, thresher and tubewell were indivisible and small farmers were not able to use these factors as efficiently as large farmers on account of their adverse land area. Other items of material cost like seed, manure, fertilizer, pesticide and implements repair did not have such indivisibilities and didn't pose any such economies of scale as depicted by Table 5.6.

The break up of the percentage value of different farm inputs is given in Table 5.7 (total of Sirsa and Kaithal). The single largest item of total cost was manure and fertilizer, which accounted for one-fifth of total expenditure. Next to fertilizer was the cost of paid-out labour. These two factors together accounted for 35 per cent of the total cost. The other major items of total costs were leased in land, irrigation, tractor hired/diesel charges of owned tractor, pesticides and insecticides and seeds, respectively according to their percentage contribution. The item of least cost were threshing and transportation. It is to be mentioned that only the hired charges of threshing and transportation were included.

Comparing across various farm sizes, it is observed that bullock maintenance comprised a major item in the cost of production of the marginal farmers. It accounted for 14.7 per cent of their total cost against 2.3 per cent of large farmers. In the case of marginal farmers, under utilization of bullocks is

Table 5.6: Input cost per acre of operated area (Rs).

Kaithal						
Name of the Input	*Marginal*	*Small*	*Semi-medium*	*Medium*	*Large*	*Total*
Seed	331	315	335	320	309	319
Manure & fertiliser	1641	1190	1232	1187	1398	1290
Pesticides & insect.	255	317	370	382	426	384
Irrigation charges	1141	1034	909	739	549	749
Maintenance of bullocks	1213	709	443	255	63	305
Tractor hired (oil charges for own tractor)	645	584	561	648	684	638
Implements repair	189	369	351	491	500	443
Thresher and transportation (hired only)	386	403	376	190	68	211
Total material cost	5801	4923	4577	4213	3998	4339
Paid out labour cost	340	504	830	1198	1690	1202
Leasing-in cost	493	483	1387	1046	390	799
Total cost	6634	5909	6795	6457	6077	6340
Gross value added	2994	3361	3816	5447	7636	5617
Farm business income (FBI)	2160	2374	1598	3203	5556	3616
Sirsa						
Seed	308	294	292	283	507	374
Manure & fertiliser	711	798	821	708	725	744
Pesticides & insect.	484	607	607	554	519	552
Irrigation charges	924	746	749	541	427	567
Maintenance of bullocks	377	500	376	174	167	246
Tractor hired (oil charges for own tractor)	610	555	530	471	443	484
Implements repair	30	60	226	287	211	215
Thresher and transportation (hired only)	242	278	227	231	119	191
Total material cost	3685	3838	3827	3249	3119	3374
Paid out labour cost	31	239	481	622	907	650
Leasing-in cost	417	482	960	599	671	674
Total cost	4133	4559	5268	4469	4697	4697
Gross value added	1900	1137	2087	2472	2952	2442
Farm business income (FBI)	1453	415	646	1251	1373	1118
Total						
Seed	319	304	313	301	418	348
Manure & fertiliser	1165	984	1025	937	1029	1001
Pesticides & insect.	372	470	489	472	477	473
Irrigation charges	1030	883	828	636	482	653
Maintenance of bullocks	785	599	410	213	120	274
Tractor hired (oil charges for own tractor)	627	569	545	556	552	556
Implements repair	108	207	288	385	342	323
Thresher and transportation (hired only)	312	337	301	211	96	200
Total material cost	4718	4352	4199	3709	3516	3829
Paid out labour cost	182	365	654	897	1261	910
Leasing-in cost	454	482	1172	812	544	733
Total cost	5354	5199	6025	5419	5320	5471
Gross value added	2434	2191	2944	3893	5067	3938
Farm business income (FBI)	1798	1344	1118	2184	3262	2296

Table 5.7: Percentage of input cost of total households (%).

Name of the input	*Marginal*	*Small*	*Semi-medium*	*Medium*	*Large*	*Total*
Seed	6.0	5.8	5.2	5.6	7.8	6.4
Manure & fertilizer	21.8	18.9	17.0	17.3	19.3	18.3
Pesticides & insect.	6.9	9.0	8.1	8.7	9.0	8.6
Irrigation charges	19.2	17.0	13.7	11.7	9.1	11.9
Maintenance of bullocks	14.7	11.5	6.8	3.9	2.3	5.0
Tractor hired (oil charges for own tractor)	11.7	10.9	9.1	10.3	10.4	10.2
Implements repair	2.0	4.0	4.8	7.1	6.4	5.9
Thresher and transportation (hired only)	5.8	6.5	5.0	3.9	1.8	3.7
Total material cost	88.1	83.7	69.7	68.5	66.1	70.0
Paid out labour cost	3.4	7.0	10.9	16.6	23.7	16.6
Leasing-in cost	8.5	9.3	19.4	15.0	10.2	13.4
Total cost	100	100	100	100	100	100

evident from the table, as despite the high bullock maintenance costs, these farmers also paid a substantial amount for hiring tractors. To take advantage of multiple cropping, these farmers hired a tractor for quick sowing, but kept bullocks as a standby (and for transportation purpose). Out of the total cost, paid out labour cost was only 3.4 per cent in case of marginal farmers but significantly high of 23.7 per cent in case of large farmers. This is due to the higher use of family labour by small and marginal farmers and hired labour by the large farmers (see Appendix Table 5.1A).

Thus, an examination of cost structure shows that the higher proportion of cost contributed by fertilizer, pesticides, irrigation and tractor, points to the importance of bio-technology and mechanical technology in the state's agriculture. Moreover, the constituents of new technology, namely, HYV seeds, chemical fertilizers, pesticides, irrigation and tractor are being utilized by all size of farms, showing no significant differences.

Output and Income

Gross farm output is a function of the area sown and yield rate per unit of area. Table 5.8 shows the value of gross output, value added and farm business income, per household per acre and per capita. Per household value of all these three variables rose with the rise in farm size. Output per acre, on the other hand, fell from marginal to small farmers and rose in the category of medium and large farmers, and thereby clearly ruled out the famous inference of inverse farm size productivity relationship.

The value added in the production process was derived by deducting the value of total material cost from gross value of output. In our calculations no provision was made for

Table 5.8: Gross farm output* and income (Rs.).

Name of the input	*Marginal*	*Small*	*Semi-medium*	*Medium*	*Large*	*Total*
		Kaithal				
Output per household	14153	33047	66530	149735	452080	96751
Output per acre	8794	8284	8393	9660	11633	9956
Gross value added per household	4818	13408	30246	84427	296732	54586
Gross value added per acre	2994	3361	3816	5447	7636	5617
FBI per household	3476	9472	12666	49648	215927	35142
FBI per acre	2160	2374	1598	3203	5556	3616
FBI per capita	654	1460	1679	4913	24599	4777
		Sirsa				
Output per household	9426	21557	47650	102328	245566	62762
Output per acre	5586	4975	5914	5720	6071	5815
Gross value added per household	3207	4925	16812	44214	119409	26351
Gross value added per acre	1900	1137	2087	2472	2952	2442
FBI per household	2452	1800	5201	22379	55551	12069
FBI per acre	1453	415	646	1251	1373	1118
FBI per capita	523	304	775	2759	4196	1732
		Total				
Output per household	11790	27242	57090	126672	340880	79672
Output per acre	7152	6544	7143	7602	8583	7767
Gross value added per household	4012	9122	23529	64864	201250	40398
Gross value added per acre	2434	2191	2944	3893	5067	3938
FBI per household	2964	5596	8933	36382	129570	23548
FBI per acre	1798/	1344	1117	2184	3262	2296
FBI per capita	593	903	1254	3983	11590	3288

Note: * Gross farm output implies Gross Value of Output including imputed value of fodder crops and by-products.

depreciation and therefore all income and its related concepts are in gross terms. As material cost per acre was inversely related with farm size, value added per acre attributes a direct relationship with farm size, thereby showing a higher profitability for the large holdings in farming activities.

Farm Business Income (FBI) was calculated by deducting from the gross value of output, the total cost including the cost of hired labour and of leasing in land. However, no imputed value of owned labour as well as owned land and depreciation for capital was included in this analysis and therefore, they are not deducted from gross output to calculate FBI. Like gross output, FBI per acre also fell with the rise in farm size in the beginning but increased for medium and large farmers. FBI per capita, however, rose consistently and rapidly with the rise in farm size, thereby indicating unequal distribution of income across different farm size categories.

Summing up the discussion, there was a direct relationship between farm size and family size. While all size holdings had a tendency to lease in land, large farmers proportionately leased in more land as compared to small and marginal farmers. Although, many crops were grown in the two districts but wheat, paddy and cotton were the main crops grown by all sizes of farmers. There was an increasing use of constituents of modern technology, *i.e.* fertilizer, pesticides, irrigation and tractor by all size of holdings. Among the farm sizes, bullocks, maintenance constituted a major item of cost for small and marginal farmers, while paid out labour cost was significantly higher for large and medium farmers. Institutional loans were accessible to large as well as small farmers but their per household amount far exceeded in case of large farmers compared to marginal and small farmers. Finally, inverse farm size productivity relationship was not observed in the analysis of output.

APPENDIX

Table 5.1A: Total family labour days (per acre).

Farm size	*Kaithal*	*Sirsa*	*Total*
Marginal	78	41	59
Small	64	35	49
Semi-medium	45	30	38
Medium	41	27	34
Large	24	15	19
Total	40	24	32

6

Farm Size and Marketed Surplus Crop-wise Analysis

I

Increasing market surplus in an economy is one of the significant indices of economic development. Surplus from agriculture has been used as a lever for promoting industrialization in almost all the developed countries. Maurice Dobb (1955) has rightly observed, "In the first place there is reason to suppose that it will be the marketed surplus of agriculture which plays the crucial role in underdeveloped countries in setting the limits to the possible rate of industrialization, and that this marketed surplus does not rise automatically as a result of an increase in productivity". Marketed surplus in the agricultural sector is important in the following ways: First, it would contribute to the much needed capital formation in agriculture and would generate additional income in farming occupations. Second, it would enable the generation of capital formation in the non-agricultural sector and thus, repudiate the process of industrialization. Third, it would help in relocating labour force from the agricultural sector to non-agricultural sector by increasing the availability of food at affordable prices. Fourth, it would contribute to an improved standard of living in the vast rural population engaged in agriculture and would make it possible for them to purchase industrial consumer goods. Last, it would also result in the improvement of agricultural marketing via better transportation, storage and sale facilities.

The increase of production in agriculture is a pre-requisite for increasing market surplus. However, increase in production would not lead to an automatic increase in the market surplus. Along with increased production, distribution of foodgrains may thus be an equally important aspect for developing economies (Bansil 1961). This relationship between production and distribution is of great importance to government for creating adequate market infrastructure. In this context, Ruttan and Hayami (1971) have shown that if a simultaneous increase in marketing services is not ensured, disequilibrium between demand and supply for marketing services may arise. This disequilibrium can create serious problems in the smooth functioning of the marketing system. Any interruption in the supply of market surplus will constitute a fundamental limiting factor in the tempo of development by reducing the supplies necessary as a source of funds for capital formation and for increasing foreign exchange earnings through the export of surplus produce.

Marketable and Marketed Surplus

Often 'Marketable Surplus' and 'Marketed Surplus' are used as synonyms. The two terms, however, are different in economic literature and theoretically cannot be used interchangeably. According to Moore *et al.* (1973, Chapter 3),

> "Marketable surplus is the residual left with the producer after meeting his requirements for family consumption, farm needs and payment-in-kind to casual and permanent labour, the landlord, artisans and others. Marketed surplus is the quantity of produce the producer actually sells irrespective of his needs for home consumption and other requirements."

In case of marketable surplus, there is a need to ascertain whether the farm household has produced the output in excess of all its compulsory retentions. In fact, this is the 'real surplus' generated on the farm. Marketed surplus, on the other hand, does not take into account the kind disposal patterns of the farm households. It thus includes the distress grains, which are sold by the farmer under the pressure of immediate cash needs. He may have to later repurchase some of the same product from the market to meet his domestic needs.

In a situation where there are no distress sales, the marketable surplus and marketed surplus might be equal. In a nutshell, the marketable surplus may be termed as an *ex-ante* concept referring to the surplus planned to be marketed and marketed surplus can be an *ex-post* concept referring to the actual amount marketed during a certain period. In view of the inherent difficulties in precisely estimating the real surplus of farm households, studies in the past have relied on the estimates of marketed surplus rather than on the estimates of marketable surplus. In order to avoid any controversy the concept of marketed surplus has been used in this study.

The proportion of output actually marketed is determined largely by the consumption habits of the people within the producing areas, the nature of the crop, the relative price levels of different farm products, government taxation policy and the economic status of the farm population. The most outstanding factor in determining the size of the marketed surplus is the size of output. In the long run, a permanent increase in marketed surplus would be feasible only with increased production. Besides the size of output, the other most important factors considered in this study are: size of holdings, size of family, level of debt, distance of the village located from the market, proportion of area irrigated, area under tenancy and total assets holding of the farmers. The analysis is being carried out by presenting the desired tables, as well as, by fitting the regression for different functional forms separately in the following pages. In fact, the regression analysis is used to verify and strengthen the results obtained from the tabular analysis. The data used in this chapter are obtained from the primary field survey, details of which have already been given in the introductory chapter.

Marketed Surplus—The Results

The present study analyses marketed surplus in relation to farm size. The farmers of the villages surveyed grow many food and non-food crops. To make the analysis easy and meaningful, all crops have been grouped into six categories, namely, (1) Wheat, (2) Paddy, (3) Coarse cereals, (4) Pulses, (5) Oilseeds, and (6) Cotton. Wheat includes all varieties of wheat while paddy includes basmati and other coarse varieties. Coarse cereals include bajra, barley, maize and guar. Oilseeds comprise of mustard-seed, sunflower seed, toria and sesamum. Pulses include gram, *masar, arhar* and *moong*. Cotton includes American and *desi* cotton. The marketed surplus of the above group of crops is discussed in physical terms. The individual crops are preceded by the value of marketed surplus of all crops (aggregate) in relation to the value of aggregate output (of all crops) and other factors mentioned above. The value of the aggregate output here excludes the value of fodder crops and by-products.

Aggregate Marketed Surplus (All Crops)

Tables 6.1 to 6.5 present the aggregate marketed surplus (of all crops). Table 6.1 shows that both the value of output per acre as well as output marketed per acre are directly related to farm size. The same relationship holds for marketed surplus as a percentage of output and farm size. Whereas, marginal farmers marketed 68 per cent of their output, large farmers marketed 91 per cent of their output. On an average, the farmers marketed 87 per cent of aggregate output. The dominant role of large farmers in the total marketed surplus is very clear from the table. The largest size class alone accounted for 45 per cent of the marketed surplus, whereas it accounted for only 10 per cent of the total households. Further, it is interesting to note that the percentage of marketed surplus was lower than the percentage of area operated up to 25 acres of land. Beyond that one finds that the share of marketed surplus was significantly higher than the share of area operated. Thus, the rise in marketed surplus over operated area for large farmers compared to other categories suggests that there is a direct and more than proportionate relationship between holding size and marketed surplus.

Table 6.2 portrays the relationship between family size and the marketed surplus of all crops. As expected, the table reveals a negative relationship between marketed surplus and family size. The negative relationship holds for all categories except for small farmers in which case after declining from 76 per cent to 72 per cent, marketed surplus rose to 77 per cent with the rise in family size. This rise in marketed surplus in the latter case might be due to a rise in per household output on account of the higher area operated as is evident from the table.

For credit generally farmers depend on institutional as well as non-institutional sources. Credit provided by institutional sources like, cooperative societies and commercial banks is generally for a short period for the purpose of seeds and fertilizers. Similarly, loans provided by money-lenders and *arhatias* are also for the duration of one crop and are to be paid back to avail of the facility again during the next crop. The loans provided by the *arhatias* and money-lenders have a pressure component on the farmers to sell their produce as soon as possible after the harvest to return the amount of debt. The high level of debt compels the farmers to sell a higher proportion of their produce to repay the loans. The small and marginal farmers especially are an easy prey to such loans.

Table 6.3 presents the marketed surplus of all crops in relation to total debt, institutional as well as non-institutional. It is clear from the table that with the rise in debt, there was a rise in the proportion of output marketed in the case of marginal and small farmers. This proportion rose from 72 per cent in case of no debt to 75 per cent for Rs. 50,000 and further to 82 per cent for above Rs. 50,000 debt for the category of small farmers. However, it seems that the sale of large farmers is not affected by the level of debt. Because of their higher operated area and higher production, these farmers are able to pay back the amount of loan without falling prey to the pressures of money-lenders. Table 6.3 shows that large farmers who did not take any loan marketed 96 per cent of their output. The percentage, however, fell to 88 for those large farmers who took loans up to Rs. 50,000 and further to 87 for those who were indebted to the extent of more than Rs. 50,000.

Access to irrigation increases the output and hence the marketed surplus. Among the households surveyed for this study, it was observed that a significantly high proportion of the area operated was irrigated. It was observed from the sample data that 65 per cent of total operated area was fully irrigated, 24 per cent was irrigated between 50 and 100 per cent and the remaining 11 per cent was less than 50 per cent irrigated. Generally, marketable crops are preferred on irrigated land as it enables the farmers to use purchased inputs like HYV seeds, chemical fertilizers, pesticides and use of machines. Land which has little access to irrigation is generally used for subsistence crops, like gram, bajra, jowar, etc. Table 6.4 presents the relationship between the proportion of area irrigated and marketed surplus. The table shows that with the rise in unirrigated area, there is a fall in the percentage of output marketed by all categories of farmers. On an average, the output marketed fell from 88 per cent on fully irrigated land to 76 per cent on less than 50 per cent irrigated land. The fall in marketed surplus at a higher level of unirrigated area is partly due to the cropping of subsistence crops on such areas and partly due to low productivity. The value of output per acre declined from Rs. 7,807 on fully irrigated land to Rs. 3,584 on less than 50 per cent irrigated land.

Bhoothalingam (1969) concluded that the farmers sowing commercial crops on their field spend relatively more on agricultural implements than the farmers who sow subsistence crops. The implication of the above statement is that the rise in farm assets should lead to a rise in marketed surplus. This is the natural outcome as rich farmers who own tractors and other capital implements will be induced to produce more for the market and even sell a higher proportion of food crops as compared to the poor farmers. The adoption of new technology, for example, has given rise to a capitalistic form of production leading to mechanical farming with the higher use of capital assets and a higher proportion of output produced for the market.

Table 6.5 presents marketed surplus with respect to assets other than land. Here, assets include all agricultural implements like tubewell, tractor, trolley, thresher, harrow, bullocks, fodder cutter, animal house, grain storage, etc. The results of the table are quite interesting. Whereas 55 per cent of marginal farmers owned assets up to Rs. 20,000, no marginal farmer fell in the category of above Rs. 1,00,000. On the other hand, no large farmer lay in the category of up to Rs. 20,000 and 77 per cent of them owned assets above Rs. 1,00,000 while most of them had their own tractors. However, as high as 51 per cent of total farmers were in the category of Rs. 20,000 to Rs. 1,00,000. The table shows a positive relationship between assets holding and the proportion of output marketed. In all the categories, with a few exceptions, every increase in asset holding led to a rise in percentage of marketed surplus to output. The percentage of output marketed rose from 78 to 91 per cent as assets holding rose from below Rs. 20,000 to above Rs. 1,00,000 for all size of holdings.

From the above discussion, one concludes that at the aggregate level of all crops the farm size and marketed surplus are directly related. Family size and marketed surplus, on the other hand, show an inverse relationship. The small and marginal farmers market a higher proportion of their output with the rise in indebtedness but the relationship does not hold in the case of large farmers. As the area under irrigation declines the percentage of marketed surplus also falls. The assets held by the cultivators are a symbol of their economic strength and have a positive relationship with marketed surplus. This is because of the lower retention requirement of seeds, kind wages and consumption on the field by the rich farmers. A crop-wise analysis of the market surplus is given below.

Wheat

In the regions surveyed wheat is the most important staple diet of the people. Rice was also used for consumption but not very often, *i.e.*, once or twice a week. Wheat is also the most important crop of both the districts as it occupied the highest percentage of gross cropped area (38 per cent) and was sown in both the districts surveyed.

Table 6.6 shows that marketed surplus per acre as well as percentage of output marketed have a positive relationship with farm size. The positive relation is due to the fact that wheat being a paramount item of diet is required more for family consumption by marginal and small farmers. This requirement falls with the rise in farm size because of higher output at an absolute level. Table 6.6 also presents the share of different size classes in the marketed surplus and in the operated area. The first three categories had a higher proportion in the operated area compared to their share in marketed surplus, while the last two categories had a higher share in the marketed surplus compared to their share in operated area. This suggests that large and medium farmers were able to generate a higher marketed surplus of wheat than the small and marginal farmers. Around 73 per cent of the total marketed surplus of wheat was contributed by the large and medium farmers alone.

The marketed surplus of wheat in relation to family size, indebtedness, unirrigated area and assets holding is given in Tables 6.7 to 6.10. With a few exceptions, the percentage of output marketed and family size were inversely related (see Table 6.7). Nadkarni's (1980) contention that the behaviour of a cultivator indebted to a bigger farmer or money-lender may not be identical to that of a debt-free cultivator is fully supported by our case of marginal and small farmers (see Table 6.8). With the rise in debt, their percentage of marketed surplus also increased. However, indebtedness did not affect the sale proportion of medium and large farmers.

However, at the aggregate level of all farmers a clear negative relationship holds between the percentage of output marketed and unirrigated area and productivity and unirrigated area (see Table 6.9). The farmers use more inputs in terms of fertilizers, pesticides and insecticides on irrigated land and so intend to sell more in order to recover the cost of these inputs. In comparison, these inputs are hardly used on unirrigated land and most of the produce is not sold in the market. Finally, Table 6.10 presents the relationship between assets holding and marketed surplus of wheat. It is perceived from the table that with a few exceptions, there is a rise in the percentage of output marketed with the rise in assets holding due to reasons similar to those mentioned in the case of aggregate marketed surplus.

Paddy

As stated above, in the study area rice was also used for consumption but it was not a staple diet like that of wheat. Growing paddy requires a lot of assured water either by canals or by tubewells. Therefore, in most of the villages in Kaithal district where assured bore-well water supply was available by electric pump paddy crop was grown while it was grown in a few villages in Sirsa district where assured water supply was not available.

Table 6.11 presents the marketed surplus of paddy. It is discernible from the table that the output per acre as well as marketed surplus per acre rise with the rise in farm size till the level of medium farms and slightly declines with large farms. The proportion of output marketed, however, increased throughout with the rise in farm size. On an average, 96 per cent of output was marketed by all size classes. Such a high percentage of marketed surplus indicates that paddy is no more a subsistence crop in Haryana. Even marginal farmers sold 91 per cent of their output of paddy. As pointed out earlier rice was not the staple diet of the cultivators because the percentage of marketed surplus to output does not fall with the rise in family size (see Table 6.12).

Table 6.13 presents the marketed surplus of paddy in relation to indebtedness. No unique relationship turns out between marketed surplus and debt burden on the farmers. As paddy has become a commercial crop, all the farmers, large as well as small, grew paddy for the market irrespective of the level of debt. As paddy requires a lot of water availability, Table 6.14 shows that 88 per cent of area under paddy was fully irrigated. Hence, the irrigation level does not seem to have any relationship with marketed surplus. Similarly, being a highly marketed crop, assets holding did not have any influence on the marketed surplus of paddy (see Table 6.15).

Coarse Cereals

Coarse cereals here include four crops, *viz*., bajra, barley, maize and guar. Jowar as a fodder crop was also produced in the regions. However, consumption of jowar was limited to own animals and therefore, it was not included in the analysis. Coarse grains being arid crops were generally preferred on unirrigated land, as that land was not suitable for the cultivation of main cereals. A higher proportion of coarse cereal production was used for home consumption as well as for cattle. Only 5.7 per cent of the total net sown area was devoted to these crops and only 17 per cent households grew these crops. Table 6.16 shows that 68 per cent of the total output of coarse cereals was marketed. Thus, their proportion of marketed surplus was even lesser than the main food crop like wheat of which 80 per cent was marketed. The table shows that there is no unique relationship between the marketed surplus per acre and the size of holdings. The percentage of output marketed, on the other hand, rises with the rise in farm size with the exception of the semi-medium class.

Coarse cereals are used for home consumption by poor farmers and for animal feed by rich farmers. Therefore no unique relationship turns out between family size and marketed surplus (see Table 6.17). As mentioned above, coarse cereals are preferred on unirrigated land, as out of the total area under coarse cereals, only 36 per cent was fully irrigated while the remaining 64 per cent was either unirrigated or partially irrigated. Due to a higher proportion of area being unirrigated and a very few households cultivating coarse cereals, the results of the tables pertaining to marketed surplus are not very consistent. The only clear statement, which can be made from Tables 6.18 to 6.20 is that the productivity of coarse cereals is much higher on irrigated land as compared to unirrigated land. For example, the productivity per acre on fully irrigated land was 4.5 quintals, while it was 2.2 quintals per acre on less than 50 per cent irrigated land. The tabular analysis fails to establish any clear relationship between marketed surplus and indebtedness, irrigated area and assets holding.

Pulses

Gram, *masar, arhar* and *moong* are the main crops, which constitute pulses in the present analysis. The retention requirement of these crops was also quite high as they also formed the major food item along with cereals. Sixty-eight per cent of total output was marketed by the farmers as is shown by Table 6.21. Marketed surplus per acre as well as the proportion of output marketed did not rise consistently over farm size. Although, pulses form part of food crops, they do not show any significant association between family size and the proportion of output marketed. This behaviour of the farmers can be explained by the fact that pulses are not as important a food item for farmers as wheat and their consumption is supplementary to the latter and form part of their food only if financially affordable. To meet a higher amount of debt, the cultivators sell a larger proportion of output. As in case of coarse cereals, unirrigated land, which could not be used for other crops like paddy or wheat, was used for growing pulses. On account of the higher area, output

Table 6.1: Output and marketed surplus by farm size (aggregate of all crops).

Farm size	*Output per acre (Rs.)*	*Marketed Surplus*		*Percentage of*			
		Per acre (Rs.)	*As % of output*	*Output*	*Marketed surplus*	*House-holds*	*Area operated*
Marginal	5904	3998	67.73	3.3	2.6	24.0	3.9
Small	5478	4051	73.95	7.7	6.5	23.7	9.6
Semi-med.	6004	5103	84.99	16.4	16.0	24.0	18.7
Medium	6680	5864	87.79	29.3	29.6	18.5	30.0
Large	7876	7150	90.78	43.3	45.3	9.8	37.8
Total	6859	5961	86.90	100.0	100.0	100.0	100.0

Table 6.2: Family size and marketed surplus of all crops (per household) (value in Rs.).

Farm size	*Up to 5 members*						*5 to 10 members*						*10 to 15 members*					
	Output (Q)	*MS*	*Area*	*MS as % of Q*	*% of hh*	*Family size*	*Output (Q)*	*MS*	*Area*	*MS as % of Q*	*% of hh*	*Family size*	*Output (Q)*	*MS*	*Area*	*MS as % of Q*	*% of hh*	*Family size*
M	9829	682	1.6	69.5	68	3.7	10073	6569	1.8	65.2	29	7.3	4433	1633	1.8	36.8	3	12.7
S	21537	16279	4.0	75.6	47	4.3	23397	16784	4.3	71.7	44	7.1	26853	20590	4.6	76.7	9	12.5
SM	47524	40417	7.9	85.0	36	4.4	48268	41237	8.0	85.4	49	7.4	48167	40169	8.2	83.4	15	13.0
M	123110	112314	18.7	91.2	13	4.2	104884	91575	16.2	87.3	53	7.7	116577	101440	16.6	87.0	34	13.3
L	755000	742966	54.0	98.4	8	4.3	296260	274283	38.0	92.6	46	7.7	255722	217183	39.1	84.9	46	15.8
T	42832	37614	5.7	87.8	40	4.1	74463	65147	11.0	87.5	43	7.4	123821	105548	18.8	85.2	17	13.0

Table 6.3: Indebtedness and marketed surplus of all crops (per household) (value in Rs.).

Farm size	*Zero debt*					*Debt up to Rs.50,000*					*Debt above Rs. 50,000*				
	Output (Q)	*MS*	*Area*	*MS as % of Q*	*% of hh*	*Output (Q)*	*MS*	*Area*	*MS as % of Q*	*% of hh*	*Output (Q)*	*MS*	*Area*	*MS as % of Q*	*% of hh*
M	8482	5552	1.5	65.5	54	11367	7923	1.8	69.7	45	4400	3300	2.0	75.0	1
S	21388	15316	4.2	71.6	36	23312	17389	4.1	74.6	60	27675	22575	4.1	81.6	4
SM	38595	30655	7.9	79.4	25	52639	45789	8.0	87.0	59	45306	37961	8.3	83.8	16
M	122429	108130	17.0	88.3	23	102566	89144	16.2	86.9	50	117987	104702	17.3	88.7	27
L	494783	475920	45.2	96.2	26	189366	167104	31.8	88.2	31	292968	253580	41.9	86.6	43
T	66596	59435	8.4	89.2	34	52841	44881	8.5	84.9	52	142718	123988	21.0	86.9	14

Table 6.4: Proportion of area irrigated and marketed surplus of all crops (per household).

Farm size	*100 % irrigated*					*Between 50 – 100 % irrigated*					*Less than 50 % irrigated*				
	Output (Q)	*MS*	*Area*	*MS as % of Q*	*% of hh*	*Output (Q)*	*MS*	*Area*	*MS as % of Q*	*% of hh*	*Output (Q)*	*MS*	*Area*	*MS as % of Q*	*% of hh*
M	11264	7842	1.7	69.6	77	11725	6475	2.0	55.2	1	4235	2186	1.5	51.6	22
S	23950	17701	4.1	73.9	76	20956	16527	4.5	78.9	13	17345	11765	4.4	67.8	11
SM	53979	46864	8.0	86.8	72	38242	30389	8.2	79.5	15	26645	19697	7.9	73.9	13
M	124474	110370	15.7	88.7	61	101466	88327	18.3	87.0	26	70682	58570	18.2	82.9	13
L	350158	320533	38.5	91.5	66	280791	252082	45.7	89.8	26	96218	73543	30.0	76.4	8
T	73384	64297	9.4	87.6	71	98828	86237	17.4	87.3	14	27959	21340	7.8	76.3	15

Table 6.5: Assets other than land and marketed surplus of all crops (per household) (value in Rs.).

Farm size	*Up to Rs. 20,000*					*Rs. 20,000 – 1,00,000*					*Above Rs. 1,00,000*				
	Output (Q)	*MS*	*Area*	*MS as % of Q*	*% of hh*	*Output (Q)*	*MS*	*Area*	*MS as % of Q*	*% of hh*	*Output (Q)*	*MS*	*Area*	*MS as % of Q*	*% of hh*
M	6975	4212	1.5	60.4	55	13129	9523	1.9	72.5	45	-	-	-	-	-
S	18974	14246	4.3	75.1	35	24274	17726	4.1	73.0	63	42050	34250	5.0	81.5	2
SM	35036	28975	7.6	82.7	20	48540	40281	7.9	83.0	69	66998	64186	9.3	95.8	11
M	74505	65373	18.2	87.7	10	90964	77686	15.0	85.4	35	130473	115930	17.4	88.8	55
L	-	-	-	-	-	173051	151416	33.8	87.5	23	354774	323752	41.5	91.3	77
T	19491	15192	4.4	77.9	28	44839	36834	7.5	82.2	51	200163	181431	24.7	90.6	21

Table 6.6: Output and marketed surplus by farm size (Wheat).

Farm size	*Output per acre (Qtls.)*	*Marketed Surplus*		*Percentage of*			
		Per acre (Qtls.)	*As % of output*	*Output*	*Marketed surplus*	*House-holds*	*Area operated*
Marginal	12.6	6.1	48.46	3.9	2.3	22	4.0
Small	12.2	8.3	67.65	9.3	7.9	23	10.0
Semi-med.	11.5	8.2	71.66	18.9	17.1	26	21.8
Medium	13.2	10.8	82.19	30.7	31.7	19	30.8
Large	14.7	12.9	87.66	37.2	41.0	10	33.4
Total	13.2	10.5	79.58	100.0	100.0	100.0	100.0

Table 6.7: Family size and marketed surplus of wheat (per household) (Quintals).

Farm size	*Up to 5 members*						*5 to 10 members*						*10 to 15 members*					
	Output (Q)	*MS*	*Area*	*MS as % of O*	*% of hh*	*Fam-ily size*	*Output (Q)*	*MS*	*Area*	*MS as % of O*	*% of hh*	*Fam-ily size*	*Output (Q)*	*MS*	*Area*	*MS as % of O*	*% of hh*	*Fam-ily size*
M	17.8	8.6	1.4	48.3	66	3.7	16.4	8.2	1.4	49.9	32	7.3	19.0	7.0	1.3	36.8	2	13.0
S	34.8	27.6	3.0	79.3	46	4.2	41.6	24.6	3.3	59.2	46	7.1	43.0	26.0	3.3	60.5	8	12.3
SM	62.2	45.1	5.2	72.4	36	4.4	72.8	51.0	6.5	70.0	49	7.4	88.6	66.2	7.9	74.7	15	13.2
M	179.3	152.0	12.6	84.6	13	4.2	139.1	117.1	11.1	84.2	53	7.7	172.3	135.6	12.6	78.7	34	13.3
L	461.3	445.3	21.3	93.5	8	4.3	387.9	349.4	27.9	90.7	46	7.8	341.1	282.4	23.4	81.9	46	15.8
T	53.3	41.4	3.9	77.7	37	4.1	103.2	82.9	8.1	80.3	45	7.4	178.4	142.1	13.0	79.7	18	13.8

Table 6.8: Indebtedness and marketed surplus of wheat (per household) (Quintals).

Farm size	*Zero debt*					*Debt up to Rs.50,000*					*Debt above Rs. 50,000*				
	Output (Q)	*MS*	*Area*	*MS as % of Q*	*% of hh*	*Output (Q)*	*MS*	*Area*	*MS as % of Q*	*% of hh*	*Output (Q)*	*MS*	*Area*	*MS as % of Q*	*% of hh*
M	16.2	7.6	1.3	47.3	55	18.9	9.4	1.5	49.6	45	-	-	-	-	-
S	35.4	20.7	2.9	58.3	35	39.3	28.1	3.3	71.5	61	53.0	41.0	3.[illegible]	77.4	4
SM	58.9	40.3	5.2	68.3	25	72.1	52.5	5.9	72.8	58	86.9	62.3	8.[illegible]	71.7	17
M	167.5	135.2	11.6	80.7	23	143.7	114.3	10.8	79.5	51	167.4	147.2	13.9	87.9	26
L	418.0	384.5	24.1	92.0	27	266.4	222.6	20.7	83.5	32	426.6	370.7	29.7	86.9	41
T	80.8	63.7	5.6	78.8	34	78.4	59.7	6.2	76.1	52	204.9	174.2	15.9	85.0	14

Table 6.9: Irrigation and marketed surplus of wheat (per household) (Quintals).

Farm size	*100 % irrigated*					*Between 50 – 100 % irrigated*					*Less than 50 % irrigated*				
	Output (Q)	*MS*	*Area*	*MS as % of Q*	*% of hh*	*Output (Q)*	*MS*	*Area*	*MS as % of Q*	*% of hh*	*Output (Q)*	*MS*	*Area*	*MS as % of Q*	*% of hh*
M	18.2	9.1	1.4	50.2	87	20.0	5.0	2.0	25.0	1	11.5	3.8	1.0	33.0	12
S	40.5	28.5	3.4	70.3	80	28.4	17.6	2.2	61.8	11	33.9	15.5	2.5	45.8	9
SM	83.0	60.5	7.0	73.0	72	55.0	39.2	4.8	71.3	14	26.2	13.2	3.5	50.2	14
M	176.3	148.1	13.0	84.0	60	143.3	114.5	11.3	79.9	26	86.5	63.1	7.3	73.0	14
L	446.5	400.2	29.1	89.6	65	278.6	229.1	21.1	82.2	27	91.7	60.0	8.5	65.5	8
T	101.5	82.2	7.5	80.9	74	121.9	96.2	9.6	78.9	14	42.4	26.0	3.9	61.3	12

Table 6.10: Assets other than land and marketed surplus of wheat (per household) (Quintals).

Farm size	Up to Rs. 20,000					Rs. 20,000 – 1,00,000					Above Rs. 1,00,000				
	Output (Q)	MS	Area	MS as % of O	% of hh	Output (Q)	MS	Area	MS as % of O	% of hh	Output (Q)	MS	Area	MS as % of O	% of hh
M	15.6	6.5	1.2	41.6	46	19.0	10.1	1.5	53.3	54	-	-	-	-	-
S	34.2	21.2	2.9	62.1	33	40.1	28.1	3.3	70.0	65	57.0	39.0	4.5	68.4	2
SM	43.2	29.4	4.4	68.1	19	70.1	51.1	5.8	72.9	67	119.8	83.7	11.1	69.9	14
M	109.3	88.3	10.2	80.8	9	132.3	103.0	10.1	77.8	36	178.5	150.7	13.2	84.5	55
L	-	-	-	-	-	231.0	183.8	17.7	79.6	24	417.8	372.2	27.7	89.1	76
T	34.1	21.9	3.1	64.3	24	65.5	48.2	5.2	73.5	54	247.1	212.3	17.6	85.9	22

Table 6.11: Output and marketed surplus by farm size (Paddy).

Farm size	Output per acre (Qtls.)	Marketed Surplus		Percentage of			
		Per acre (Qtls.)	As % of output	Output	Marketed surplus	Hous holds	Area operated
Marginal	10.4	9.5	90.82	2.6	2.5	17	3.0
Small	10.6	9.6	90.73	6.3	5.9	20	7.1
Semi-med.	11.8	11.1	94.39	17.6	17.2	27	17.9
Medium	12.7	12.2	96.39	29.4	29.5	23	27.8
Large	11.9	11.7	98.14	44.1	44.9	13	44.2
Total	12.0	11.5	96.31	100.0	100.0	100.0	100.0

Table 6.12: Family size and marketed surplus of paddy (per household) (Quintals).

Farm size	Up to 5 members						5 to 10 members						10 to 15 members					
	Output (Q)	MS	Area	MS as % of Q	% of hh	Family size	Output (Q)	MS	Area	MS as % of Q	% of hh	Family size	Output (Q)	MS	Area	MS as % of Q	% of hh	Family size
M	16.9	15.8	1.4	93.2	59	3.9	12.7	11.0	1.5	86.3	41	7.1	-	-	-	-	-	-
S	28.0	24.7	2.5	88.4	45	4.7	31.1	28.7	3.0	92.4	43	7.1	33.3	30.8	3.3	92.5	12	12.3
SM	80.3	77.8	6.0	96.6	27	4.6	60.1	56.2	5.2	93.6	55	7.5	45.9	42.1	4.8	91.8	18	13.3
M	176.0	174.0	6.5	98.9	5	4.5	126.5	121.9	10.5	96.4	49	7.8	118.4	113.6	9.6	96.0	46	12.9
L	346.0	336.0	28.7	97.1	14	4.3	347.6	343.1	26.2	98.7	59	7.5	232.3	225.7	26.0	97.1	27	16.2
T	63.4	60.6	4.8	95.6	29	4.4	110.2	106.6	8.9	96.8	49	7.5	111.6	107.0	10.6	95.9	22	13.5

Table 6.13: Indebtedness and marketed surplus of paddy (per household) (Quintals).

Farm size	Zero debt					Debt up to Rs.50,000					Debt above Rs. 50,000				
	Output (Q)	MS	Area	MS as % of Q	% of hh	Output (Q)	MS	Area	MS as % of Q	% of hh	Output (Q)	MS	Area	MS as % of Q	% of hh
M	14.4	13.5	1.6	93.6	52	16.1	14.2	1.3	88.2	48	-	-	-	-	-
S	22.8	19.6	2.0	86.3	24	32.6	30.0	3.1	91.9	70	28.0	25.0	2.5	89.2	6
SM	67.3	62.5	5.7	92.9	18	61.6	58.5	5.2	94.9	73	66.0	61.5	5.8	93.2	9
M	98.8	94.3	8.5	95.4	22	123.6	119.0	9.6	96.2	51	150.2	145.9	11.5	97.1	27
L	594.8	591.5	40.5	99.5	18	217.5	212.8	2.5	97.8	27	272.3	264.9	24.8	97.3	55
T	97.4	94.4	7.5	96.9	26	70.8	67.5	6.0	95.4	57	181.8	176.2	15.7	96.9	17

Table 6.14: Proportion of area irrigated and marketed surplus of paddy (per household) (Quintals).

Farm size	100 % irrigated					Between 50 – 100 % irrigated					Less than 50 % irrigated			
	Output (Q)	MS	Area	MS as % of Q	% of hh	Output (Q)	MS	Area	MS as % of Q	% of hh	Output (Q)	MS	Area	MS as % Q
M	15.2	13.8	1.5	90.8	100	-	-	-	-	-	-	-	-	-
S	30.9	28.1	2.9	90.9	94	8.0	7.0	2.5	87.5	3	22.0	19.0	2.0	86.4
SM	66.4	63.0	5.4	94.9	91	34.0	30.0	5.3	88.2	7	16.0	8.0	2.0	50.0
M	129.2	124.3	10.4	96.2	81	123.3	120.5	8.7	97.7	16	24.0	22.0	2.0	91.7
L	311.9	305.4	27.7	97.9	82	334.3	331.0	20.8	99.0	18	-	-	-	-
T	92.6	89.0	7.9	96.1	90	156.2	153.1	11.0	98.0	8	20.7	16.3	2.0	79.0

Table 6.15: Assets other than land and marketed surplus of paddy (per household) (Quintals).

Farm size	Up to Rs. 20,000					Rs. 20,000 — 1,00,000					Above Rs. 1,00,000				
	Output (Q)	MS	Area	MS as % of Q	% of hh	Output (Q)	MS	Area	MS as % of Q	% of hh	Output (Q)	MS	Area	MS as % of Q	% of hh
M	19.7	18.8	1.8	95.3	22	13.9	12.4	1.3	89.0	78	-	-	-	-	-
S	47.3	44.7	2.8	94.4	9	29.1	26.2	2.9	90.1	85	16.0	14.5	1.5	90.6	6
SM	-	-	-	-	-	66.0	62.3	5.6	94.3	86	44.2	41.9	4.0	94.9	14
M	218.0	216.0	9.5	99.1	3	103.2	98.8	8.6	95.8	30	131.5	126.8	10.5	96.4	67
L	-	-	-	-	-	362.5	360.0	22.0	99.3	9	311.3	305.1	26.9	98.0	91
T	13.7	12.3	1.7	98.6	6	54.1	51.3	4.5	94.9	61	192.7	187.3	16.0	97.2	33

Table 6.16: Output and marketed surplus by farm size (Coarse cereals).

Farm size	*Output per acre (Qtls.)*	*Marketed Surplus*		*Percentage of*			
		Per acre (Qtls.)	*As % of output*	*Output*	*Marketed surplus*	*House-Holds*	*Area operated*
Marginal	3.22	1.89	58.62	1.8	1.6	7	1.9
Small	3.95	2.37	59.95	10.8	9.5	18	9.3
Semi-med.	3.78	1.79	47.39	18.3	12.8	26	16.4
Medium	2.71	1.68	61.81	23.1	21.1	33	28.8
Large	3.56	2.89	81.34	45.9	55.0	16	43.6
Total	3.38	2.29	67.87	100.0	100.0	100.0	100.0

Table 6.17: Family size and marketed surplus of coarse cereals (per household) (Quintals).

Farm size	*Up to 5 members*						*5 to 10 members*						*10 to 15 members*					
	Output (Q)	*MS*	*Area*	*MS as % of Q*	*% of hh*	*Family size*	*Output (Q)*	*MS*	*Area*	*MS as % of Q*	*% of hh*	*Family size*	*Output (Q)*	*MS*	*Area*	*MS as % of Q*	*% of hh*	*Family size*
M	2.6	2.1	0.9	81.0	80	4.0	4.0	0	1.0	0	20	6.0	-	-	-	-	-	-
S	6.2	3.4	1.5	55.7	61	4.4	8.6	6.0	1.4	69.6	31	6.5	2.0	0	4.0	0	8	14.0
SM	9.3	5.8	2.3	63.1	33	4.5	7.6	3.8	2.1	49.1	44	8.0	7.3	1.0	1.9	13.8	23	12.0
M	11.2	6.3	2.5	56.6	13	4.3	7.9	5.2	3.1	50.2	70	7.6	6.5	2.8	2.6	42.3	17	15.5
L	-	-	-	-	-	-	35.2	31.5	6.8	89.6	27	7.3	32.0	25.3	10.2	78.9	73	15.8
T	7.1	4.3	1.8	60.4	30	4.3	10.4	7.2	2.9	69.8	46	7.5	18.4	12.8	6.1	69.3	24	14.7

Table 6.18: Indebtedness and marketed surplus of coarse cereals (per household) (Quintals).

Farm size	Zero debt					Debt up to Rs.50,000					Debt above Rs. 50,000				
	Output (Q)	MS	Area	MS as % of Q	% of hh	Output (Q)	MS	Area	MS as % of Q	% of hh	Output (Q)	MS	Area	MS as % of Q	% of hh
M	2.8	2.2	0.8	76.5	60	3.0	1.0	1.0	33.3	40	-	-	-	-	-
S	4.8	1.9	2.0	40.4	54	8.8	6.3	1.3	72.4	46	-	-	-	-	-
SM	9.7	5.7	2.8	58.6	33	7.2	2.6	1.7	35.6	50	7.7	4.0	2.3	52.2	17
M	7.3	3.8	2.1	51.7	39	8.4	5.8	3.2	69.2	39	8.4	5.4	4.1	64.3	22
L	31.5	20.0	10.0	63.5	18	20.7	15.0	7.3	72.6	27	39.9	35.3	10.1	88.3	55
T	8.5	4.7	2.7	56.0	39	9.0	5.5	2.6	61.5	41	21.8	17.9	6.3	82.3	20

Table 6.19: Proportion of area irrigated and marketed surplus of coarse cereals (per household) (Quintals).

Farm size	100 % irrigated					Between 50 — 100 % irrigated					Less than 50 % irrigated				
	Output (Q)	MS	Area	MS as % of Q	% of hh	Output (Q)	MS	Area	MS as % of Q	% of hh	Output (Q)	MS	Area	MS as % of Q	% of hh
M	3.7	1.7	1.0	45.5	60	1.5	1.5	0.5	100	20	2.0	2.0	1.0	100.0	20
S	4.7	1.2	1.7	25.5	38	5.9	3.8	1.6	63.6	46	13.5	11.5	1.8	85.2	16
SM	5.9	1.0	2.1	17.0	44	11.1	6.9	2.2	62.2	39	6.8	4.2	2.0	61.0	17
M	9.2	5.8	2.6	62.8	39	7.5	4.4	2.5	58.1	35	6.8	4.4	4.0	65.4	26
L	43.8	39.0	6.5	89.0	46	30.9	25.4	13.6	82.2	36	11.0	0.0	7.8	0.0	18
T	12.8	8.9	2.8	69.4	43	11.5	8.0	3.9	70.0	37	8.0	4.6	3.6	57.1	20

Table 6.20: Assets other than land and marketed surplus of coarse cereals (per household) (Quintals).

Farm size	Up to Rs. 20,000					Rs. 20,000 – 1,00,000					Above Rs. 1,00,000				
	Output (Q)	MS	Area	MS as % of Q	% of hh	Output (Q)	MS	Area	MS as % of Q	% of hh	Output (Q)	MS	Area	MS as % of Q	% of hh
M	2.2	1.8	0.8	84.6	60	4.0	1.5	1.0	37.5	40	-	-	-	-	-
S	8.4	6.1	2.1	72.0	62	3.7	0.6	1.0	16.2	38	-	-	-	-	-
SM	7.0	3.5	2.4	49.8	22	8.3	3.6	2.1	43.3	72	9.0	8.0	2.0	88.9	6
M	7.8	6.7	2.5	85.8	13	6.0	2.9	2.5	47.9	30	9.1	5.7	3.3	62.0	57
L	-	-	-	-	-	24.7	15.0	10.8	60.8	27	36.3	31.4	8.8	86.6	73
T	7.0	4.9	2.0	70.2	26	8.4	3.9	2.8	47.1	43	19.0	15.1	5.2	79.7	31

Table 6.21: Output and marketed surplus by farm size (Pulses).

Farm size	Output per acre (Qtls.)	Marketed Surplus		Percentage of			
		Per acre (Qtls.)	As % of output	Output	Marketed surplus	House-holds	Area operated
Marginal	1.88	0.92	48.71	4.7	3.3	11.0	3.7
Small	1.45	0.92	63.66	4.8	4.5	12.1	5.0
Semi-med.	1.25	0.73	58.43	14.5	12.5	27.5	17.4
Medium	1.43	0.95	66.75	29.1	28.6	29.7	30.4
Large	1.61	1.19	73.77	46.9	51.0	19.8	43.5
Total	1.49	1.01	67.85	100.0	100.0	100.0	100.0

Table 6.22: Family size and marketed surplus of pulses (per household) (Quintals).

Farm size	Up to 5 members						5 to 10 members						10 to 15 members					
	Output (Q)	MS	Area	MS as % of Q	% of hh	Family size	Output (Q)	MS	Area	MS as % of Q	% of hh	Family size	Output (Q)	MS	Area	MS as % of Q	% of hh	Family size
M	2.8	1.4	1.5	50.0	60	3.3	3.5	1.7	1.9	47.1	40	7.5	-	-	-	-	-	-
S	2.5	1.4	2.1	56.9	73	4.6	3.5	2.5	1.3	71.4	18	7.0	5.0	4.0	3.0	80.0	9	12.0
SM	2.4	1.3	3.4	50.4	48	4.0	5.3	3.2	2.9	60.5	40	7.5	4.4	3.0	2.5	68.2	12	14.0
M	19.3	17.1	8.1	89.0	15	4.0	4.9	2.4	4.7	48.7	63	7.1	5.5	3.3	3.8	60.7	22	13.5
L	-	-	-	-	-	-	16.7	12.2	12.8	73.0	33	7.0	17.7	13.1	9.7	74.1	67	15.9
T	4.8	3.5	3.3	71.9	33	4.0	6.6	4.0	5.0	61.1	43	7.2	12.0	8.6	6.8	72.3	24	14.8

Table 6.23: Indebtedness and marketed surplus of pulses (per household) (Quintals).

Farm size	Zero debt					Debt up to Rs.50,000					Debt above Rs. 50,000				
	Output (Q)	MS	Area	MS as % of Q	% of hh	Output (Q)	MS	Area	MS as % of Q	% of hh	Output (Q)	MS	Area	MS as % of Q	% of hh
M	2.5	0	1.8	0	40	3.4	2.4	1.5	71.2	50	4.0	3.0	2.0	75.0	10
S	2.8	1.6	2.3	59.3	64	3.2	2.3	1.6	70.3	36	-	-	-	-	-
SM	4.9	3.3	5.0	68.0	24	3.1	1.3	2.3	42.3	56	4.6	3.6	3.1	76.7	20
M	10.1	7.4	4.1	73.2	37	6.1	3.6	6.1	58.9	52	2.2	1.5	3.2	70.8	11
L	20.1	16.0	7.2	79.7	28	18.5	12.8	17.0	69.9	22	15.3	11.0	9.9	72.1	50
T	8.1	5.8	4.0	71.3	35	5.7	3.4	1.8	60.5	45	9.5	6.9	6.5	72.7	20

Table 6.24: Proportion of area irrigated and marketed surplus of pulses (per household) (Quintals).

Farm size	*100 % irrigated*					*Between 50—100 % irrigated*					*Less than 50 % irrigated*				
	Output (Q)	*MS*	*Area*	*MS as % of Q*	*% of hh*	*Output (Q)*	*MS*	*Area*	*MS as % of Q*	*% of hh*	*Output (Q)*	*MS*	*Area*	*MS as % of Q*	*% of hh*
M	1.7	0.8	1.3	50.0	30	-	-	-	-	-	3.7	1.8	1.8	48.5	70
S	-	-	-	-	-	3.4	2.4	1.7	69.3	63	2.1	1.0	2.6	47.7	37
SM	3.0	1.4	1.7	45.9	32	3.4	1.4	2.2	40.7	32	5.0	3.8	5.1	75.6	36
M	2.0	0.0	1.3	0.0	30	4.7	2.5	4.1	52.3	41	15.7	12.8	9.9	81.3	29
L	12.6	9.8	2.8	78.3	33	20.0	15.0	14.1	74.8	50	18.7	12.0	16.7	64.3	17
T	4.8	2.9	1.8	60.2	28	8.1	5.4	5.8	67.0	38	8.4	6.1	6.4	72.3	34

Table 6.25: Assets other than land and marketed surplus of pulses (per household) (Quintals).

Farm size	*Up to Rs. 20,000*					*Rs. 20,000 — 1,00,000*					*Above Rs. 1,00,000*				
	Output (Q)	*MS*	*Area*	*MS as % of Q*	*% of hh*	*Output (Q)*	*MS*	*Area*	*MS as % of Q*	*% of hh*	*Output (Q)*	*MS*	*Area*	*MS as % of Q*	*% of hh*
M	3.1	1.4	1.8	46.0	80	3.0	1.8	1.3	60.0	20	-	-	-	-	-
S	2.8	1.6	2.2	59.3	64	3.2	2.3	1.8	70.3	36	-	-	-	-	-
SM	3.0	2.3	3.6	75.3	36	4.3	2.1	2.8	49.7	56	4.5	3.0	2.5	66.7	8
M	15.3	12.5	8.9	81.8	19	7.1	4.9	4.8	68.0	37	3.8	1.5	3.6	39.5	44
L	-	-	-	-	-	18.8	13.8	16.0	73.4	28	16.8	12.4	8.7	73.9	72
T	5.1	3.7	3.7	71.6	32	7.0	4.6	1.4	65.5	38	10.1	6.9	6.0	67.9	30

Table 6.26: Output and marketed surplus by farm size (Oilseeds).

Farm size	*Output per acre (Qtls.)*	*Marketed Surplus*		*Percentage of*			
		Per acre (Qtls.)	*As % of output*	*Output*	*Marketed surplus*	*House-Holds*	*Area operated*
Marginal	3.2	3.1	95.80	3.5	3.5	13.3	4.3
Small	2.5	2.3	94.61	4.6	4.5	16.7	7.5
Semi-med.	3.7	3.5	96.38	16.2	16.2	24.2	17.6
Medium	3.7	3.5	96.23	31.6	31.4	30.0	34.3
Large	4.8	4.7	97.19	44.1	44.4	15.8	36.3
Total	4.0	3.8	96.59	100.0	100.0	100.0	100.0

Table 6.27: Family size and marketed surplus of oilseeds (per household) (Quintals).

Farm size	*Up to 5 members*						*5 to 10 members*						*10 to 15 members*					
	Output (Q)	*MS*	*Area*	*MS as % of Q*	*% of hh*	*Family size*	*Output (Q)*	*MS*	*Area*	*MS as % of Q*	*% of hh*	*Family size*	*Output (Q)*	*MS*	*Area*	*MS as % of Q*	*% of hh*	*Family size*
M	3.7	3.7	1.1	99.0	69	3.9	3.2	2.8	1.2	87.5	31	7.0	-	-	-	-	-	-
S	3.0	2.8	1.4	93.0	50	4.0	4.6	4.4	1.7	95.7	50	7.1	-	-	-	-	-	-
SM	9.2	8.7	2.4	94.7	45	4.5	9.9	9.6	2.6	97.5	41	7.1	6.8	6.7	2.6	99.3	14	12.3
M	13.8	13.4	2.7	96.8	17	4.2	14.7	14.3	4.3	97.4	58	7.8	13.9	12.9	3.8	93.1	25	13.7
L	30.0	30.0	5.0	100.0	5	4.0	50.7	49.6	9.9	97.8	37	6.9	30.7	29.5	6.8	96.3	58	15.5
T	7.4	7.1	1.9	96.2	34	4.1	15.3	14.9	3.9	97.3	46	7.3	20.4	19.5	5.0	95.6	20	14.3

Table 6.28: Indebtedness and marketed surplus of oilseeds (per household) (Quintals).

Farm size	*Zero debt*					*Debt up to Rs.50,000*					*Debt above Rs. 50,000*				
	Output (Q)	*MS*	*Area*	*MS as % of Q*	*% of hh*	*Output (Q)*	*MS*	*Area*	*MS as % of Q*	*% of hh*	*Output (Q)*	*MS*	*Area*	*MS as % of Q*	*% of hh*
M	3.1	2.8	1.1	90.8	44	3.9	3.9	1.1	95.8	56	-	-	-	-	-
S	3.6	3.4	1.6	95.3	45	4.0	3.8	1.5	94.1	55	-	-	-	-	-
SM	10.3	9.9	2.6	96.3	24	8.1	7.8	2.3	95.3	62	11.8	11.8	3.0	100.0	14
M	11.6	10.7	2.8	92.6	33	11.4	11.0	3.2	95.8	42	22.9	22.7	6.6	99.1	25
L	69.7	69.0	12.3	99.0	37	12.7	12.0	3.3	94.8	26	24.4	22.7	6.7	93.0	37
T	17.9	17.4	3.8	97.1	35	7.9	7.6	2.3	95.6	48	21.2	20.5	5.9	96.7	17

Table 6.29: Proportion of irrigated area and marketed surplus of oilseeds (per household) (Quintals).

Farm size	*100 % irrigated*					*Between 50 – 100 % irrigated*					*Less than 50 % irrigated*				
	Output (Q)	*MS*	*Area*	*MS as % of Q*	*% of hh*	*Output (Q)*	*MS*	*Area*	*MS as % of Q*	*% of hh*	*Output (Q)*	*MS*	*Area*	*MS as % of Q*	*% of hh*
M	3.6	3.4	1.2	95.5	94	-	-	-	-	-	3.5	3.5	0.5	100.0	6
S	3.8	3.7	1.4	97.4	70	2.1	1.7	1.6	83.7	25	12.0	11.0	3.0	91.7	5
SM	9.4	9.1	2.6	96.8	86	9.5	8.8	2.0	93.0	10	2.0	2.0	1.3	100.0	4
M	16.8	16.5	4.6	98.1	53	11.3	10.4	3.7	92.2	30	12.3	11.7	2.2	94.9	17
L	43.7	42.3	8.5	96.9	63	32.2	31.7	7.8	98.4	32	4.8	4.0	1.0	83.3	5
T	14.0	13.6	3.4	97.1	71	14.2	13.6	4.0	95.4	21	9.6	9.1	1.9	94.2	8

Table 6.30: Assets other than land and marketed surplus of oilseeds (per household) (Quintal).

Farm size	*Up to Rs. 20,000*					*Rs. 20,000 – 1,00,000*					*Above Rs. 1,00,000*				
	Output (Q)	*MS*	*Area*	*MS as % of Q*	*% of hh*	*Output (Q)*	*MS*	*Area*	*MS as % of Q*	*% of hh*	*Output (Q)*	*MS*	*Area*	*MS as % of Q*	*% of hh*
M	2.8	2.7	0.9	97.1	31	3.9	3.8	1.2	95.4	69	-	-	-	-	-
S	4.4	4.0	1.8	91.4	20	3.7	3.5	1.5	95.6	80	-	-	-	-	-
SM	10.2	10.0	2.8	97.4	31	8.5	8.1	2.4	96.1	62	10.6	10.0	1.5	94.3	7
M	21.7	21.2	4.2	97.9	8	9.7	8.8	2.5	90.7	36	16.3	16.0	4.8	98.1	56
L	-	-	-	-	-	9.6	9.0	2.6	94.0	21	45.6	44.4	9.3	97.4	79
T	9.0	8.7	2.4	97.0	17	6.8	6.4	2.0	94.1	52	27.9	27.2	6.4	97.5	31

Table 6.31: Output and marketed surplus by farm size (Cotton).

Farm size	*Output per acre (Qtls.)*	*Marketed Surplus*		*Percentage of*			
		Per acre (Qtls.)	*As % of output*	*Output*	*Marketed surplus*	*House-holds*	*Area operated*
Marginal	2.82	2.82	100.0	4.3	4.3	15.5	3.7
Small	1.90	1.87	98.30	8.5	8.3	24.9	10.9
Semi-med.	2.47	2.467	99.78	18.0	18.1	24.9	17.9
Medium	2.33	2.31	99.17	30.2	30.1	22.6	31.8
Large	2.68	2.68	100.0	39.0	39.2	12.1	35.7
Total	2.45	2.44	99.57	100.0	100.0	100.0	100.0

and proportion of output marketed rose with the rise in unirrigated area (see Table 6.24). However, assets did not give any significant push to the marketed surplus.

Both oilseeds and cotton were the cash crops of the region as they were produced only for the market. A small quantity of oilseeds like mustard or toria was retained for home consumption. Similarly, a very little amount of cotton was also retained for household use. This is clear from the Tables 6.26 to 6.31. Ninety-seven per cent of oilseeds output and 99.6 per cent of cotton output was sold in the market. There was no great difference in the marketed surplus of small and large farmers. In other words, these crops were produced completely for the market by all size classes of holdings and their surplus was not much affected by the factors like family size, indebtedness or assets holding.

To sum up the crop-wise analysis, the marketed surplus of wheat as a percentage of output was found to be directly related with farm size and assets held by the households. It was inversely related with family size and unirrigated area, while indebtedness affected positively the sale pattern of only the small and marginal farmers. In the case of coarse cereals and pulses, no systematic association was possible as these crops were not the main crops and were grown only on the marginal unirrigated land. The results of the tables for these crops were not very consistent and possibly the results would be better by regression analysis. In the case of paddy, oilseeds and cotton, it was found that a very high proportion of output of these crops was marketed. As these crops were grown only for the market, their sale was hardly affected by factors like family size, indebtedness, etc. Thus, the above discussion supports the fact that not only the large farmers but also the small and marginal farmers were producing for the market in the survey area, *i.e.*, in the Kaithal and Sirsa districts of Haryana.

II

Functional Analysis of Marketed Surplus

The analysis of tables presented in the previous section gives us an idea of the behaviour of marketed surplus for the total agricultural output as well as for different crops, across various farm size groups. However, the tabular analysis so attempted suffers from limitations because it takes into consideration the aggregate impact of all the variables. Nonetheless, the multiple regression analysis gives us the direction of the relationship as well as the quantum effect of each of the individual variables affecting the marketed surplus.

Regression analyses is carried out on the pooled data for all the categories rather than separate regressions for each farm size category. Before running the regression analysis the zero-order correlation matrix was examined. Those variables that presented a very high value of inter-correlation amongst the independent variables were either dropped or taken alternatively to avoid the problem of multi-colinearity. The zero-order correlation matrix of dependent and independent variables is presented for various crops separately in Appendix Table 6.1A.

As mentioned at the outset, the analysis of marketed surplus attempted by earlier studies, regressed marketed surplus on output[1] or net operated area (NOA)[2]. This study uses both output as well as NOA as explanatory variables. In addition, marketed surplus as a proportion of output has also been regressed upon the NOA. The analysis has been attempted for the aggregate marketed surplus of all the crops in value terms as well as marketed surplus of individual crops in physical terms. In addition to output and NOA, the other independent variables tried in the study are: Average household size (numbers); Distance of the village from the main market (kms); Unirrigated area as a proportion of gross cropped area; Total loans per acre of area operated (Rs.); and Area leased in as a proportion of net operated area. Both linear and double log forms were tried and the results of linear regressions are presented in Table 6.32 as linear form makes the best fit in terms of significance of β coefficients and the value of R^{-2}.

Analysing the results of all crops (aggregate output), it is observed from the table that the value of output was the most important variable determining the value of marketed surplus. The coefficient of output was positive and significant at one per cent indicating that a one rupee rise in output led to an increase in marketed surplus worth 96 paise of the aggregate agricultural output. Household size was the other important variable significant at one per cent with a negative coefficient, indicating that an additional member in the family reduced marketed surplus by raising the retention requirement by Rs. 1,003. Replacing the value of output by NOA, it is observed that NOA and marketed surplus also have a significant positive relationship. One acre increase in NOA raised the marketed surplus by Rs. 8,084. However, household size and unirrigated area as a proportion of GCA in this model turned significant at one per cent with negative signs. This is partially because a rise in unirrigated area results into low productivity (as was seen in the previous section), leading to lower marketed surplus.

In the third model, the value of marketed surplus as a proportion of output was taken as the dependent variable. One encounters some interesting results, for example, the household size in this model was not significant in determining the proportion of output marketed although NOA and un-irrigated area as a proportion of GCA remained significant at one per cent with signs as earlier. The area under tenancy as a proportion of NOA turned out significant at 5 per cent with a positive sign, thereby indicating a higher proportion of output marketed by those who took land on lease. The main reason for such a significant positive relationship seems to be that the land under tenancy bears a direct paid out cost to the cultivators and this cost has to be borne by producing for the market, irrespective of the nature of crop grown on such land.

The variables observed as insignificant in all the three equations were, distance of village from the market and loans per acre of operated area. The reason for the non-significance of distance could be the availability of infrastructure facilities like road and transportation in the study area. All the eight villages surveyed were well connected to the *mandis* by *pucca* roads. All the cultivators had sufficient owned or hired resources available to transport their produce to the *mandis*. So the distance factor does not play a big role in the marketing decisions of farmers. In the case of borrowing, it was observed in the tabulation analysis that only the small and marginal farmers were selling higher proportion of output under the pressure of indebtedness. Large farmers were not affected by indebtedness. However, the coefficient of indebtedness, though insignificant, had a positive sign in all the three equations, thereby indicating its positive influence on the marketed surplus. To sum up the discussion, significant variables identified with a positive effect on marketed surplus were, value of output, NOA and area under tenancy. The variables with a negative effect were household size and unirrigated area.

The value of R^{-2} presents a very interesting comparison in the three equations presented here. The value of R^{-2} was higher in the first equation where output was the explanatory variable rather than in the second equation where NOA was taken as an explanatory variable. It suggests that marketed surplus was more closely related with output than with the

Table 6.32: Regression results (Marketed surplus).

Dependent Variable	*Constant*	*Output*	*NOA*	*House-hold size*	*Distance located*	*Un-irrigated area / GCA*	*Loan per acre*	*Leased in area as % of NOA*	R^2	*F value*
Aggregate (All crops) (No of observations = 399)										
MS	-1563 (-0.8)	0.965* (176.0)	-	-1003* (-6.0)	92.3 (0.9)	1707 (0.7)	0.051 (0.4)	1113 (0.6)	0.988	5691*
MS	18935 (1.9)		8084* (28.7)	-3912* (-4.3)	-382 (-0.7)	-51171* (-4.0)	0.117 (0.2)	-9892 (-1.1)	0.703	158*
MS/OUT	0.642 (17.5)		0.007* (6.4)	0.003 (0.9)	0.0006 (0.3)	-0.291* (-5.9)	0.000002 (0.8)	0.071** (2.2)	0.200	17.3*
Wheat (No of observations: 372)										
MS	-3.9 (-1.1)	0.925* (94)		-1.41* (-4.3)	0.130 (0.7)	-3.80 (-0.6)	0.00007 (0.3)		0.966	2123*
MS	-8.9 (-1.3)		13.3* (45.6)	-1.48** (-2.3)	0.21 (0.6)	-23.8** (-2.0)	-0.00005 (-0.1)		0.872	508*
MS/OUT	0.43 (4.3)		0.017* (4.2)	0.002 (0.2)	0.008 (1.6)	-0.31 (-1.9)	0.000004 (0.6)		0.064	6.0*
Paddy (No of observations: 162)										
MS	-0.91 (-1.0)	0.995* (577.0)		-0.18** (-2.4)	-0.06 (-1.2)	0.18 (0.1)	-0.00003 (-0.4)		0.999	68760*
MS	6.4 (0.3)		13.1* (16.7)	-3.49 (-1.7)	1.06 (0.7)	26.0 (0.3)	-0.001 (-0.7)		0.641	58.6*
MS/OUT	0.94 (26.0)		0.003** (2.3)	-0.001 (-0.4)	-0.002 (-1.2)	-0.18 (-1.5)	-0.000004 (-1.4)		0.042	2.4**
Coarse cereals (No of observations: 70)										
MS	-1.8 (-1.1)	0.966* (31.3)		-0.24** (-2.4)	0.03 (0.4)	-1.09 (-0.5)	0.00009 (0.7)		0.942	224*
MS	-5.9 (-1.1)		2.17* (5.6)	-0.16 (-0.5)	0.61** (2.4)	-12.0 (-1.7)	0.000007 (.02)		0.365	8.9*
MS/OUT	0.32 (1.6)		0.04* (2.6)	-0.02 (-1.8)	0.009 (0.9)	0.04 (0.2)	0.00003 (1.4)		0.081	2.21
Pulses (No of observations: 91)										
MS	5.3 (1.5)	0.16* (4.8)		0.50* (2.5)	-0.47** (-2.1)	3.66 (1.1)	-0.0002 (-0.9)		0.279	7.97*
MS	3.5 (1.2)		1.09 (9.6)	0.22 (1.4)	-0.37** (-2.1)	-0.85 (-0.3)	-0.00003 (-0.3)		0.554	23.5*
MS/OUT	0.33 (0.8)		0.0099 (0.6)	0.042 (1.8)	-0.02 (-0.8)	0.03 (0.1)	0.00001 (0.7)		0.002	1.04
Oilseeds (No of observations: 119)										
MS	-0.34 (-1.5)	0.99* (299.0)		-0.06* (-3.8)	0.03* (2.6)	-0.14 (-0.3)	0.000005 (0.3)		0.999	19629*
MS	1.75 (0.6)		5.22* (22.5)	-0.26 (-1.2)	-0.25 (-1.8)	1.94 (0.4)	-0.0003 (-1.2)		0.826	112.9*
MS/OUT	0.76 (10.6)		0.02* (2.9)	-0.01** (-2.1)	0.01* (3.1)	-0.06 (-0.5)	0.000004 (0.6)		0.111	3.9*
Cotton (No of observations: 179)										
MS	0.04 (0.4)	0.999* (670.0)		0.003 (0.4)	-0.006 (-1.4)	-0.12 (-.9)	0.000002 (0.2)		0.9997	110093*
MS	-0.48 (-0.2)		2.34* (14.1)	0.16 (0.6)	0.07 (0.5)	4.93 (1.0)	-0.0008* (-2.9)		0.611	57*
MS/OUT	1.04 (53.0)		0.0007 (0.7)	-0.003 (-1.6)	-0.001 (-1.7)	-0.10* (-3.6)	-0.0000007 (-0.4)		0.074	3.9*

Notes: Figures in parentheses are respective 't' values.
* Significant at 1% level. ** Significant at 10% level.

operated area. With the change in farm size, productivity may change due to the different inputs used, thereby making the relationship between marketed surplus and farm size less sound. Further, in the third equation, when the proportion of output marketed was regressed, the value of R^{-2} fell to 0.20 (from 0.99 in the first equation). However, even with low value of R^{-2} the equation has a very important economic significance. It is always better if in place of the absolute value of marketed surplus, the relationship is seen in terms of proportion of output marketed. The latter is more relevant in policy formulation.

Chattopadhyay and Sen (1988: A156) while analyzing the pattern of marketable surplus of rice, state, "It is indeed surprising that earlier authors hold that marketable surplus goes up with the increase in farm size either for subsistence crop or for all the crops as a whole. As such, there is no basis whatsoever for establishing such kind of relationship. Per capita availability of cultivated land among the larger farms is certainly higher compared to the smaller ones, but per capita availability of land under a specific crop need not be higher in the larger size groups than the smaller farms". They further state, "The larger size groups prefer to choose commercial crops, *viz.*, potato, jute, cotton, etc. with greater intensity for higher return. Small farmers, on the other hand, have no such kind of choice for the very nature of their holdings and therefore, try to cultivate the whole amount of land for the main subsistence crop only, like rice or wheat to meet their consumption needs."

From this empirical reality, the marketed surplus of individual crops have been examined in physical terms by regressing MS on output and operated area of the respective crops, along with the other explanatory variables as taken earlier. However, the area under tenancy is excluded from the explanatory variable list as it is not known whether any specific crop was planted on such an area or not. Three regression models were fitted as earlier for each crop and the results are presented in Table 6.32.

The data in the table reveals that the output of each crop is the most significant variable affecting the marketed surplus of the respective crop. Except pulses, the magnitude of the coefficient of output exceeded 0.90 indicating a rise in output by one kilogram leads to a rise in marketed surplus by more than 0.90 kilograms. Paddy, oilseeds and cotton were highly commercial crops as their coefficients of output exceeded 0.990. Regressing marketed surplus on the cultivated area of the crop instead of output shows that area was also highly significant in all the crops with a positive coefficient. The crop-wise area coefficient shows that a one acre increase in net operated area leads to a thirteen quintal rise in the marketed surplus of wheat and paddy each, two quintals rise in coarse cereals and cotton each, and a five and one quintal increase in the marketed surplus of oilseeds and pulses, respectively. However, because of the reasons stated above, the value of R^{-2} was much higher when the output was taken as an independent variable rather than the area under the crop. In the case of pulses, however, the area had a better fit as compared to output. This may be due to the fact that pulses being irregular crops of the region are mostly grown on unirrigated land and exert pressure on the farmers to sell a higher amount when grown on a higher area, irrespective of the level of output and retention requirements.

There was a significant negative relationship between household size and marketed surplus for all the crops except cotton and pulses. Cotton being a commercial crop had no reason to be associated with family size. In the case of pulses, household size and marketed surplus were positively related, though significant only in one equation. As stated above, the marketed surplus of pulses was more closely related with the area operated. When this variable was not included among the explanatory variables, its effect might have been captured by the household size as both were positively correlated (see Appendix Table).

Marketed surplus fell significantly with a rise in the proportion of unirrigated area to gross cropped area only in the case of wheat and cotton. However, for the remaining crops, it was mostly negative but insignificant. The distance located from the village was insignificant in all the main crops, like wheat, paddy, cotton and coarse cereals. In the case of irregular crops like oilseeds and pulses, the coefficient was significant with alternate signs. The reason might be their irregular nature as well as a scarcity of the wide network of competent markets available in the region to sell the product. Last, the loan per acre turned out insignificant in almost all the crops thereby ruling out any possibility of extra pressure on the sale pattern of farmers due to indebtedness[3]. Thus, the most important variables affecting the marketed surplus crop wise were output and area cultivated of the respective crops with a positive or direct effect and family size with negative or indirect effect.

An important question raised about the behaviour of marketed surplus has remained whether its relationship with output is proportionate and linear or non-proportionate and non-linear. Dharam Narain (1961) in his pioneering study on the rural economy of India found that the marketed surplus as a proportion of value of output declines up to size class 10-15 acres and then rises with the size of holdings. Thus, he found that the marketed surplus as a proportion of output makes a U shape curve across farm size. Raj Krishna (1965) in his study of the subsistence crop of rice or wheat observed that in most cases there exists a strong linear and in some cases, non-linear relation between the marketable surplus and output by different peasant families. Ashoke Hati (1976) fitted two non-linear equations and grafted them into one. The results were revealing when presented graphically. Marketable surplus was found to be negative for the first part of the curve, which included land holdings up to 0.66 hectares. For holdings between 0.66 and 1.98 hectares, the curve flattened at about 5 per cent of marketable surplus. In the case of farm holdings above 1.98 hectares, the proportion of marketable surplus rose at an increasing rate as farm size increased. Nadkarni (1980) in his micro-level study based on farm management data on the millet region of Maharashtra found that the marketable surplus was negative for jowar and bajra and for total foodgrains in the smallest two size classes of below two hectares and 2 to 4 hectares and in the case of jowar even for the next size class of 4 to 6 hectares. However, in case of wheat, the marketable surplus was positive for all the size classes. Baredhan (1970) using the village level cross-section data observed that the volume of marketed surplus was a quadratic function (with positive second order derivative) of the average level of foodgrain production. In addition to this, some other studies have fitted log linear and semi-log forms.

It is to be pointed out here that a very few studies are available with farm level data on the market surplus of all crops (aggregate level), as well as individual crops. Most of the studies make their generalizations on the basis of one or two subsistence crops[4]. The present study makes an attempt to find out the relationship between marketed surplus and output produced on the basis of value of all crops (aggregate) as well as the physical quantity of individual crops. As stated above, there was no significant distress sale prevalent in the regions under study and so, no distinction is made between the marketable surplus and marketed surplus. The amount, which was made available for sale by the farmers, is taken to be the marketed surplus. We tried the various forms, *viz.*, linear, log linear, quadratic, cubic, etc., for all and individual crops. On the basis of plot and significance of coefficients, it was observed that the quadratic form was best fitted to the functions except oilseeds and cotton for which the linear form was found better. As the quadratic form is also consistent with economic interpretation, its results are presented in Table 6.33. The average and marginal propensity to sell and the elasticity of marketed surplus (calculated) with respect to output are presented in Table 6.34. The quadratic equation may be written as:

$$MS = a + bQ + CQ^2$$

where Q denotes the total quantity produced and MS the marketed surplus.

Table 6.33 reveals that the coefficient of Q^2 was significant in all the crops except oilseeds and cotton. Barring pulses, the sign of the coefficient was also positive. The significant positive coefficient of Q^2 indicates that there was a rise in rate or proportion of output marketed with a successive increase in output. This is also clear from the marginal propensity to sell (MPS). Rising MPS with a rise in output was found in the case of all crops (aggregate) as well as wheat, paddy and coarse cereals. In the case of oilseeds and cotton, the coefficient of Q^2 was insignificant, thereby indicating a linear relationship between their output and marketed surplus. Therefore, the proportion of output marketed remained constant with the rise in output of these two crops (see Table 6.34). The reason for constant MPS over all ranges of output for oilseeds and cotton was that being cash crops they were generally produced for the market by all size classes of farmers.

In the case of pulses, the coefficient of Q^2 was significant with a negative sign, indicating a fall in its marginal propensity to sell (MPS) with the rise in output. As pointed out earlier, pulses are subsistence crops and form a significant part of the food basket along with wheat and rice. However, they were not affordable equally by all the farmers. Generally, rich farmers and other classes who had a higher level of output of these crops, retained a proportionately higher amount for home consumption. Therefore, one finds that the proportion of output marketed was higher for the small and marginal farmers. A higher MPS at lower levels of output indicates the pressure of other obligations on the small farmers to sell a higher amount of additional output of pulses[5]. APS, *i.e.* the ratio of output marketed, rises with the rise in output initially but declines subsequently, thereby supporting the above contention[6]. The last column of Table 6.33 shows the minimum subsistence output. The table shows that the minimum subsistence output *i.e.* the output level below which sale becomes zero, was positive in all the crops without any exception. It implies that at a very low level of output, the whole amount was kept for self-consumption and nothing was sold in the market.

The results of elasticity of marketed surplus with respect to output are presented crop-wise in Table 6.34. It is evident from the table that the magnitude of elasticity of all crops as well as wheat, paddy, coarse cereals, oilseeds and cotton exceeded unity and was positive for all levels of output above the subsistence level. The economic implication of more than unit elasticity of marketed surplus is that, above the subsistence level, any increase in output leads to more than a proportionate increase in its volume of sale. Further, initially when the output was at the subsistence level, the value of elasticity was very high. Elasticity declined rapidly towards unity with the rise in output level above the subsistence output. However, before reaching unity, at a sufficiently high level of output, it again started rising with a further increase in output.

Table 6.33: Marketed surplus—quadratic functions.
(MS = $\alpha + \beta$ output + γ Output^2)

Name of the crop	*No. of obser-vations*	*Constant (α)*	*Output (β)*	*Output² (γ)*	R^2	*Minimum subsistence output where MS = 0*
All crops (value Rs.)	400	-2887 (-3.7)	0.878* (86.0)	0.0000001* (8.4)	0.989	3287 (7.2)
Wheat (quintals)	374	-6.5 (-3.9)	0.823* (41.0)	0.00016* (4.7)	0.967	7.9 (7.3)
Paddy (quintals)	163	-2.4* (-6.7)	0.984* (293.0)	0.0000099* (3.4)	0.999	2.4 (7.8)
Coarse cereals (quintals)	70	-1.98 (-3.0)	0.769* (10.0)	0.0029** (2.5)	0.944	2.55 (8.3)
Pulses (quintals)	91	-1.06 (-1.7)	0.899* (16.0)	-0.0043* (-14.0)	0.752	1.20 (8.0)
Oilseeds (quintals)	119	-0.37 (-3.7)	0.995* (134.0)	-0.000054 (-1.0)	0.999	0.37
Cotton (quintals)	181	-0.01 (-0.3)	0.995* (308.0)	0.00004 (1.4)	0.9997	0.01
Oilseeds (quintals)	119	-0.32 (-3.8)	0.989* (294.0)		0.999	0.32
Cotton (quintals)	181	-0.05 (-1.4)	0.999* (753.0)		0.9997	0.05

Notes: Figures in parentheses in first three columns are respective 't' values and in the last columns are average family size.
* significant at 1% level. ** significant at 5% level.

The simple interpretation of the above behaviour of elasticity is that initially when output starts rising above the subsistence level, farmers try to fulfil their basic needs of home consumption, feeds, seeds and gifts, etc. This tendency of farmers causes a falling elasticity due to the lower proportionate output sold. Once a sufficiently high level of output is achieved, despite all these obligations, the farmers sell a higher percentage of output. So, the elasticity along with APS and MPS, starts increasing at such high levels of output. This critical level of output was achieved at more than 15 acres of operated area[7]. Dharam Narain (1961) observed during the fifties that marketable surplus as a proportion of

Table 6.34: APS, MPS and output elasticity of marketed surplus.

S.N.	*Output (Q) (Rs.)*	*Marketed surplus (MS) (Rs.)*	$\hat{MS}$ *(Rs.)*	*APS* = $(\hat{MS})/Q$	*MPS* = $\Delta(\hat{MS})/\Delta Q$	*Elasticity* = *MPS* * $(Q / \hat{MS})$
All crops (aggregate)						
1	1750	0	-1350	-	-	-
2	4200	2100	802	0.19	0.879	4.60
3	6600	3100	2912	0.44	0.879	1.99
4	11400	8600	7135	0.63	0.880	1.41
5	19600	14000	14360	0.73	0.882	1.20
6	42800	31600	34875	0.81	0.887	1.09
7	67200	53200	56566	0.84	0.891	1.06
8	107850	87350	92968	0.86	0.900	1.04
9	773500	751800	736076	0.95	1.03	**1.09**
10	1133000	1126000	1120256	0.99	1.10	**1.12**
Wheat						
1	6	0	-1.6	-	-	-
2	15	9	5.9	0.39	0.83	2.10
3	30	17	18.3	0.61	0.83	1.36
4	42	26	28.3	0.67	0.84	1.24
5	80	68	60.4	0.75	0.85	1.12
6	140	100	111.9	0.80	0.87	1.09
7	200	180	164.5	0.82	0.89	1.08
8	470	450	415.7	0.88	0.97	**1.10**
9	600	520	544.9	0.91	1.01	**1.12**
10	982	962	956.0	0.97	1.14	**1.17**
Paddy						
1	4	4	1.5	0.38	0.984	2.62
2	12	10	9.4	0.78	0.984	1.26
3	32	28	29.1	0.91	0.985	1.08
4	50	49	46.8	0.94	0.985	1.05
5	112	109	107.9	0.96	0.986	1.02
6	152	150	147.4	0.97	0.987	1.02
7	240	220	234.3	0.98	0.989	1.01
8	352	350	345.2	0.98	0.991	1.01
9	672	668	663.3	0.99	0.997	1.01
10	1492	1487	1487.8	0.997	1.01	**1.02**
Coarse cereals						
1	2	0	-0.4	-	-	-
2	4	3	1.1	0.29	0.79	2.88
3	8	4	4.4	0.54	0.81	1.48
4	23	23	17.2	0.75	0.90	1.21
5	45	40	38.5	0.85	1.03	1.20
6	80	78	78.1	0.98	1.23	**1.26**
Pulses						
1	2.4	0	1.0	0.45	0.88	1.97
2	6	6	4.2	0.70	0.85	1.21
3	16	15	12.2	0.76	0.76	1.00
4	32	29	23.3	0.73	0.62	0.86
5	40	30	28.0	0.70	0.55	0.79
6	52	48	34.1	0.66	0.45	0.69
Oil seeds						
1	2	2	1.7	0.83	0.989	1.19
2	6	6	5.6	0.94	0.989	1.05
3	10	10	9.6	0.96	0.989	1.03
4	38	36	37.3	0.98	0.989	1.01
5	50	48	49.1	0.98	0.989	1.01
6	90	88	88.7	0.99	0.989	1.00
Cotton						
1	1	1	0.95	0.949	0.999	1.05
2	6	6	5.9	0.991	0.999	1.02
3	20	20	19.9	0.997	0.999	1.00
4	44	44	43.9	0.998	0.999	1.00
5	99	99	98.9	0.998	0.999	1.00

output, *i.e.*, APS decreases with the increase in farm size up to the size class of 10-15 acres. Above this size class, it starts increasing steadily.

The following crops, *viz.*, oilseeds, cotton and pulses show somewhat different trends in terms of elasticity. Oilseeds and cotton were represented by linear regressions and therefore, elasticity did not show any rising trend. At all levels of output, the value of elasticity was near unity and did not differ much across farm size. This indicates that these two crops belong to the category of cash crops and any increase in output leads to a proportionate increase in marketed surplus, irrespective of the farm size. Further, since the intercept was negative in the linear regression and b coefficient positive in both the cases, elasticity never fell below unity. In the case of pulses, like MPS and APS, elasticity too fell steadily from 1.97 to 0.69 and thereby fell below unity. It indicates that with higher output, the farmers in case of falling MPS, put proportionately lower amount for sale.

Thus the findings of upward movements of elasticity and rising MPS have far reaching implications. Rising MPS contradicts Raj Krishna's assertion that the small as well as large farmers producing above the subsistence level sell the same additional quantity out of additional output. Rising MPS points out that the supply behaviour of farmers is not similar and it differs from small to large farmers. To understand the supply behaviour of farmers, one also needs to understand their land distribution. The upward movement of elasticity at a substantially high level of output implies that generally the large farmers sell a proportionately higher amount of increased output, as compared to the small farmers. The policy implication is that to foster a high growth of market surplus, the holding size should increase. However, it will have very serious consequences for employment in the rural areas.

Pattern of Market Disbursement

Before concluding the chapter the quarterly distribution of the marketed surplus of the field data is presented in Table 6.35. The total sale during the year has been divided into four quarters. For Rabi, the first quarter consists of April, May and June and for Kharif it consists of September, October and November. The subsequent second, third and fourth quarters consist of the next three months each, respectively.

It is clear from the table that most of the output was sold in the first quarter, *i.e.* after the harvest. Taking for example, the case of all crops (aggregate) as shown by the Table 6.35, 95 per cent of output by marginal farmers and 98 per cent of output by large farmers was sold immediately in the first quarter after the harvest. Other farmers also sold around 96 per cent of their output in the first quarter and the remaining 4 per cent was disposed of in the second and third quarters.

Crop-wise, the whole quantity of wheat and coarse cereals were disposed of in the first quarter. Pulses and oilseeds entirely were sold in the first two quarters and only in case of paddy and cotton, a little amount was carried till the third quarter. On an average, 90 to 95 per cent of the output of all the individual crops was sold in the first quarter and mostly immediately after the harvest.

Thus, the above analysis contradicts the general belief that there is a tendency to hoard produce by large farmers for speculative and other purposes. Small as well as large farmers in the regions surveyed, tried to dispose of their produce immediately after the harvest. In this respect large farmers were hastier than the small farmers. The reasons for farmer's sales in the first quarter might be lack of appropriate storage facilities, uncertainty of prices or demonstration effect (as will be seen in detail in the next chapter).

Table 6.35: Quarterly distribution of marketed surplus of different crops (%).

Farm size	*First quarter*	*Second quarter*	*Third quarter*	*Fourth qurter*	*Total*
All crops (aggregate)					
Marginal	95.08	3.97	0.95	0.00	100.0
Small	96.99	3.01	0.00	0.00	100.0
Semi-medium	93.84	6.16	0.00	0.00	100.0
Medium	96.34	3.66	0.00	0.00	100.0
Large	98.39	1.29	0.32	0.00	100.0
Total	96.88	2.95	0.17	0.00	100.0
Wheat					
Marginal	100.0	0.00	0.00	0.00	100.0
Small	100.0	0.00	0.00	0.00	100.0
Semi-medium	100.0	0.00	0.00	0.00	100.0
Medium	100.0	0.00	0.00	0.00	100.0
Large	100.0	0.00	0.00	0.00	100.0
Total	100.0	0.00	0.00	0.00	100.0
Paddy					
Marginal	95.71	4.29	0.00	0.00	100.0
Small	95.98	4.02	0.00	0.00	100.0
Semi-medium	96.49	3.51	0.00	0.00	100.0
Medium	94.55	5.45	0.00	0.00	100.0
Large	99.27	0.00	0.73	0.00	100.0
Total	97.12	2.55	0.33	0.00	100.0
Coarse cereals					
Marginal	100.0	0.00	0.00	0.00	100.0
Small	100.0	0.00	0.00	0.00	100.0
Semi-medium	100.0	0.00	0.00	0.00	100.0
Medium	100.0	0.00	0.00	0.00	100.0
Large	100.0	0.00	0.00	0.00	100.0
Total	100.0	0.00	0.00	0.00	100.0
Pulses					
Marginal	100.0	0.00	0.00	0.00	100.0
Small	65.85	34.15	0.00	0.00	100.0
Semi-medium	87.57	12.43	0.00	0.00	100.0
Medium	90.70	9.30	0.00	0.00	100.0
Large	100.0	0.00	0.00	0.00	100.0
Total	94.24	5.76	0.00	0.00	100.0
Oil seeds					
Marginal	100.0	0.00	0.00	0.00	100.0
Small	88.19	11.81	0.00	0.00	100.0
Semi-medium	93.75	6.25	0.00	0.00	100.0
Medium	94.77	5.23	0.00	0.00	100.0
Large	95.87	4.13	0.00	0.00	100.0
Total	94.98	5.02	0.00	0.00	100.0
Cotton					
Marginal	89.91	6.73	336	0.00	100.0
Small	100.0	0.00	0.00	0.00	100.0
Semi-medium	81.32	18.68	0.00	0.00	100.0
Medium	94.45	5.55	0.00	0.00	100.0
Large	92.21	7.79	0.00	0.00	100.0
Total	91.47	8.39	0.14	0.00	100.0

Summing up the chapter, the variable that most important affected the marketed surplus was the output level. The other significant variables were operated area, family size, unirrigated area and area under tenancy in that order. While output, operated area and area under tenancy fostered the marketed surplus, family size and unirrigated area had a negative relationship with marketed surplus. Not only output and output marketed were directly related, they established a direct and more than proportionate relationship, thereby having rising MPS over all ranges of output. Moreover, elasticity of marketed surplus with respect to output declined initially but at a subsequently higher level of output, it started increasing. The rising elasticity indicates that to increase marketed surplus, increase in output of large farmers becomes more important and should be encouraged. Finally, farmers had a tendency to sell their produce immediately after the harvest and nearly 90 to 95 per cent of output was sold in the first quarter after the harvest.

Turning to the original hypotheses as mentioned in the first chapter—

- H_1: Proportion of output marketed is directly related with the farm size.
- H_2: Marginal propensity to sell rises with the rise in output.
- H_3: Marketed surplus and distance of the village from the market are inversely related.
- H_4: The larger the size of holdings, the larger the times lag in marketing the produce.

The first two hypotheses are accepted as except pulses, almost all other crops showed a rising APS and MPS with the rise in output. In addition to APS, the marketed surplus as a proportion of output had a positive significant coefficient with respect to operated area for all the crops, except pulses and cotton. The third hypothesis cannot be accepted as the coefficient of distance remained insignificant in all of the important regular crops of the regions. The fourth hypothesis is also rejected as large farmers sold a higher proportion of their output than small farmers in the first quarter.

NOTES

1. See, for example, Parthasarathy and Rao (1964), Krishna (1965), Rao (1965), Bhargava and Rastogi (1972), and Prasad (1989).
2. See, for example, Muthiah (1964), Hati (1976), and Chattopadhyay and Sen (1988).
3. Insignificant coefficient of loans rules out any possibility of distress sales even in the case of paramount food crop like wheat.
4. Raj Krishna's study has been criticized because of making generalization on the basis of one or two subsistence crops like rice or wheat. See, for example, Rao Hanumantha, Krishnaji, Manoranjan Mazumdar and Brahmananda Prasad, Economic Weekly, February 1965.
5. This cannot be termed as distress sales as farmers sell under the pressure of cash requirements but never repurchase from the market. Moreover, the low level of output of pulses does not necessarily represent the small farmers. Large farmers might also have sown pulses in a small area.
6. The conflicting results in Table 6.21, where the proportion of output marketed rises with the rise in farm size may be due to this initial rise in APS and the table fails to point out the subsequent fall in APS at high levels of output.
7. This size of holding is calculated by dividing the level of output where the elasticity takes an upward turn by the productivity per acre.

APPENDIX-6A

Table 6.1A: Zero-order correlation matrix.

Variables	*MS*	*Output*	*NOA*	*HH size*	*Distance*	*UA/ GCA*	*Loan per acre*	*ALI/ NOA*	*MS/ OUT*
All crops (aggregate)									
MS	1.00								
Output	0.99	1.00							
Net operated area	0.83	-	1.00						
HH size	0.27	0.30	0.44	1.00					
Distance	-0.06	-0.07	-0.05	-0.06	1.00				
UA / GCA	-0.14	-0.15	-0.05	-0.05	0.08	1.00			
Loan per acre	-0.08	-0.08	-0.09	-0.00	0.04	0.06	1.00		
ALI / NOA	-0.00	-0.01	0.01	-0.03	0.03	-0.13	-0.02	1.00	
MS / Output	-	0.36	0.35	0.20	-0.01	-0.29	-0.01	0.13	1.00
Wheat									
MS	1.00							-	
Output	0.98	1.00						-	
Net operated area	0.93	-	1.00					-	
HH size	0.36	0.41	0.43	1.00				-	
Distance	-0.08	-0.09	-0.10	-0.06	1.00			-	
UA / GCA	-0.15	-0.15	-0.12	-0.01	0.04	1.00		-	
Loan per acre	-0.05	-0.05	-0.05	-0.01	0.04	0.03	1.00	-	
MS / Output	-	0.18	0.25	0.11	0.05	-0.1	0.02	-	1.00
Paddy									
MS	1.00							-	
Output	1.00	1.00						-	
Net operated area	0.80	-	1.00					-	
HH size	0.14	0.14	0.27	1.00				-	
Distance	-0.04	-0.04	-0.10	-0.14	1.00			-	
UA / GCA	-0.05	-0.05	-0.08	0.06	-0.05	1.00		-	
Loan per acre	-0.08	-0.08	-0.06	0.01	-0.06	-0.11	1.00	-	
MS / Output	-	0.25	0.20	0.03	-0.10	-0.12	-0.10	-	1.00
Coarse cereals									
MS	1.00							-	
Output	0.97	1.00						-	
Net operated area	0.57	-	1.00					-	
HH size	0.27	0.34	0.43	1.00				-	
Distance	0.23	0.22	-0.03	0.06	1.00			-	
UA / GCA	-0.12	-0.12	0.10	-0.26	-0.09	1.00		-	
Loan per acre	0.05	0.04	-0.01	0.14	0.12	-0.22	1.00	-	
MS / Output	-	0.43	0.24	-0.07	0.11	0.06	0.17	-	1.00
Pulses									
MS	1.00							-	
Output	0.49	1.00						-	
Net operated area	0.74	-	1.00					-	
HH size	0.22	0.08	0.15	1.00				-	
Distance	-0.17	-0.04	-0.05	0.18	1.00			-	
UA / GCA	0.10	0.13	0.22	-0.27	-0.01	1.00		-	
Loan per acre	-0.10	-0.07	-0.12	-0.01	-0.02	0.11	1.00	-	
MS / Output	-	0.01	0.10	0.20	-0.05	-0.0/2	0.07	-	1.00
Oilseeds									
MS	1.00							-	
Output	0.999	1.00						-	
Net operated area	0.91	-	1.00					-	
HH size	0.23	0.24	0.31	1.00				-	
Distance	-0.10	-0.10	-0.02	0.08	1.00			-	
UA / GCA	-0.06	-0.06	-0.09	0.05	-0.04	1.00		-	
Loan per acre	-0.10	-0.10	-0.04	0.07	0.07	-0.23	1.00	-	
MS / Output	-	0.17	0.20	-0.09	0.26	-0.10	0.06	-	1.00
Cotton									
MS	1.00							-	
Output	1.00	1.00						-	
Net operated area	0.77	-	1.00					-	
HH size	0.40	0.40	0.48	1.00				-	
Distance	-0.02	-0.02	-0.05	0.05	1.00			-	
UA / GCA	-0.02	-0.02	-0.12	-0.02	-0.10	1.00		-	
Loan per acre	-0.16	-0.16	-0.02	-0.03	0.03	-0.23	1.00	-	
MS / Output	-	0.07	0.03	-0.11	-0.11	-0.26	0.03	-	1.00

APPENDIX-6B

Table 6.2A: Marketable Surplus of Important Crops (All India).

S.N.	*Commodity*	*Marketable surplus as a % of production*[1]	*Reference year*[1]	*Marketable surplus as a % of production*[2]	*Reference year*[2]
1	Paddy	42.71	1981-82	59.20	1988-89
2	Wheat	52.44	"	54.47	"
3	Jowar	32.85	"	60.20	"
4	Bajra	33.29	"	54.23	"
5	Maize	27.19	"	61.30	"
6	Ragi	18.20	"	56.84	"
7	Barley	28.00	"	-	
8	Mung	-		73.50	"
9	Urd	-		75.20	"
10	Arhar	50.88	"	53.70	"
11	Gram	40.30	"	53.00	"
12	Ground nut	82.30	1982-83	82.35	"
13	Caster-seed	94.00	"	87.90	"
14	Seasamum	77.60	"	68.10	"
15	Rape-seed & Mustard	92.70	"	63.50	"
16	Lin seed	88.80	"	66.50	"
17	Niger seed	97.50	"	92.77	"
18	Safflower	87.70	"	-	
19	Sunflower	86.50	"	93.75	"
20	Soyabean	90.00	"	83.80	"
21	Coriander seed	95.00	Avg of 1961-62 to 1965-66	94.00	"
22	Garlic	90.00	"	79.40	"
23	Cotton seed	-		94.70	"
24	Sugarcane	-		92.50	"
25	Jute	-		87.30	"
26	Sann hemp	-		96.50	"
27	Tobacco	-		96.80	"
28	Fodders	-		23.30	"

Sources: (1) Report of the High Power Committee on Agricultural Marketing, Government of India, Ministry of Rural Development, Directorate of Marketing and Inspection, Faridabad, 1992.
(2) NCAER (1990).

7

Marketing Efficiency of the Households Surveyed

Generally farm output is not produced at the time, place and form in which the consumer requires it. Since the purpose of all production is to satisfy consumer's demand, agricultural output is of no use until supply and demand of these products are brought together. Agricultural marketing is the combination of activities by which agricultural produce is made available for consumption to the final consumer in a suitable form, at a right time and right place. According to the National Commission on Agriculture, "Agricultural Marketing includes all aspects of market structure and systems, both functional and institutional, pre and post-harvest operations, assembling, grading, storage, transport and distribution"[1]. Thus, agricultural marketing is a composite and specialized economic process, the principal function of which is the determination of equilibrium prices of different agricultural products over space and time.

To a large extent the determination of these prices depends upon the availability of marketing infrastructure between the point of production and point of consumption. In any region, if the marketing services are well provided, the marketing operations would be carried out smoothly and effectively. Important among these services are—availability of well furnished regulated markets with efficient functionaries;

standardized weights and measures; adequate transport and communication facilities; proper storage facilities, well connected market information system. In addition, the cultivators would be able to harness the benefits of the marketing network only if they are not heavily indebted to private agencies, money-lenders or *arhatias* and they participate in the market with some marketed surplus, after satisfying their home needs.

While marketing efficiency was analysed by means of the cointegration technique using the secondary data of wholesale prices in the *mandis* of Haryana in Chapter 4. An attempt is made in this chapter to work out the marketing efficiency of the sampled households in the light of data generated by our survey. The chapter has been sub-divided into four sections. The first section presents the marketing infrastructure available to the households surveyed. The second section presents the cost of marketing the produce by different farm size categories. Variations in the price received by various classes of farmers are discussed with the help of simple tabular analysis in the third section. The variations in prices because of factors like value of output, marketed surplus, distance from the market, indebtedness, time of sale, etc., are analysed with the help of a multiple regression analysis in the last section of the chapter.

Marketing Infrastructure Available to the Households

Regulated Markets

The main purpose in creating regulated markets was to standardize the sale and purchase of agricultural products, create conditions for fair competition and ensure a square deal to the farmers. Thus to make agricultural marketing more orderly and efficient, the institution of the regulated market has a role to play. In the two districts under study, which were well connected with the marketing network, there were 7 regulated markets and 18 sub-yards operating in Kaithal district and 6 regulated markets and 13 sub-yards operating in Sirsa district in 1993-94. Both Kaithal and Sirsa were the largest *mandis* in the respective districts and all the farmers in each district could approach these *mandis* with ease. The sub-yards generally operated as purchasing centres for their respective *mandis* and could provide marketing opportunities to the farmers at their doorsteps in the village or nearby towns. As these sub-yards operate mostly for wheat farmers got this facility for marketing of wheat within a radius of 5 to 7 kilometres of their production point. For other crops, even the farthest farmer had to cover a maximum of 20 to 25 kilometres to find a *mandi* for the produce[2] in both the districts.

Table 7.1: Percentage of sale through regulated markets.

Name of the crop	*Percentage of farmers selling through regulated markets*	*Percentage of quantity sold through regulated markets*
Wheat	99.70	99.98
Paddy (Basmati)	98.50	98.65
Paddy (PR)	100.0	100.0
Cotton (American)	99.40	99.96
Cotton *(Desi)*	100.0	100.0
Mustard	100.0	100.0
Gram	100.0	100.0

The result of such a widespread market network was that the majority of the farmers were able to sell all the different commodities that they produced in the regulated markets. Table 7.1 presents the percentage of sale in regulated markets by the households surveyed. It is clear from the table that the sale outside the regulated *mandis* was just negligible. Almost all the farmers sold their products in the regulated *mandis* and the whole quantity was sold through these *mandis*.

An important contribution of the regulated markets consisted in their system of uniform market charges. Generally farmers had to bear three types of charges in the regulated market, namely, (i) Unloading at the market place, (ii) Cleaning and dressing, and (iii) Weighment charges. The unloading, cleaning and dressing charges were at the rate of Rs. 1.20 per bag and weighment charges were at the rate of Rs. 1.12 per bag[3]. One bag included 95 kgs. of wheat, 65 kgs. of paddy and 45 kgs. of sunflower. The farmers didn't have to pay any commission, brokerage or market fee, which were charged from the buyers by the commission agents.

Regulated markets have brought considerable benefits to the producer-sellers by preventing trading malpractices such as unauthorized market charges, falsification of weights and measures, etc. In the regulated markets, only the legal market charges were taken and these were fixed and strictly enforced by the market committees. The practice of over-weighing of farmer's produce was not possible as the weighment was allowed only to the licensed weighmen in the presence of the cultivators. Moreover, market committees regularly checked the scales and weights.

However, some malpractices were observed in the markets of the regions surveyed. All categories of farmers in both the districts were found heavily indebted to *arhatias* or commission agents. As a result, the farmers lost their bargaining power and were compelled to sell their produce to the same commission agents (to whom they were indebted) even if it meant getting a lower price for their produce. Moreover, farmer's positive balance with *arhatias* was not subject to any interest. However, the negative balance (or loan provided by *arhatias*) to the farmers was subject to the rate of interest of 24 to 36 per cent per annum. Regulated markets of both the districts had little or no facility for grading and most of the products were exchanged without any sort of grading. Thus, the farmers with better quality of produce were deprived of a higher price due to lack of grading practices.

Transport System

An important constituent of efficient marketing is the developed system of transportation and communication. Lack of proper transport causes an imperfect market structure and disparities in prices across different places. Autarky or isolated markets are subject to various exploitations by traders and other intermediaries, while market centres, which are well connected with neighbouring markets, enjoy the advantage of wider competition and benefit both to the buyers and the sellers.

To provide the gains of competition to the farmers, not only should market centres be well connected, but they should also have a good connectivity with the villages where the production takes place. In other words, the widespread marketing network would enable efficient marketing only if developed inter and intra-regional transport facilities are present.

The districts studied had a very developed transportation system. About 99.3 per cent villages in Kaithal and about 98.7 per cent villages in Sirsa were connected to the market centres by *pucca* or metalled roads. Thereby, all the households or cultivators had easy access to market centres. With the developed transportation, quicker means of transport replaced to some extent the traditional bullock and horse carts.

In both the districts, tractor-trolley and tempos had become the more popular means for bringing in the produce from the village to the market centres.

Among the households surveyed, generally the tractor-trolley was observed to be the main source of transportation for produce. Large farmers used their own tractor-trolley for transportation while small and marginal farmers generally hired this facility from the large farmers to transport their produce. Table 7.2 shows the ownership of tractors among the households surveyed. It is clear from the table that as high as 77 per cent of large farmers and 41 per cent of medium farmers had the facility of their own tractor. However, no small and marginal farmer owned any tractor and they had to hire this facility from other farmers.

Table 7.2: Ownership of tractor among the households surveyed.

Farm size	*Number of households having their own tractor*	*Percentage of households having their own tractors*
Marginal	0	0.00
Small	0	0.00
Semi-medium	9	9.37
Medium	30	40.54
Large	30	76.92
Total	69	17.25

The bullock cart was also used as a source of transportation but usually for a short distance. Farmers who covered a long distance in search of a better *mandi* to gain a higher price for their produce were seen using tempos for marketing their produce. For example, some farmers from Kaithal district sold paddy-basmati in Trori *mandi* which is better known for paddy-basmati located in Karnal district and used the services of tempos. Similarly, many farmers from

Sirsa district sold cotton in better-known Barnala *mandi* in Punjab using the facility of tempos and trucks.

The unit cost of transportation varies from market to market or even from village to village depending upon the conditions of road, distance to be covered and mode of transport used. Transportation cost for each crop by farm size is discussed in the next section of this chapter. It will be seen that average transportation cost in the villages varied from Rs. 5 to Rs. 10 per quintal according to the distance covered. It was observed in the field survey that the tractor-trolley has turned out to be the least cost transportation source. However, because of the low opportunity cost of the bullock cart, this source was common among the small and marginal farmers for short distances.

Storage and Warehousing

Availability of suitable and adequate storage is an integral part of an efficient marketing strategy. The seasonal character of agricultural production and its continuous consumption throughout the year increases the importance of storage in agricultural marketing. As is well known, agricultural production due to its biological nature is subject to fluctuations, thus influencing the agricultural prices. If the farmers are provided with the appropriate storage facilities, it would help them to weather these fluctuations in production by increasing their withholding capacity. Thus, storage can enable farmers to have more desirable and competitive prices and set them free from the vagaries of glut sale.

Among the households surveyed, it was observed that the farmers were completely lacking in scientific storage facilities. After disposal in the post-harvest season, whatever was left over was stored in *kachha kothies, bharolas* made of mud or bricks, earthen pots, mobile oil drums, metallic bins and *pucca kothies*. The produce was stored either in the open or in the bags, which were stacked in rooms and *verandahs* of the *kachha* or *pucca* house.

Among the villages surveyed, it was found that all the households stored wheat for their personal consumption, for seed and for feeding the cattle. Wheat being a prime consumption commodity was stored for the whole year. Generally to save it from insects, it was filled in bags and kept in *bhusa* or in a *tuda* house. However, steel drums, being a better storage method, were increasing by the choice for storing wheat, paddy and other agricultural products for home consumption. Primary cooperative societies operating in the village supplied steel drums to the farmers at a subsidized rate. Table 7.3 shows the figures for farmers with the facility of steel drums.

Table 7.3: Number of farmers having the facility of steel drums.

Farm size	*Number of households having steel drums*	*Percentage of households having steel drums*
Marginal	23	24.0
Small	26	27.4
Semi-medium	26	27.1
Medium	30	40.5
Large	20	51.3
Total	125	31.3

The table shows that steel drums were popular not only among the large farmers but also among the small and marginal farmers. Because of their higher requirement of home consumption, many of large and medium farmers owned two or more than two steel drums.

Table 7.4 shows crop wise time of sale after the harvest. It is clear from the table that all the farmers sold wheat, paddy PR and cotton *desi* immediately within a week of harvest. However, in the case of other crops, some cultivators did avoid sales at harvest and waited for better prices, utilizing whatever domestic facilities were available for storage. Nonetheless, in case of other crops also, 82 per cent of paddy basmati, 87 per cent of cotton American and 93 and 95 per cent of mustard and gram, respectively were sold within a week of harvest (see Table 7.4). Moreover, an immediate sale after harvest was prevalent not only among small farmers who were in dire need of cash but also among the large farmers.

Large farmers on account of their sound financial position were capable of maintaining better storage facilities than the small farmers and could withhold their stocks for a longer time period. However, the tendency of large farmers to sell immediately after the harvest shows that the immediate sale was not due to the lack of storage facility alone but also due to other factors. The possible explanation for an immediate disposal by large farmers could be the following: (i) the price support by the government insured that there was no major rise in prices in the later period (wheat and rice being the principal ones), thus not yielding enough returns on storage of these commodities; (ii) indebtedness of farmers to the *arhatias*; and (iii) need of cash for buying inputs for the next seasonal crop, for consumption and for other purposes.

Table 7.4. Pattern of sale (crop-wise) (percentage of sale).

Time Period of Sale	*Marginal*	*Small*	*Semi-med.*	*Medium*	*Large*	*Total*
Wheat						
Immediately after harvest	100.0	100.0	100.0	100.0	100.0	100.0
Within 7-30 days of harvest	-	-	-	-	-	-
Within 30-60 days of harvest	-	-	-	-	-	-
After 60 days of harvest	-	-	-	-	-	-
Paddy (PR)						
Immediately after harvest	100.0	100.0	100.0	100.0	100.0	100.0
Within 7-30 days of harvest	-	-	-	-	-	-
Within 30-60 days of harvest	-	-	-	-	-	-
After 60 days of harvest	-	-	-	-	-	-
Paddy (Basmati)						
Immediately after harvest	90.8	91.7	79.2	62.5	95.5	81.6
Within 7-30 days of harvest	2.5	0.0	14.6	15.3	0.0	7.3
Within 30-60 days of harvest	6.7	8.3	6.1	21.0	0.0	8.9
After 60 days of harvest	0.0	0.0	0.0	1.2	4.5	2.2
Cotton *(Desi)*						
Immediately after harvest	100.0	100.0	100.0	100.0	100.0	100.0
Within 7-30 days of harvest	-	-	-	-	-	-
Within 30-60 days of harvest	-	-	-	-	-	-
After 60 days of harvest	-	-	-	-	-	-
Cotton (American)						
Immediately after harvest	86.4	97.0	77.8	88.0	87.6	86.8
Within 7-30 days of harvest	0.0	0.0	0.0	4.4	0.0	1.3
Within 30-60 days of harvest	0.0	0.0	10.9	2.9	0.0	2.7
After 60 days of harvest	13.6	3.0	11.3	4.7	12.4	9.2
Mustard						
Immediately after harvest	100.0	100.0	88.4	96.0	92.2	93.0
Within 7-30 days of harvest	0.0	0.0	0.0	0.0	0.0	0.0
Within 30-60 days of harvest	0.0	0.0	0.0	0.0	5.1	2.4
After 60 days of harvest	0.0	0.0	11.6	4.0	2.7	4.6
Gram						
Immediately after harvest	100.0	65.9	100.0	90.7	100.0	95.3
Within 7-30 days of harvest	0.0	0.0	0.0	0.0	0.0	0.0
Within 30-60 days of harvest	0.0	0.0	0.0	0.0	0.0	0.0
After 60 days of harvest	0.0	34.1	0.0	9.3	0.0	4.7

Table 7.5 shows the percentage of sale in different quarters at different levels of storage investment. The table strengthens the above argument that instantaneous sale after harvest was not solely due to lack of storage facilities. It is evident from the table that as high as 94 to 99 per cent of the produce was sold in the first quarter after harvest irrespective of the level of storage investment. It is to be pointed out here that the

storage investment includes expenditure made on metallic bins, *kachha kothies* and *pucca kothies*. These methods of storage were unscientific and the end result was a deterioration in the quality of produce stored. Similarly, produce kept in gunny bags or left open in *kachha* or *pucca* house was liable to damage by insects, moisture and rodents. In addition, there was a risk on the price front also. In some of the crops, the price was quite high in the first quarter and declined or remained stagnant in subsequent quarters. In some other crops the price rose in the subsequent quarters but not in proportion to the storage losses. Under the circumstances, farmers generally sold their major produce immediately after the harvest and avoided the risk involved in storing the products.

Thus, non-availability of proper scientific storage facilities and stagnant prices (*e.g.* wheat and paddy) led to an immediate sale after the harvest. It is, therefore, desirable that farmers should be furnished with scientific godown facilities at reasonable rates. There should also be certain price incentives in the post-harvest season that would help farmers to gain prices that are more reasonable for their produce. In addition to helping the farmers it would also release *mandis* from the burden of glut sales after harvest.

Table 7.5: Pattern of quarterly sale at different levels of storage investment (all crops).

Storage investment	*1st quarter*	*2nd quarter*	*3rd quarter*	*4th quarter*	*Total*
Up to Rs. 5,000	96.9	3.0	0.1	0.0	100.0
Rs. 5,000-10,000	97.9	2.1	0.0	0.0	100.0
Rs. 10,000-20,000	94.2	5.8	0.0	0.0	100.0
Above Rs. 20,000	99.1	0.4	0.5	0.0	100.0

Market Information

Market information means communication of knowledge or intelligence. It includes all facts, estimates, opinions and other information used in marketing decisions that affect the marketing of goods and services (Tousley *et al.*, 1968: 496). The information needed for decision-making in marketing is varied and relates to arrivals, sales, demand and prices for certain commodities from important centres in country or outside. Efficient marketing in agriculture depends to a great extent upon the availability and dissemination of accurate, adequate and timely market information among the traders and cultivators (Gupta, 1975: 110).

Market information is very useful to cultivators in planning the sale of their produce. Farmers can base the pattern of their sale through a successful interpretation of trends depicted by market data. Guided by such correct and timely information, they can choose the appropriate time and space to market their produce to maximize their returns. However, the real advantage of market information lies in its correct use, which is determined by the accurate interpretation of the available information.

With the advancement of science and technology, information technology is being widely implemented in agricultural marketing. Installation of computers at the State Agricultural Marketing Boards are being utilized for creating a database of trade at the state level and enhancing it by getting information at the national and international level. The National Informatics Centre has been the focal organization for creating a national level database through its District Computer Centres. Information regarding the local trading is being disseminated to the producers and traders through the mass media, such as television, radio and newspapers. However, installations of computers at the market yards to capture the basic details of local trade have yet to be undertaken on a wider scale.

The advantage of market intelligence was not available to these cultivators who had limited means and were generally ill-equipped in terms of modern means of communication. For market information, they relied on a number of sources, only a few of which were accurate and reliable. These sources included radio broadcast, daily newspaper, telephone messages from the market centres, personal visit to the market centres, information received from neighbouring villages and information from agents, brokers and buyers who visited their village.

In the regions surveyed, the most prevalent source of information was observed to be the personal visit of the farmers to the market yard. As most of the farmers sold their product immediately after the harvest, they kept in touch with the market during harvest days either via personal visits to the nearby towns or through their neighbours. Some farmers who were more conscious about the price in other markets used to get this information from the daily broadcast of prices at the All India Radio. Some educated farmers had a direct correspondence with the markets and were able to get this information through post. A few large farmers owing telephone connections were in direct touch with the markets for price information.

However, it was observed that in many cases the farmers hardly bothered about the price prevailing in other markets and brought their product to the pre-determined *arhatia* and sold it at whatever price was determined by open auctioning. This was due to the following reasons: indebtedness of farmers to the *arhatia*; supply of materials by *arhatia* like bags, transportation means and other implements, fertiliser, pesticides, etc.; consumption loans provided by the *arhatia* to the farmers; and also due to personal relations or support established by the *arhatia* to the cultivators.

To sum up, among the households surveyed, there was a complete lack of market intelligence. On the one hand, there was a lack of consciousness among the farmers about the prevailing price in different markets and on the other hand, there was the financial compulsiveness to sell in a single pre-determined market. Thus, these factors created hurdles in the equalization of prices in different markets.

Indebtedness

Efficient marketing requires that the producer-seller should be free to choose a market for his product. If the producer is in debt, his decision of how much output is to be disposed of, the place and time of disposal and other related aspects are affected to a great extent, by the nature and source of borrowings.

Farmers who borrow from non-institutional sources are generally compelled to sell their produce to the creditors at lower prices. In addition, untimely pressure from the creditors to repay the loan may also force the farmers to dispose of their produce at a lower price immediately after the harvest. The latter phenomenon is more common among the farmers who are indebted to *arhatias* or commission agents. In contrast, the farmers who borrow from the government or public institutions sell their produce independently, at a suitable time and place and to a suitable agency and gain an appropriate price for their produce.

The households surveyed in both the districts had a high tendency of borrowing. It is apparent from Table 5.4 (see Chapter 5) that per household borrowing of large farmers was much more than small farmers in both the districts. Moreover, large farmers were taking more loans from both the sources, institutional as well as non-institutional as compared to small farmers. The following tables show the break-up of institutional and non-institutional credit by farm size categories.

Table 7.6: Source of borrowing (No. of farmers).

Farm size	*No. of farmers surveyed*	*Source of borrowing*				
		Commercial banks	*Co-operative societies*	*Land mortgage banks*	*Arhatias*	*Money-lenders and others*
Marginal	96	8	20	6	13	1
Small	95	6	31	12	38	2
Semi-medium	96	12	38	11	42	2
Medium	74	15	29	6	40	1
Large	39	17	16	3	17	0
Total	400	58	134	38	150	6

Table 7.6 reveals that in terms of all size categories a larger number of farmers took loans from institutional sources than non-institutional sources. However, the percentage of amount provided by non-institutional sources was much higher as compared to institutional sources (see Table 7.7). The results of the tables rule out the general contention that institutional credit is not available to the small and marginal

Table 7.7: Percentage of amount borrowed from different sources.

	Institutional				*Non-institutional*			
	Commercial banks	*Co-operative societies*	*Land mortgage banks*	*Total*	*Arhatias*	*Money-lenders and others*	*Total*	*Sum Total*
Marginal	29.1	17.0	20.7	66.8	26.6	6.6	33.2	100.0
Small	6.5	18.7	11.7	36.9	59.9	3.2	63.1	100.0
Semi-medium	21.0	16.5	7.4	44.9	52.5	2.5	55.0	100.0
Medium	19.1	14.0	3.6	36.7	62.9	0.4	63.3	100.0
Large	28.5	10.4	13.0	51.9	48.2	0.0	48.2	100.0
Total	21.4	14.1	9.4	44.9	53.6	1.4	55.0	100.0

farmers and is generally appropriated by the large farmers. Table 7.7 shows that the marginal farmers borrowed 67 per cent amount from institutional sources and only 33 per cent from non-institutional sources. The corresponding figures for large farmers were 52 and 48 per cent, respectively. Nonetheless, the credit provided by the *arhatias* was still very high for small as well as large farmers. More than half of the credit to all size of farmers was provided by *arhatias* at a rate of interest, which was two to three times higher than the institutional credit.

To sum up, the above discussion, it is clear from the analysis that all the farmers sold their produce in the regulated markets. Thus, the farmers of the state have been almost free from the clutches of traders and intermediaries who cause inefficiency in the marketing system by increasing the difference between the price received by the producers and the price paid by the consumers. With the availability of approachable *pucca* roads and transport facilities, farmers were able to choose a market, which could fetch them the highest possible price. Agricultural marketing efficiency has increased to a greater extent with the regulated marketing system and with the elimination of intermediaries who were the subject of excessive exploitation. However, the marketing system of the regions can still be improved by providing the farmers with scientific storage facilities, proper grading and standardization of their produce, by providing them the proper market intelligence and making provision for more institutional credit to all the farmers.

Marketing Cost

Generally speaking, the costs of marketing the produce are the expenses incurred in bringing the goods and services from the producer, *i.e.* farmer at the field, to the consumer. These costs generally include handling, packing and loading charges at the farm place, storage and transportation charges, charges for unloading, cleaning and weighing at the market place and other retail charges to the consumers. However, the present study looks at the expenses incurred by the producers in selling their produce to the traders through the services of commission agents in the regulated *mandis*. From the traders how the produce moves to the hands of consumers is beyond the purview of this study. Therefore, in this study retail charges are not included in the marketing cost.

The main items included in the marketing cost in the present study are transportation cost (only the paid up charges), unloading, cleaning and weighing charges at the *mandi*, storage cost and other charges including the personal expenses incurred by the farmers during their stay in the *mandi* to sell the produce. Handling, packing and loading at the farm place are done by the producers themselves and therefore, these items do not figure in the marketing cost in the present analysis.

Crop-wise marketing cost is given in Tables 7.8 to 7.14. Marketing cost can be divided into regulated and unregulated cost. Regulated cost includes the cost of unloading, cleaning and weighing at the market place. With the regulation of markets, these charges are generally fixed per unit. Therefore, crop-wise, these charges do not vary across farm size as is seen in the tables. Unregulated cost includes the cost of transportation, storage and other charges in selling the produce. In the latter category, economies of scale were in operation in the case of transportation charges. As is clear from Tables 7.8 to 7.14, for all the crops, the transportation cost had an inverse relationship with farm size[1]. Per unit transportation cost declined with the rise in total output sold. In the case of the other two items of unregulated cost, namely, storage cost and other charges, there were no such economies of scale observed (see Tables 7.8 to 7.14). Because of the high weight of transportation costs in the total marketing cost, the total marketing cost was also found to have an inverse relationship with farm size for all the crops. Concluding the debate, one can say that with the regulation of the market, the exploitation of farmers especially the small farmers by the traders and intermediaries in terms of excessive unauthorized charges has completely been eradicated.

Table 7.8: Marketing cost of total produce sold—Wheat.

(Rs. per quintal).

Items of marketing costs	*Marg-inal*	*Small*	*Semi-medium*	*Medium*	*Large*	*Total*
Transportation cost (only paid out)*	7.66	5.66	4.99	2.86	1.14	2.82
Unloading, cleaning and weighing	2.38	2.11	2.45	2.58	2.29	2.39
Other charges	0.00	0.04	0.02	0.03	0.04	0.03
Storage cost	0.00	0.00	0.00	0.00	0.00	0.00
Total marketing cost	10.04	7.81	7.47	5.47	3.47	5.25

Note: * Includes only the hired charges of transportation and no imputed cost was included for transportation by own tractor.

Table 7.9: Marketing cost of total produce sold—Paddy (PR).

(Rs. per quintal).

Items of marketing costs	*Marg-inal*	*Small*	*Semi-medium*	*Medium*	*Large*	*Total*
Transportation cost (only paid out)*	7.02	5.83	3.43	1.56	0.00	1.43
Unloading, cleaning and weighing	3.49	3.63	3.63	3.74	3.90	3.79
Other charges	0.00	0.47	0.14	0.12	0.00	0.08
Storage cost	0.00	0.00	0.00	0.00	0.00	0.00
Total marketing cost	10.51	9.94	7.20	5.42	3.90	5.30

Note: * Includes only the hired charges of transportation and no imputed cost was included for transportation by own tractor.

Table 7.10: Marketing cost of total produce sold—Paddy (Basmati).

(Rs. per quintal).

Items of marketing costs	*Marg-inal*	*Small*	*Semi-medium*	*Medium*	*Large*	*Total*
Transportation cost (only paid out)*	8.85	7.32	6.49	3.50	1.27	3.56
Unloading, cleaning and weighing	3.82	3.41	3.63	3.48	3.52	3.53
Other charges	1.00	2.20	0.70	0.55	0.26	0.60
Storage cost	2.80	5.42	2.55	3.27	1.10	2.44
Total marketing cost	16.47	18.34	13.37	10.81	6.15	10.13

Note: *Includes only the hired charges of transportation and no imputed cost was included for transportation by own tractor.

Table 7.11: Marketing cost of total produce sold—Cotton *(Desi)*

(Rs. per quintal).

Items of marketing costs	*Marg-inal*	*Small*	*Semi-medium*	*Medium*	*Large*	*Total*
Transportation cost (only paid out)*	8.67	9.83	5.82	4.76	6.91	6.07
Unloading, cleaning and weighing	4.27	3.92	4.57	4.53	4.63	4.50
Other charges	1.33	1.74	0.00	0.00	0.00	0.21
Storage cost	0.00	0.00	0.00	0.00	0.00	0.00
Total marketing cost	14.27	15.49	10.39	9.29	11.54	10.77

Note: *Includes only the hired charges of transportation and no imputed cost was included for transportation by own tractor.

Table 7.12: Marketing cost of total produce sold—Cotton (American).

(Rs. per quintal)

Items of marketing costs	*Marg-inal*	*Small*	*Semi-medium*	*Medium*	*Large*	*Total*
Transportation cost (only paid out)*	10.69	9.91	7.31	5.59	3.07	5.38
Unloading, cleaning and weighing	4.66	4.47	4.59	4.31	4.12	4.30
Other charges	0.57	0.25	0.52	0.22	0.00	0.19
Storage cost	7.05	2.22	10.78	2.56	2.32	4.04
Total marketing cost	22.97	16.84	23.19	12.69	9.51	13.92

Note: *Includes only the hired charges of transportation and no imputed cost was included for transportation by own tractor.

Table 7.13: Marketing cost of total produce sold—Mustard seed.

(Rs. per quintal).

Items of marketing costs	*Marg-inal*	*Small*	*Semi-medium*	*Medium*	*Large*	*Total*
Transportation cost (only paid out)*	6.13	9.21	7.80	6.10	2.09	4.60
Unloading, cleaning and weighing	4.41	2.69	3.64	3.21	3.20	3.28
Other charges	0.00	0.00	0.73	0.00	0.00	0.13
Storage cost	0.00	0.00	1.63	0.52	1.26	1.04
Total marketing cost	10.54	11.89	13.79	9.83	6.54	9.05

Note: *Includes only the hired charges of transportation and no imputed cost was included for transportation by own tractor.

Table 7.14: Marketing cost of total produce sold—Gram.

(Rs. per quintal).

Items of marketing costs	*Marg-inal*	*Small*	*Semi-medium*	*Medium*	*Large*	*Total*
Transportation cost (only paid out)*	10.00	10.00	7.07	8.02	3.56	5.91
Unloading, cleaning and weighing	3.71	4.63	4.07	4.08	3.84	3.98
Other charges	0.00	0.00	0.00	0.00	0.00	0.00
Storage cost	0.00	9.76	0.00	0.93	0.00	0.79
Total marketing cost	13.71	24.39	11.14	13.04	7.40	10.68

Note: *Includes only the hired charges of transportation and no imputed cost was included for transportation by own tractor.

Pricing Efficiency of the Households Surveyed

A common feature of the agricultural market set up in the state is the predominance of sales in the regulated *mandis*. The price in the regulated *mandi* is determined by the open auctioning. Therefore, the farmer's exploitation by intermediaries in terms of low price and excessive un-authorized market charges seems to be a thing of the past. However, even in a regulated marketing system, the price received by farmers of the same commodity need not be equal. Imperfect knowledge of the market among sellers, differences in the time of sale and other factors accounting for the bargaining power of farmers would manifest themselves in interpersonal differences in the price received by the farmers for a homogeneous product offered for sale.

The economic environment affects the bargaining power of the groups differently resulting in a wider price spread among different groups of farmers. Studies on agricultural markets indicate that the poor and small peasants are paid lesser for their produce than are large peasants. A study by Sarkar (1981) on marketing in West Bengal and Bihar revealed such price discrimination in the commodity market not only within similar crops but also by similar market channels. Nadkarni (1985) observed more price differentials across size classes in less commercialized and underdeveloped villages than in highly commercialized and developed villages. Harriss (1984) observed big farmers receiving higher prices than small farmers only in the case of commercial crops like cotton and groundnut in Southern India. Similarly, Subbarao (1978) revealed that in the case of paddy, the price gross as well as net of market expenses was lower for small cultivators operating 7 acres of land as compared to large cultivators operating more than 15 acres of land.

This section presents the tabular analysis of factors influencing the price for the crop received by farmers by size class of holdings. The main factors, which play an important role in the formation of price in the market, are:

(i) Economic status of the farmer determined in terms of the land area operated or the value of total output produced and sold;

(ii) Source of borrowing, *i.e.*, the percentage of institutional and non-institutional borrowing;

(iii) Availability of storage facility reflected in storage investment;
(iv) Point of time at which produce is sold; and
(v) Distance covered to market the produce.

Crop-wise gross and net prices received by the farmers are given in Tables 7.15 to 7.27. The net price is the price net of market expenses in terms of charges paid in the market, namely transport, storage and other expenses incurred by the farmers in selling the produce. Net price as a percentage of gross price is also given in the respective tables. It is clearly evident from the tables that gross, as well as net price did not have any unique relationship with farm size. However, net price as a percentage of gross price, increased with the rise in farm size in almost all the crops. It reflects the economies of scale in marketing the produce. As mentioned above, the per unit marketing cost falls with the rise in farm size and as a result, differences between gross and net price decline as farm size increases.

Marginal farmers obtained the minimum gross as well as net price for all crops, except paddy PR and wheat. On the other hand, small farmers competed well with medium and large size farmers. Overall, semi-medium and medium farmers, *i.e.* the cultivators operating 5 to 25 acres of land obtained the highest gross and net price of almost all the crops. Thereby, the gross and net price obtained by large farmers was less than what medium and semi-medium farmers received for all the crops except wheat and paddy PR.

The reason for a low price for the highest and lowest categories appears to be that in the lowest category, *i.e.* marginal farmers, the size of operated land was very small and so was the volume of surplus. It was not economical to move the small volume to the big *mandis* to gain a higher price, while the lack of transportation facilities and higher indebtedness of these farmers to *arhatias* were the other factors influencing an uneconomical disposal of produce. In the case of large farmers, due to the big size of their holdings, these farmers generated a large amount of surplus but because of lacking a godown or scientific means of storage, they faced the problem of disposing the surplus after harvest. Under the circumstances, they sold immediately after the harvest when the prices in the market were not very favourable. This is also clear from Table 7.4, in most of the crops, the highest sale within a week of harvest was by large farmers.

In the casé of wheat and paddy PR, due to government support prices, the gross price in the market was almost fixed and farmers sold the whole of their produce immediately after the harvest. For wheat, all the farmers received a fixed price of Rs.350 per quintal (see Table 7.15). Due to differences in per quintal marketing cost, the net price had an inverse relationship with farm size. However, the difference in net price across farm size was not very pronounced. Similarly, in the case of paddy PR, the net price was not very different across the farm size. The other factors influencing prices are discussed below.

The bargaining power of the producer seller is best reflected by the value of their marketed surplus as marketed surplus bears not only the area operated but also the differences in fertility of land. It is clear from the tables that in all the crops *viz*., paddy basmati, cotton American, cotton *desi* and mustard, gross as well as net price, were higher when value of the marketed surplus was above Rs. 20,000 compared to the prices when the marketed surplus was below this amount for all size of farms. The above-mentioned amount was sufficient to strengthen the economic position of the farmers to sell their produce at the most profitable place and point of time.

Most of the large and medium farmers above this amount had their own tractor facility to transport their produce to get a better price. Even small and marginal farmers having a marketed surplus above Rs. 20,000 were in a position to hire transportation for a better *mandi* to get a more competitive price for their produce. However, in some exceptional cases the gross and net price fell with the rise in value of marketed surplus, which may be due to an incidental rise or fall in prices or because of some arbitrary factors. The above discussion suggests that small as well as large farmers were at a disadvantage when they had weak bargaining power in terms of lower marketed surplus.

Another important factor responsible for the weak bargaining power of the farmers was indebtedness, especially to non-institutional sources. The important sources of credit in the regions under study were *arhatias*, besides, institutional sources like cooperative societies and commercial banks. Being indebted to *arhatias*, farmers were forced to sell their produce immediately after harvest and at a price deliberately kept low by the combined actions of the *arhatias* and the buyers (who were mostly private traders or *pucca arhatias*).

The data in the tables support this as the price of all of the crops except gram fell as producers became indebtors to non-institutional sources. The results of paddy, cotton and mustard show a lower price for those farmers who were indebted to non-institutional sources and a higher price for those who did not take a loan from non-institutional sources. With a few exceptions, all farmers, *i.e.* small as well as large, also exhibited the same trend[5].

Hence, when the seller was free from the financial commitments, he was in a position to realize a better price for his produce. When he was in debt, it was the non-institutional source of his borrowings, which had an adverse effect on the price offered for his crop and sometimes even a small borrowing from such sources affected the price very adversely.

Proper storage facilities available with the farmers was another factor which enhanced their bargaining power in marketing the produce. It helped farmers to hold their surplus for some time and saved them from bulk selling after the harvest, which yielded them low prices. However, for crops for which procurement was done by the government, storage did not have any impact on their prices, for example wheat and paddy. Nonetheless, for other crops, storage could help the farmers to realize a higher price by withholding the stock for some time period.

In the villages surveyed, there was a total lack of appropriate means of storage and farmers were forced to sell immediately after the harvest. Some farmers still tried to hold their produce by whatever means available. In this analysis, farmers whose storage investment exceeded Rs. 5,000 are considered to have better opportunities of storage. It is clear from the tables that except for mustard and gram, all other crops showed a rise in the price realized by the farmers with the better storage opportunities available to them. The rise in prices occurred not only in case of large farmers but also in the case of small and marginal farmers. Thus, if farmers were provided with scientific storage facilities, it helped them to realize higher prices for their produce and also saved consumers from sharp hikes in prices in the off-season.

Storage facility helps farmers to gain higher price via delaying the time of sale, as immediately after the harvest prices are low. In the regions surveyed, most of the crops were sold within a week of harvest. Only in case of Basmati paddy, cotton American, mustard and gram, a few farmers held back their crops for more than two months. Apart from a lack of storage facility, the fear of a fall in prices in the later period also compelled them to sell their produce immediately after the harvest. The latter phenomenon had occurred in case of Basmati paddy. The net price of Basmati paddy fell from Rs. 660 per quintal after harvest to Rs. 645 per quintal after two months of harvest. Thus, two farmers who stored their produce had to bear a loss of Rs. 15 per quintal. In the case of cotton the price rise was quite sharp and the farmers who stored their crop for two months had a net gain of Rs. 81 per quintal and those who held more than two months gained by Rs. 144 per quintal. Similarly, the net gain in mustard and gram stood Rs. 202 and Rs. 163 per quintal, respectively for more than two months of storage.

However, one should not be misled by these results, as the price rise seems to be quite encouraging especially in the case of mustard and gram. One should not ignore the fact that making generalizations on the basis of only a few farmers who stored their produce for a short period would not be appropriate. Moreover, the two crops, namely, mustard and gram were not the main crops of the region as they accounted for a small proportion of the area devoted to these crops. Wheat and paddy PR, the two main crops were sold immediately after the harvest and farmers did not find it lucrative to store these crops. Nevertheless, the results point out the importance of storage in yielding the more desired price to the farmers.

Table 7.15: Price received by the farmers—Wheat.

(Rs. per quintal).

Farm size	*No. of households*	*Gross price*	*Net price*	*Net price as a % of gross price*
Marginal	79	350	340	97.1
Small	89	350	342	97.8
Semi-medium	96	350	343	97.9
Medium	73	350	345	98.4
Large	37	350	347	99.0
Total	374	350	345	98.5

Table 7.16: Price received by the farmers—Paddy (PR).

(Rs. per quintal)

Farm size	*No. of households*	*Gross price*	*Net price*	*Net price as a % of gross price*
Marginal	6	362	351	97.1
Small	14	358	348	97.2
Semi-medium	27	340	333	97.8
Medium	20	349	343	98.5
Large	13	350	346	98.9
Total	80	348	343	98.5

Table 7.17: Price received by the farmers—Paddy (Basmati).

(Rs. per quintal)

Farm size	*No. of households*	*Gross price*	*Net price*	*Net price as a % of gross price*
Marginal	22	653	637	97.5
Small	23	650	632	97.2
Semi-medium	32	685	671	98.6
Medium	33	671	660	98.4
Large	18	671	665	99.0
Total	127	671	660	98.5

Table 7.18: Differences in net price due to different factors of sale—Paddy (Basmati).

(Rs. per quintal)

Category	*Marginal*	*Small*	*Semi-medium*	*Medium*	*Large*	*Total*
Surplus up to Rs. 20,000	622	642	682	-	-	633
Surplus above Rs. 20,000	681	631	671	660	665	662
No borrowing from Non-inst.	629	660	645	686	677	670
Cases of borrowing from NI	705	577	703	641	641	647
No proper storage facility	612	626	634	737	546	658
Better storage facility	664	634	687	646	669	661
Sale within 7 days	632	637	671	659	665	660
Sale 7 to 60 days	679	571	673	666	-	663
Sale after 60 days	-	-	-	553	666	645

Table 7.19: Price received by the farmers—Cotton (American).

(Rs. per quintal)

Farm size	*No. of households*	*Gross price*	*Net price*	*Net price as a % of gross price*
Marginal	24	1270	1247	98.2
Small	40	1276	1259	98.7
Semi-medium	42	1344	1320	98.3
Medium	36	1321	1308	99.0
Large	22	1299	1290	99.3
Total	164	1310	1296	98.9

Table 7.20: Differences in net price due to different factors of sale—Cotton (American).

(Rs. per quintal)

Category	*Marginal*	*Small*	*Semi-medium*	*Medium*	*Large*	*Total*
Surplus up to Rs. 20,000	1247	1247	1321	-	-	1272
Surplus above Rs. 20,000	-	1305	1320	1308	1290	1300
No borrowing from Non-inst.	1268	1294	1322	1320	1316	1316
Cases of borrowing from NI	1181	1234	1319	1297	1254	1275
No proper storage facility	1272	1237	1268	1259	1123	1244
Better storage facility	1208	1285	1380	1330	1303	1316
Sale within 7 days	1191	1255	1271	1316	1271	1280
Sale 7 to 60 days	-	-	1483	1249	-	1361
Sale after 60 days	1595	1410	1502	1242	1424	1424

Table 7.21: Price received by the farmers—Cotton *(Desi)*.

(Rs. per quintal)

Farm size	*No. of households*	*Gross price*	*Net price*	*Net price as a % of gross price*
Marginal	6	1010	996	98.6
Small	11	1068	1053	98.5
Semi-medium	10	1139	1129	99.1
Medium	15	1151	1142	99.2
Large	7	1071	1059	98.9
Total	49	1117	1106	99.0

Table 7.22: Differences in net price due to different factors of sale—Cotton *(Desi)*.

(Rs. per quintal)

Category	*Marginal*	*Small*	*Semi-medium*	*Medium*	*Large*	*Total*
Surplus up to Rs. 20,000	996	1046	1143	-	-	1036
Surplus above Rs. 20,000	-	1085	1128	1142	1059	1116
No borrowing from Non-inst.	1024	1035	1160	1225	1021	1135
Cases of borrowing from NI	810	1065	1094	997	1056	1056
No proper storage facility	726	1073	1140	927	885	1039
Better storage facility	1094	1021	1082	1209	1069	1138

Table 7.23: Price received by the farmers—Mustard seed.

(Rs. per quintal)

Farm size	*No. of households*	*Gross price*	*Net price*	*Net price as a % of gross price*
Marginal	4	1000	989	98.9
Small	7	1018	1006	98.8
Semi-medium	18	1053	1039	98.7
Medium	22	1027	1017	99.0
Large	15	1019	1013	99.4
Total	66	1027	1018	99.1

Table 7.24: Differences in net price due to different factors of sale—Mustard seed.

(Rs. per quintal)

Category	*Marginal*	*Small*	*Semi-medium*	*Medium*	*Large*	*Total*
Surplus up to Rs. 20,000	989	1015	975	-	-	990
Surplus above Rs. 20,000	-	885	1060	1017	1013	1021
No borrowing from Non-inst.	991	1011	1051	1040	1021	1027
Cases of borrowing from NI	987	1006	1037	1000	997	1010
No proper storage facility	991	962	1081	1051	-	1058
Better storage facility	986	1091	877	1003	1013	1004
Sale within 7 days	989	1006	1021	1006	999	1005
Sale 7 to 60 days	-	-	-	-	1186	1186
Sale after 60 days	-	-	1181	1282	1171	1207

Table 7.25: Price received by the farmers—Black gram.

(Rs. per quintal)

Farm size	*No. of households*	*Gross price*	*Net price*	*Net price as a % of gross price*
Marginal	10	1160	1147	98.8
Small	11	1240	1216	98.0
Semi-medium	21	1158	1146	99.0
Medium	24	1128	1115	98.8
Large	17	1058	1051	99.3
Total	83	1104	1093	99.0

Table 7.26: Differences in net price due to different factors of sale—Black gram.

(Rs. per quintal)

Category	*Marginal*	*Small*	*Semi-medium*	*Medium*	*Large*	*Total*
Surplus up to Rs. 20,000	1147	1193	1125	-	-	1156
Surplus above Rs. 20,000	-	1269	1156	1115	1051	1086
No borrowing from Non-inst.	1121	1180	1154	1124	1042	1085
Cases of borrowing from NI	1185	1360	1136	1093	1103	1122
No proper storage facility	1164	1278	1138	1083	-	1112
Better storage facility	1132	1135	1152	1186	1051	1085
Sale within 7 days	1147	1142	1146	1108	1051	1085
Sale 7 to 60 days	-	-	-	-	-	-
Sale after 60 days	-	1357	-	1185	-	1248

Table 7.27: Difference in price and storage cost across different periods of sale.

(Rs. per quintal)

Name of the crop	*Sale within 10-60 days harvest*			*Sale after 60 days of harvest*		
	No. of HH	*Increase in price over the harvest price*	*Storage cost*	*No. of HH*	*Increase in price over the harvest price*	*Storage cost*
Paddy Basmati	12	14.38	18.26	2	3.96	37.18
Cotton American	5	121.08	46.97	10	169.15	36.94
Mustard	1	186.84	12.00	3	214.62	16.50
Gram	0	-	-	3	178.28	16.84

Note: Storage cost includes transportation cost from field to the storage place and from storage place to the market, damage to the product during the time of storage, loss in weight and loss by insects.

The above tables present the crop-wise price differentials across the farm size. It is observed that in the case of cotton, gram and mustard, the marginal farmers obtained the minimum average net price whereas they obtained the maximum net price of paddy PR. Similarly, the results are not uniform for the other size of farmers and crops. Therefore, to reach some general conclusion it becomes necessary to club the price of all the crops together to get some aggregate price index. It is not appropriate to take a simple average of the prices of different crops because price is already an average figure. The following procedure is adopted to club the price of different crops :

$$P_j = \frac{\Sigma P_{ij} Q_{ij}}{\Sigma Q_{ij}}, \quad \begin{matrix} i = 1, 2, ..., 7 \text{ (wheat, paddy, cotton, etc.)} \\ j = 1, 2, ..., 400 \text{ (no. of households),} \end{matrix}$$

where,

P = price obtained by the farmer,
Q = quantity sold by the farmer.

The price index of jth household is obtained by multiplying jth farmer's price obtained for each crop by the quantity sold of each crop and dividing the sum of all the crops by the sum of quantity sold of all crops. This is the indirect weighted price, weight being the quantity sold. One can also apply direct weights to calculate the weighted price index. The weighted price index is calculated here by giving weight to the above price index in terms of arca undcr a particular crop divided by the gross cropped area. The weighted price index is calculated as under:

$$P_j = \frac{\Sigma P_{ij} Q_{ij} W_{ij}}{\Sigma Q_{ij} W_{IJ}}$$

where,

W_{ij} represents weight for jth farmer for the ith crop. The results are given in Table 7.28.

Table 7.28: Aggregate price index (all crops).

(Rs. per quintal)

Farm size	*Gross price*	*Net Price*	*Weighted GP*	*Weighted NP*
Marginal	509	497	509	496
Small	457	447	444	434
Semi-medium	459	450	438	429
Medium	463	456	431	425
Large	454	450	432	428
Total	459	453	436	430

The above index at the aggregate level makes it very clear that there was no price discrimination against the marginal farmers. Rather, if any discrimination was prevalent, it was against the large farmers who obtained less than the average price. Both, gross as well as net and weighted as well as unweighted price was highest for the marginal farmers. The marginal farmers obtained a net price of Rs. 497 while large farmers obtained Rs. 450 only.

As in Haryana, all the farmers sell their produce in the regulated *mandis*, the circumstances which were earlier compelling the marginal and small farmers to sell their produce at lower prices are now completely non-existent. In the case of large farmers on the other hand, due to lack of storage facilities and due to the higher volume of their marketed surplus, they dispose of their produce immediately after the harvest when the price is low. Thus, the above results refute the general belief that the marginal and small farmers are discriminated against while the large farmers are the major gainers in the agricultural product markets.

Regression Results

The results of multiple regression analysis carried out to ascertain the volume and direction of factors entering into price formation are presented in Tables 7.29 and 7.30. Net price defined as the (gross) price received by the farmers minus the cost incurred to market the produce, was taken as the dependent variable. Independent variables in Table 7.29 are: Total value of marketed surplus (of all crops) Rupees; Total Net Operated Area Acres; Value of Total Output Produced (excluding fodder crop and by-product) Rupees; Total Storage Investment Rupees; Distance Covered to market the produce kms; Dummy for non-institutional loans with value zero for those who do not take non-institutional loans and one for those who take and finally, dummy for time of sale with value zero for those who sell immediately after harvest and one for those who hold down and sell later. In the next table (Table 7.30), in place of regressing the net price on total marketed surplus, total area and total output, it is regressed upon the marketed surplus (quintals) of the respective crop, area operated in acres of the respective crop and output produced in quintals of the same crop. The other independent variables remain the same as that in Table 7.29.

It is clear from the tables that the value of total marketed surplus and the value of total output, the two, also represent the economic status of the farmers, had significant coefficients for the crops of cotton American and paddy Basmati with a positive sign, thereby indicating a rise in the net price received by the farmers, with a rise in their economic status. Cotton *Desi*, on the other hand, shows a significant positive relationship with the size of output produced and sold of the respective crop. The reason for a positive relationship seems to be that with a higher value of output and marketed surplus, the farmers were in a better position to choose the appropriate *mandi* (supported by the better transportation facilities) where they could get a more competitive price for their product.

The above fact is also supported by the significant positive coefficient of distance covered to market the produce in the case of paddy PR, paddy Basmati and cotton *Desi*. As farmers covered a greater distance to sell at a larger or more competitive *mandi*, they got a comparatively higher net price. In the case of paddy Basmati, it was observed during the survey that farmers who could have better transportation facilities and those who were more conscious about the price were selling their produce in more profitable markets, *e.g.* Trori *mandi* in Karnal district which is better known for Basmati rice. This *mandi* was at distance of 50 kilometres or more from the villages surveyed.

Mustard on the other hand, displayed significant coefficient of distance with a negative sign, thereby indicating a fall in price with the rise in distance covered. The reason for the above dichotomy was that in Kaithal and Sirsa districts of Haryana, mustard was not a significant crop. One does not come across any big market dealing in the product, except Kaithal *mandi* and Sirsa *mandi* in the respective districts. Therefore, the farmers had to travel a long average distance to sell the produce and thus end up with a relatively lower net price due to transportation and other costs.

The other most important factor affecting the net price was time of selling the produce. The coefficient of dummy time of sale was significant and positive for all crops except paddy Basmati. The value of the coefficient indicates that there was a considerable increase in the net price received by the farmers if they delayed their sale by a month or more. It is clear from Table 7.29 that delaying of sale by 10 days to 6 months resulted in an increase in net price by Rs. 175 for cotton American, Rs. 234 for mustard and Rs. 187 for gram. In the case of paddy Basmati, the coefficient was negative (–Rs. 12) but insignificant. The negative coefficient was due to the fact that there was a fall in average net price from Rs. 660 to Rs. 645 when the sale was delayed by more than two months (see Table 7.22). However, in the case of the remaining crops, a significant positive coefficient implied that the rise in gross price over time was much more than the storage and other costs and so the net price (*i.e.* gross price-marketing cost) rose with the delay in sale of these crops. The above results are also supported by Table 7.27, which presents the rise in price received by the farmers and storage cost incurred over the storage period[6]. It is clear from the table that only in case of paddy Basmati, the rise in gross price was less than the storage cost for the delayed sale. In case of all the other crops, rise in gross price far exceeded the storage cost when sale was delayed by 10 days or more and so yielded higher net price for such sales.

While analysing the tables in the last section, it was observed that the non-institutional loans exert a negative influence on net prices in all the crops except gram. However, the coefficient of non, institutional loans remained insignificant for all the crops in both the tables, except cotton *Desi*. A part of the effect of non institutional loans might have been taken away by the variable of distance covered as farmers who were free from indebtedness and especially those who were free from the clutches of *arhatias* sold their produce independently to the markets where they got a higher price. Whereas farmers who were heavily indebted to *arhatias* of neighbouring *mandis* were bound to sell in the same *mandis* at their doorsteps and so covered less distance, while obtaining a lower price (as most of the crops had negative correlation between the distance covered and indebtedness).

Table 7.29: Regression results (Net price received by the farmers).

Dependent Variable	*Constant*	*Aggregate MS*	*Aggregate NOA*	*Aggregate Output*	*Storage investment*	*Distance covered*	*Dummy Non-inst. Loans*	*Dummy Time of Sale*	R^2	*F value*
Paddy Basmati (No.of observations = 126)										
Net Price	636 (30.0)	0.0001** (2.2)			-0.001 (-1.1)	2.2* (2.8)	0.04 (0.002)	-12.5 (-0.4)	0.057	2.5**
Net Price	637 (30.0)		1.1 (1.4)		-0.001 (-0.9)	2.2* (2.7)	-3.6 (-0.2)	-12.6 (-0.4)	0.036	1.9***
Net Price	636 (30.0)			0.0001** (2.2)	-0.001 (-1.1)	2.2* (2.8)	0.14 (0.01)	-12.0 (-0.4)	0.058	2.5**
Paddy PR (No of observations: 79)										
Net Price	337 (43.0)	0.00002 (0.7)			-0.0006 (-1.5)	1.3*** (1.7)	10.05 (1.4)		0.041	1.8
Net Price	338 (43)		0.04 (0.1)		-0.0005 (-1.2)	1.3*** (1.7)	10.1 (1.4)		0.036	1.7
Net Price	337 (43.0)			0.00002 (0.7)	-0.0006 (-1.5)	1.3*** (1.7)	10.5 (1.4)		0.041	1.8
Cotton American (No.of observations: 164)										
Net Price	1211 (33.0)	0.0003*** (1.8)			0.001 (0.7)	2.0 (1.1)	-18.0 (-0.8)	175.2* (4.7)	0.147	6.6*
Net Price	1209 (33.0)		0.61 (0.6)		0.002 (1.3)	2.1 (1.2)	16.1 (-0.7)	176.0* (4.6)	0.131	5.9*
Net Price	1210 (33.0)			0.0003*** (1.8)	0.001 (0.8)	2.0 (1.1)	-18.0 (-0.8)	176.1* (4.7)	0.146	6.6*
Cotton Desi (No of observations: 49)										
Net Price	810 (11.0)	0.0004 (1.5)			0.0007 (0.3)	12.3* (3.7)	69.7 (1.6)		0.207	4.1*
Net Price	823 (11.0)		0.30 (0.2)		0.002 (0.9)	11.8* (3.4)	74.8 (1.7)		0.167	3.4**
Net Price	809 (12.0)			0.003 (1.5)	0.0007 (0.3)	12.2* (3.7)	69.7 (1.6)		0.207	4.1*
Mustard (No.of observations: 61)										
Net Price	1113 (24.0)	-0.00002 (-0.1)			-0.001 (-0.8)	-6.1** (-2.4)	-11.6 (-0.5)	234.0* (4.8)	0.274	5.5*
Net Price	1120 (25.0)		-0.66 (-0.8)		-0.0006 (-0.5)	-6.1** (-2.4)	-14.2 (-0.6)	233.0* (4.9)	0.283	5.7*
Net Price	1113 (24.0)			-0.00001 (-0.1)	-0.001 (-0.8)	-6.1** (-2.4)	-11.4 (-0.5)	234.0* (4.8)	0.275	5.5*
Gram (No.of observations: 42)										
Net Price	1009 (12.0)	-0.0002 (-1.2)			0.0004 (0.2)	8.1 (1.4)	11.3 (0.4)	187.0* (3.4)	0.215	3.2**
Net Price	1012 (12.0)		-2.0** (-2.1)		0.002 (0.9)	8.3 (1.5)	18.0 (0.6)	182.0* (3.4)	0.275	4.1*
Net Price	1028 (12.0)			-0.0002 (-1.4)	0.0009 (0.5)	6.8 (1.2)	12.1 (0.4)	187.0* (3.4)	0.228	3.4**

Notes: Figures in parentheses are respective 't' values.
*Significant at 1% level.
**Significant at 5% level.
***Significant at 10% level.

Table 7.30: Regression results (Net price received by the farmers).

Dependent Variable	*Constant*	*Crop MS*	*Crop NOA*	*Crop Output*	*Storage investment*	*Distance covered*	*Dummy Non-inst. Loans*	*Dummy Time of Sale*	R^2	*F value*
Paddy Basmati (No. of observations = 126)										
Net Price	640	0.13			-0.0005	2.1*	-1.5	-19.7	0.023	1.6
	(30.0)	(0.6)			(-0.5)	(2.6)	(-0.1)	(-0.6)		
Net Price	642		-0.22		-0.0002	2.1*	-1.1	-17.0	0.020	1.5
	(30.0)		(-0.14)		(-0.2)	(2.6)	(-0.1)	(-0.6)		
Net Price	640			0.13	-0.0006	2.1*	-1.6	-19.9	0.024	1.6
	(30.0)			(0.7)	(-0.5)	(2.6)	(-0.1)	(-0.6)		
Paddy PR (No. of observations: 79)										
Net Price	337	0.007			-0.0005	1.3***	10.3		0.037	1.8
	(43.0)	(0.4)			(-1.4)	(1.7)	(1.4)			
Net Price	337		0.29		-0.0006	1.3***	10.4		0.040	1.8
	(42.0)		(0.6)		(-1.5)	(1.8)	(1.4)			
Net Price	337			0.007	-0.0005	1.3***	10.3		0.037	1.8
	(43)			(0.4)	(-1.4)	(1.7)	(1.4)			
Cotton American (No. of observations: 164)										
Net Price	1209	0.24			0.002	2.2	-14.8	179.0*	0.130	5.9*
	(33.0)	(0.4)			(1.6)	(1.3)	(0.7)	(4.7)		
Net Price	1209		0.71		0.002	2.2	-15.6	180.0*	0.130	5.9*
	(33.0)		(0.4)		(1.6)	(1.2)	(-0.7)	(4.7)		
Net Price	1209			0.23	0.002	2.2	-14.8	179.0*	0.130	5.9*
	(33.0)			(0.4)	(1.6)	(1.3)	(-0.7)	(4.7)		
Cotton Desi (No. of observations: 49)										
Net Price	773	6.9**			0.001	12.2*	93.4**		0.239	4.8*
	(10.6)	(2.0)			(0.6)	(3.7)	(2.1)			
Net Price	829		-5.9		0.003	12.1*	76.6**		0.171	3.5**
	(12.0)		(-0.5)		(1.1)	(3.5)	(1.7)			
Net Price	773			6.9**	0.001	12.1*	94.1**		0.240	4.8*
	(10.7)			(2.1)	(0.6)	(3.7)	(2.1)			
Mustard (No. of observations: 61)										
Net Price	1109*	0.23			-0.001	-6.0**	-10.3	234.0*	0.276	5.6*
	(24.0)	(0.3)			(-1.1)	(-2.4)	(-0.5)	(4.9)		
Net Price	1111		0.63		-0.001	-6.1**	-10.9	234.0*	0.275	5.5*
	(24.0)		(0.2)		(-1.0)	(-2.4)	(-0.5)	(4.9)		
Net Price	1109			0.22	-0.001	-6.0**	-10.3	234.0*	0.276	5.6*
	(24.0)			(0.3)	(-1.1)	(-2.4)	(-0.5)	(4.9)		
Gram (No. of observations: 42)										
Net Price	1035	-2.0			0.0002	6.8	5.9	184.0*	0.233	3.5**
	(12.0)	(-1.5)			(0.1)	(1.2)	(0.2)	(3.4)		
Net Price	1000		-2.2		0.0005	8.7	14.3	184.0*	0.208	3.2**
	(11.0)		(-1.0)		(0.3)	(1.5)	(0.5)	(3.3)		
Net Price	1012			0.04	0.0006	7.5	11.1	186.0*	0.184	2.9**
	(11.5)			(0.1)	(0.4)	(1.3)	(0.4)	(3.3)		

Notes: Figures in parentheses are respective 't' values.

*Significant at 1% level.

**Significant at 5% level.

***Significant at 10% level.

The coefficient of storage investment was insignificant in all the crops in both the tables indicating that storage investment was completely unsuccessful in influencing the net price obtained by the farmers. As mentioned in the first section of this chapter, the storage facility could benefit the farmers by yielding a higher price only through delaying the time of sale of the crop. However, storage investment failed completely in the latter purpose as was also clear from Table 7.5. Similarly, the farm size, *i.e.* the total area operated as well as the area operated for the respective crops did not show any significant impact upon the net price obtained. Their coefficients were insignificant in almost all the crops. Finally, the coefficients of output and marketed surplus did not differ much, indicating that the two variables were almost the same in terms of their effect on net price received by the farmers.

Before concluding the discussion, it must be pointed out that out of the significant variables discussed above, the time of sale was significant at the one per cent level. The distance covered was significant at the one per cent level in the case of paddy Basmati and cotton *Desi*, at the five per cent level in case of mustard and ten per cent level in case of paddy PR. The value of marketed surplus and the value of output were significant at the five and ten per cent levels for paddy Basmati and cotton American, respectively. The value of R^2 was quite low, especially in the case of paddy, the value of goodness of fit fell below 0.1. The low value of R^2 indicates that the explanatory variables are not able to explain much variation in the dependent variable and probably some important variables are not included in the model[7]. It is well known that the price in a regulated *mandi* is determined by the open bid of the traders which depends on many factors like the number of traders present in the *mandi*, the total amount of output under auctioning, price expectations of the traders, size and location of the *mandi*, government price policy, etc. All these explanatory variables could not be included in the regression analysis. The regressions with low R^{-2} are kept in the analysis because of their desired economic interpretation.

To sum up, the discussion of the chapter, the agricultural marketing of the districts surveyed appeared to be efficient with the full participation of large as well as small farmers in the market. There prevailed a well-connected regulated marketing system along with perfect transportation facilities for all size classes. As a result, almost all the farmers sold their products in the regulated *mandis*. Lack of storage and market intelligence among the farmers caused inefficiency in the market among all size of farmers equally. The cost of marketing the produce as a result of economies of scale in transportation, established an inverse relationship with farm size. The tabular analysis of prices revealed that the price received by the farmers did not show any definite relationship with farm size. Further, a higher amount of marketed surplus and no borrowing from *arhatias* helped the farmers in gaining a higher price. The delayed sale of all crops except paddy Basmati resulted in a higher price to the farmers. Among the explanatory variables in the regression analysis, time of sale and distance covered to market the produce were the two most important and significant variables with a positive effect on the net price received by the farmers. The value of marketed surplus and the value of output demonstrating the economic status of the farmers also had a positive effect on net price, though not significant in all the crops. Storage investment, farm size and non-institutional loans turned out insignificant in the regression analysis. From the analysis, one reaches the conclusion that though markets of the regions surveyed appeared to be efficient, they were not perfectly integrated across space and time. Positive significant coefficients of time of sale and distance covered were proof of the fact that there was always the possibility of getting a higher net price by delaying the sale and by covering a greater distance to market the produce.

Finally, coming to the basic hypotheses as mentioned in the first chapter:

H_1: Price obtained by farmers is directly related to the farm size.

H_2: Higher proportion of produce is sold to intermediaries by small farmers as compared to large farmers.

In the light of the discussion in the chapter the H_2 hypothesis is sternly rejected as all large as well as small farmers sold their produce in the regulated *mandis* and the sale to the intermediaries was zero. In the case of hypothesis H_1, though there is some evidence of large farmers having their own transportation facilities to market the produce, small and marginal farmers also had an equal approach to the market via hired transportation means and did not get price lower than that obtained by the large farmers. In no case, was the coefficient of operated area significant in affecting the net price, giving rise to a rejection of this hypothesis.

NOTES

1. National Commission on Agriculture (1976)—*Abridged Report*, Government of India, Ministry of Agriculture & Irrigation, Department of Agriculture, New Delhi, p.577.
2. Average area served by each regulated *mandi* was 713 and 400 sq. kilometres in 1993-94 in Sirsa and Kaithal districts, respectively.
3. The information was provided by the Market Committee— Kaithal.
4. Even if the imputed cost of transportation of own tractor was included in terms of diesel charges, lower per unit cost of transportation for large farmers as compared to small farmers would

still be the case. This is because per kilometre diesel cost for own tractor was much less than per kilometre hired transport charges.

5 The studies of Jasdanwala (1966) and Subbarao (1978) also highlighted that farmers indebted to non-institutional sources have to content with a lower price. In their cases, the non-institutional sources were money-lenders, traders and commission agents.

6. In the lack of private warehousing for the farmers, they use the other available methods mentioned for storing and so storage cost is a rough approximation of amount basically lost in spoilage, deterioration by insects and loss in weight.

7. According to Maddala (1977: 122), in a multiple regression, some coefficients are significant, while R^{-2} is not significant, then by including some more appropriate variables and by dropping the insignificant variables we may get the value of R^{-2} as also significant.

APPENDIX-7A

Table 7.1A: Zero order correlation matrix.

	Net price	Aggregate MS	Aggregate NOA	Aggregate output	Storage investment	Distance covered	Dummy NI loans	Dummy time sale
				Paddy Basmati				
Net price	1.00							
Aggregate MS	0.13	1.00						
Aggregate NOA	0.06	-	1.00					
Aggregate output	0.13	-	-	1.00				
Storage investment	-0.07	0.39	0.49	0.43	1.00			
Distance covered	0.24	-0.13	-0.17	-0.14	-0.16	1.00		
Dummy NI loans	-0.03	-0.04	0.05	-0.05	-0.03	-0.06	1.00	
Dummy time sale	-0.04	-0.00	0.00	0.00	0.19	0.08	0.12	1.00
				Paddy PR				
Net price	1.00							
Aggregate MS	-0.01	1.00						
Aggregate NOA	-0.04	-	1.00					
Aggregate output	-0.01	-	-	1.00				
Storage investment	-0.14	0.44	0.50	0.44	1.00			
Distance covered	0.22	-0.04	0.02	-0.04	-0.11	1.00		
Dummy NI loans	0.13	0.02	0.13	0.02	0.21	0.06	1.00	-
				Cotton American				
Net price	1.00							
Aggregate MS	0.21	1.00						
Aggregate NOA	0.17	-	1.00					
Aggregate output	0.21	-	-	1.00				
Storage investment	0.16	0.47	0.47	0.47	1.00			
Distance covered	0.06	0.01	-0.03	0.02	-0.05	1.00		
Dummy NI loans	-0.09	0.03	0.04	0.03	-0.07	-0.20	1.00	
Dummy time sale	0.35	0.10	0.20	0.09	0.09	-0.11	-0.03	1.00
				Cotton *Desi*				
Net price	1.00							
Aggregate MS	0.20	1.00						
Aggregate NOA	0.04	-	1.00					
Aggregate output	0.21	-	-	1.00				
Storage investment	0.15	0.40	0.39	0.41	1.00			
Distance covered	0.42	-0.09	-0.04	-0.07	0.10	1.00		
Dummy NI loans	0.06	0.05	-0.03	0.04	-0.15	-0.33	1.00	-
				Mustard				
Net price	1.00							
Aggregate MS	0.11	1.00						
Aggregate NOA	-0.07	-	1.00					
Aggregate output	0.11	-	-	1.00				
Storage investment	-0.01	0.58	0.54	0.59	1.00			
Distance covered	-0.16	0.12	0.08	0.13	0.10	1.00		
Dummy NI loans	-0.10	-0.33	-0.22	-0.31	-0.13	-0.14	1.00	
Dummy time sale	0.50	0.36	0.31	0.36	0.23	0.20	-0.17	1.00

APPENDIX-7B

Table 7.2A: Zero-order correlation matrix.

	Net price	Crop MS	Crop NOA	Crop output	Storage investment	Distance covered	Dummy NI loans	Dummy time sale
				Paddy Basmati				
Net price	1.00	0.00	-0.06	0.01	-0.07	0.24	-0.03	-0.04
Crop MS		1.00	-	-	0.44	-0.09	0.03	0.21
Crop NOA			1.00	-	0.47	-0.13	0.04	0.11
Crop output				1.00	0.45	-0.08	0.03	0.21
				Paddy PR				
Net price	1.00	-0.01	0.00	-0.01	-0.14	0.22	0.13	-
Crop MS		1.00	-	-	0.27	-0.03	0.01	-
Crop NOA			1.00	-	0.28	-0.09	0.04	-
Crop output				1.00	0.27	-0.03	0.01	-
				Cotton American				
Net price	1.00	0.10	0.09	0.10	0.16	0.06	-0.09	0.35
Crop MS		1.00	-	-	0.31	-0.05	-0.03	0.11
Crop NOA			1.00	-	0.33	0.00	0.05	0.05
Crop output				1.00	0.31	-0.05	-0.03	0.11
				Cotton *Desi*				
Net price	1.00	0.24	0.10	0.24	0.15	0.42	0.06	-
Crop MS		1.00	-	-	0.25	0.03	-0.23	-
Crop NOA			1.00	-	0.39	0.23	-0.05	-
Crop output				1.00	0.25	0.04	-0.24	-
				Mustard				
Net price	1.00	0.03	-0.01	0.02	-0.01	-0.16	-0.10	0.50
Crop MS		1.00	-	-	0.35	-0.09	-0.10	0.01
Crop NOA			1.00	-	0.32	-0.00	-0.03	0.01
Crop output				1.00	0.34	-0.09	-0.10	0.01
				Gram				
Net price	1.00	-0.30	-0.21	-0.04	0.21	0.19	0.10	0.48
Crop MS		1.00	-	-	0.35	-0.18	-0.16	-0.08
Crop NOA			1.00	-	0.52	0.04	0.05	-0.16
Crop output				1.00	0.31	0.01	-0.03	-0.08

8

Findings and Conclusion

Development of agricultural marketing is considered as imperative for sustaining the growth of agricultural production. An efficient marketing system must ensure the best possible returns for the produce to the farmer, minimum incidental costs, as also reasonable prices to the consumer. The system must be capable of mopping up the increasing market surplus, developing a systematic mechanism for price determination and of fostering competition. It is generally believed that the indigenous private marketing system for agricultural products is exploitative, economically inefficient and operates with high profit margins. The recent investigations into the performance of the system, however, unanimously confirmed that the private foodgrains marketing in India operates quite efficiently by the standard economic criteria of a perfect market. However, the statistical tools used in most of these studies to calculate marketing efficiency consisted of the most ambiguous bivariate correlation and regressions of the time series data, which were employed without taking care of autocorrelation and other time series properties.

The present study is undertaken with the objective of calculating marketing efficiency by using the recent developments in the theory of time series, namely, the 'Cointegration Technique'. A study of the market structure, market surplus and an analysis of prices across farm size provides additional information about marketing efficiency at the micro level. The results of cointegration analysis are based on secondary data of the wholesale monthly prices of wheat, paddy, gram and mustard in the regulated *mandis* of Haryana for two periods *viz.*, the pre-liberalization comprising of 1978-79 to 1989-90 and the post-liberalization period, *i.e.* 1990-91 to 2002-03. The rest of the study is based on primary data of 400 households that was collected from two districts namely, Kaithal and Sirsa in Haryana while selecting four villages in each district. The primary data pertains to the agricultural year 1993-94.

An analysis of the regulated marketing in the state revealed that Haryana has successfully implemented the regulated marketing system in agriculture. There exists a wide network of *mandis* spread all over the state dealing with all the agricultural commodities being produced therein. Farmers generally sold their produce in the regulated *mandis* through the services of commission agents while sale to intermediaries outside the regulated *mandis* was marginal. This was possible because of the availability of *pucca* roads connecting the villages to the *mandis* and farmer's access to transportation facilities like tractor-trolley, etc.

The market integration has been analysed using the cointegration analysis by selecting nine wholesale wheat markets, six mustard seed markets and four markets each for paddy PR and gram in Haryana. The empirical evidences suggest that all wheat markets in Haryana exhibited a long run relationship during both the periods. The farmers transferred their produce from one market to the other according to the price changes as the markets were linked together and arbitrage through trade tied their prices together. Inter-market linkages ware perfect during both the periods without any significant change. Price adjustment among wheat markets was taking place within a couple of weeks. While prices were tied together in the long run, they drifted apart in the short run. In the case of paddy, all the four markets were cointegrated and had a common long run path. Inter-market linkages were observed during both the periods albeit a little less than that of wheat in the post-liberalization period. Price adjustment among paddy markets took place within a 2-3 week time period and the adjustment process was found to be quicker in the post-liberalization period compared to the pre-liberalization period.

The analysis of cointegration in pulses (gram) revealed that although markets were integrated during both the periods, inter-market linkages were less efficient in pulses as compared to wheat and rice, especially after the implementation of reforms in the 1990s. In other words, the markets were found to be strongly integrated in the pre-liberalization period, which saw a dilution in the post-liberalization period. The time period of shock absorption and error-correction got extended from 1-2 weeks in the pre-liberalization period to 3-4 weeks in the post-liberalization period. In the case of oilseeds (mustard seed), it was observed that no long run integration existed in the post-liberalization period. In the pre-liberalization period, all markets except one were observed as cointegrated with a common sharing path. The inter-market linkages among these six price series were found perfect and comparable with that of wheat and rice during the pre-liberalization period. Price transmission, however, was found to be lacking in the short run. Price adjustment among the markets was taking a time period of around 2-3 weeks.

Thus, we can conclude that the agricultural *mandis* in Haryana were well integrated with each other in the long run. In the short run, however, price transmission was found to be lacking, because of paucity in the availability of information and the lack of a quicker dissemination of available information.

The main conclusions based on primary data analysis are given as under. It was observed that family size increased as the farm size increased, thereby showing a direct relationship between farm size and family size. Although, all classes of farmers leased in and leased out land but the relative amount of leasing in was observed to be higher among large farmers compared to small and marginal farmers. This phenomenon generally termed as switching of tenancy had evolved because large farmers who had an excess capacity of costly implements like tractors, etc., wanted to optimally utilize these resources by increasing their holding size through leasing in land.

Although many crops were grown in the two districts surveyed, wheat, paddy, cotton and fodder were the main crops in terms of area devoted to these crops by the households. Cropping intensity was higher in the Kaithal district, which was predominantly tubewell irrigated, compared to Sirsa district, which depended on canal irrigation. There was an increasing use of modern technology in agriculture, *i.e.*, fertilizer, pesticides, irrigation and tractor by all sizes of farmers. Among marginal and small farmers, manure and fertilizer, irrigation, bullocks and hired tractor charges, constituted the major items of production cost. For large farmers, paid out labour, fertilizer, tractor charges and rent on leased in land constituted the major cost of production. Institutional loans were accessible to large as well as small farmers. However, due to higher requirements, large farmers took a very high amount of non-institutional loans as well. As a result, the ratio of institutional loans to total loans turned out to be higher for marginal farmers compared to the large farmers. The farm size productivity relationship was tested and it was observed that the relationship had become constant as compared to the earlier studies, which had established an inverse relationship between farm size and productivity.

From the discussion of marketed surplus, it was observed that farmers of all sizes of holdings fully participated in the market and could be termed as commercial farmers. The analysis revealed that on an average 87 per cent of aggregate output was marketed by farmers. Across the size classes, even the marginal farmers were able to market as much as 68 per cent of their output compared to 91 per cent marketed by large farmers. The dominant share of large farmers in the total marketed surplus was evident from the fact that although, they constituted only 10 per cent of the total cultivators, they contributed around 45 per cent of total marketed surplus. At the other extreme, marginal farmers constituting 24 per cent of total households were able to contribute only 2.6 per cent of total marketed surplus.

The study shows that cultivators with small families, other things being equal, contributed more to the marketed surplus than did those with large families. The study also shows that due to indebtedness, small and marginal farmers were compelled to market a higher proportion of their output to pay back their debts. This did not hold true in the case of medium and large farmers. Due to the custom of sowing subsistence crops on unirrigated land and also because of low productivity on such land, the marketed surplus declined as the area under irrigation declined. Further, it was observed that the higher the value of farm assets held by the cultivators the higher was their proportion of output sold.

Crop-wise, the tabular analysis revealed that 80 per cent of wheat, 96 per cent of paddy, 68 per cent of coarse cereals and pulses each, 97 per cent of oilseeds and 99.6 per cent of cotton output was marketed by the farmers in the surveyed districts. Except oilseeds and cotton, a higher proportion of output of all other crops was marketed by large farmers compared to small and marginal farmers. The marketed surplus of wheat showed an indirect relationship with family size and unirrigated area and direct relationship with assets holdings. Other crops did not conform to such relationships.

The results of the multiple regression analysis showed that output, farm size and area under tenancy were the significant factors with positive effect while family size and unirrigated area had a negative effect, affecting the aggregate marketed surplus. One rupee increase in agricultural output led to a 96 paise increase in marketed surplus, while one acre increase in the net operated area increased the aggregate marketed surplus by Rs. 8,084. As villages were well connected with the towns and *mandis* in Haryana and cultivators had sufficient transportation facilities available, proximity to the market did not act as a positive determinant of marketed surplus. Further, with the elimination of intermediaries like money-lenders in the credit as well as commodity markets, the coefficient of debt burden on farmers remained insignificant indicating that debt obligations did not affect the marketing decisions of farmers.

The behaviour of surplus in individual crops differed from that of aggregate marketed surplus. Crop-wise marketed surplus was analysed in relation to output and area of the respective crops along with family size, distance, indebtedness and irrigation. It was observed that the marketed surplus of a particular crop rose with the rise in output and area under the respective crops and fell with the rise in family size. Other variables turned out insignificant thereby not affecting the marketed surplus of the crops under question.

Regarding the relationship of marketed surplus and output, it was observed to be a direct and more than proportionate relationship between the two. In the quadratic function, the coefficient of output was found to be significant and positive for aggregate output, wheat, paddy and coarse cereals and negative for pulses. The coefficient was insignificant in the case of oilseeds and cotton. Thus rising MPS was observed for all levels of output in the case of aggregate output and wheat, paddy and coarse cereals. In the case of pulses, MPS declined with a rise in output indicating that large farmers unlike small farmers were able to afford the consumption of pulses and may have marketed a lower proportion of their output because of the vegetarian preferences in the study area, which was dominated by Jat and Vishnoi farmers.

The results of elasticity of marketed surplus with respect to output were quite interesting. Except in the case of pulses, oilseeds and cotton, elasticity fell with the rise in output in all other crops but at a substantially high level of output (above 15 acres of operated area) elasticity started increasing. In 1960-61, Dharam Narain observed the same results for APS. Due to home requirements the farmers made available a lower proportion of additional output for sale. But at a very high level of output, these requirements are fulfilled and a higher proportion of increased output is sold. In the case of oilseeds and cotton, the elasticity remained constant around unity indicating that any increase in output led to a proportionate increase in the marketed surplus of these two crops. The elasticity of the marketed surplus of pulses declined with the rise in output due to their higher consumption at higher levels of output. The seasonal pattern of marketed surplus indicated that farmers in the region mostly sold their produce immediately after harvest. Nearly 90 to 95 per cent of output was sold in the first quarter by small as well as large farmers.

The existing market structure in the two regions surveyed appeared to be competitive. The farmers surveyed were free from the clutches of traders and intermediaries and sold their entire produce in the regulated *mandis*. All the villages surveyed were found to be well connected with *mandis* by approachable *pucca* roads. Moreover, adequate transport facilities for instance bullock-cart, tractor-trolley etc., were available to the farmers. However, the farmers had no scientific storage facilities on account of which they sold their produce immediately after the harvest even if it yielded them lower prices. There was no provision for proper grading and standardization in the market yards. It was observed that the institutional credit provided to the farmers was far lesser than their requirements and they were compelled to take loans from commission agents or *arhatias*. Consequently these *arhatias* charged a much higher rate of interest compared to the institutional loans.

In an analysis of the cost of marketing the produce, it was observed that there were economies of scale in operation in terms of transporting the produce from the field to the *mandi*. Because of the high weightage of transportation cost in the total marketing cost, there was observed to be an inverse relationship between farm size and total marketing cost. The price analysis undertaken by means of tables indicated that gross as well as net prices received by farmers did not rise with the rise in farm size. Except wheat and paddy PR, the gross and net prices of all the crops were at a maximum for semi-medium or medium farmers. Small farmers were found competing with other farmers in terms of price received for their produce.

All farmers, small as well as large, obtained a lower price for their product when they had weak bargaining power in terms of a low marketed surplus or indebtedness to the *arhatias*. A small number of farmers who held their produce for the crops of cotton American, gram and mustard and sold later, reaped excessive profits as the rise in prices were much greater than the storage charges. However, the most regular crops of the region namely, wheat, paddy PR and cotton *desi* were sold within a week of harvest. In the case of paddy Basmati, it incurred losses in storage as the net price after rising initially, fell subsequently in the post-harvest seasons.

The distance covered to market the produce, time of sale, value of output and value of marketed surplus turned out to be significant factors affecting the net price obtained by farmers in the multiple regression analysis. With the extra mileage covered by farmers to search out a better *mandi* for their produce a higher net price was realized. Similarly, those farmers who avoided sales immediately after harvest and delayed their sale by a month or more, generally obtained higher net prices. This phenomenon was observed for cotton American, gram and mustard while the only exception was paddy Basmati. Gross output and gross marketed surplus were observed to have positive coefficients, though significant only in the case of paddy Basmati and cotton American. The crop output and its marketed surplus had significant coefficients with positive signs in the case of cotton *desi*. The factors, which were found, having no significant influence on the net price in the regression analysis were storage investment, farm size and non-institutional loans.

Regarding the marketing efficiency at the farm size level, it was observed in the analysis that there was equal market participation by all sizes of farmers. Though, large farmers sold proportionately more than the small and marginal farmers, however a 68 and 74 per cent sale of aggregate output by marginal and small farmers, respectively despite their high consumption requirements indicated a considerably high level of commercialization of these farmers. The net prices obtained by marginal and small farmers were not lesser than those obtained by large farmers. It was seen from the price index calculated at the aggregate level that there was no price discrimination against the marginal farmers. Rather, if any discrimination was prevalent, it was against the large farmers who obtained lesser than the average price. Both, gross as well as net and weighted as well as unweighted price was highest for the marginal farmers. This fact was also proved by the regression analysis of net prices. None of the crops turned out with positive significant coefficient of farm size, thereby, indicating that the net price obtained by the marginal and small farmers did not differ from that realized by the medium and large farmers.

To sum up, the broad conclusions of the present study are, the markets in Haryana at the macro level are integrated, though a weaker rather than stronger form of integration was observed. The network of regulated markets was working well in the regions surveyed. All farmers, large as well as small, fully participated in the market. The whole of the farmer's produce was sold through the regulated *mandis* only. There were metal (*pucca*) roads connecting the villages with the markets and the farmers surveyed had sufficient transportation facilities. Intermediaries like money-lenders and traders were completely eliminated in the commodity markets of the region. The practice of excessive market charges had totally disappeared. Thus, the agricultural markets in the regions surveyed appear to be efficient. However, they were not perfectly integrated across time and space. Positive significant coefficients of time of sale and distance covered supplement this argument. There was a possibility of the farmers getting a higher net price either by delaying their sale after harvest or by selling more carefully in a *mandi*, which could fetch them a higher net price, even if this was located at a far off distant place.

Bibliography

Abbott, J.C. (1972); Marketing an Accelerator of Economic Growth, in Proceedings, Agricultural Marketing Conference (MFA); Document No.16, Ministry of Food & Agriculture, Government of Nepal, June, pp.15-28.

Acharya, S.S. and Agarwal, N.L. (1984); Efficiency in Millet Marketing: A Case Study of Rajasthan, *Indian Journal of Agricultural Economics*, 39(2), April-June, pp. 233-38.

Acharya, S.S. and D.P.Chaudhri (2001), *Indian Agricultural Policy at the Crossroads: Priorities and Agenda* (Ed.), Rawat Publications, New Delhi.

Agarwal, N.L. (1986); *Agricultural Prices and Marketing in India: An Analytical Case Study of Rajasthan*, Mittal Publication, Delhi.

Ahmed Raja and Abdul Mazid (1965); State Trading in Foodgrains in India—In *Marketing Agricultural Commodities*, Seminar Series, V, Indian Society of Agricultural Economics, Bombay; pp. 64-71.

Akaike, H. (1969); *Fitting Autoregressions for Prediction*; Annals of the Institute of Statistics and Mathematics, Vol.21, pp. 243 247.

Alderman, H. (1993); Intercommodity Price Transmittal: Analysis of Food Markets in Ghana, *Oxford Bulletin Economics and Statistics*, 55, pp. 43-64.

Ardeni, P.G. (1989); Does the Law of One Price Really Holds for Commodity Prices, *American Journal of Agricultural Economics,* 71, pp. 661-69.

Asche, F., H. Bremnes and C.R. Wessells (1999), "Product Aggregation, Market Integration and Relationships Between Prices: An Application to World Salmon Markets", *American Journal of Agricultural Economics,* Vol. 81, August, pp. 568-581.

Aulakh, H.S. (1983); *Changing Foodgrain Market Structure in India,* B.R. Publishing Corporation, Delhi.

Baffes, J. and B. Gardner (2003), "The Transmission of World Commodity Prices to Domestic Markets under Policy Reforms in Developing Countries", *Policy Reforms,* Vol. 6(3), September, pp. 159-80.

Banerjee, A., Dolado, J J., Hendry, D.F. and Smith, G.W. (1986); Explaining Equilibrium Relationships in Econometrics Through Static Models: Some Monte Carlo Evidence, *Bulletin*, Vol.48 (3); pp. 253-78.

Banerjee, A., Dolado, J.J., Galbraith, J.W. and Hendry, D.F. (1993); *Cointegration Error Correction and the Econometric Analysis of Non-Stationarity Data*, Oxford University Press, Oxford.

Bansil, P.C. (1961); Problems of Marketable Surplus, *The Indian Journal of Agricultural Economics,* Vol. XVI, No.I, Jan-March, pp. 26. p. 13.

Bardhan, Kalpana (1970); Price and Output Response of Marketed Surplus of Foodgrains : A Cross Sectional Study of Some North Indian Villages; *American Journal of Agricultural Economics,* Vol.52, No.I, pp.51-61.

Bardhan, P.K. and Bardhan Kalpana (1969); Problems of Marketed Surplus of Cereals, *Economic and Political*

Weekly, Vol.IV, No.26, June (Review of Agriculture), pp.A 103-A 110.

——, (1971); Price Response of Marketed Surplus of Foodgrains, Oxford Economic Papers, No.2, July, pp. 255-261.

Barrett, C.B. and J.R. Li (2002), "Distinguishing between Equilibrium and Inegration in Spatial Price Analysis", *American Journal of Agricultural Economics,* Vol. 84(2), May, 292-307.

Behrman, Jere, R. (1966); Price Elasticity of the Marketed Surplus of a Subsistence Crop; *Journal of Farm Economics,* Vol. 48, No. 4, Nov., pp.875-893.

Berg, Elliot (1977); 'Upper Volta' in CILSS/Club de Sahel Marketing Food Policy and Storage of Foodgrains in the Sahel: A Survey No. 2; Country Studies I, Centre for Research on Economic Development, University of Michigan/US Agency for International Development, Ann Arbor, Michigan, USA.

Bhalerao, M.M. and Kalicharan (1968); Marketing of Wheat in Varanasi, *Agricultural Situation in India*, Vol. 23(1), pp.13-16.

Bhalla, G.S. (1991); Some Issues in Agricultural Marketing in India; Presidential Address delivered at the 5th National Conference of ISAM; *Indian Journal of Agricultural Marketing*; Vol. 5, No. 3, July-December, pp. 128-137.

Bhardwaj, Krishna (1974); *Production Conditions in Indian Agriculture*; Cambridge University Press.

Bhargava, P.N. and Rustogi, V.S. (1972); Study of Marketable Surplus of Paddy in Bardwan District; *Indian Journal of Agricultural Economics*, Vol. 28, No. 3, July-September, pp. 63-68.

Bhattacharjee, J.P. (1960); Changing Characteristics of the Flow of Foodgrains Supplies from the Farmer; *Agricultural Situation in India*, Vol. 14, No.10, January, pp.1079-86.

Bhide, S., Chowdhury, A., Heady, E.A.O. and Muralidharan, M.A. (1981); Structural Changes in an Agricultural Assembling Market : A case study of Arecanut Market in Mangalore, Karnataka State; *Indian Journal of Agricultural Economics;* Vol. 36, No. 2, pp. 25-34.

Bhoothalingam, S. (1969); *Structure and Behaviour of Prices of Foodgrains*, National Council of Applied Economic Research, New Delhi.

Blyn, George (1973); Price Series Correlation as a measure of Market Integration, *Indian Journal of Agricultural Economics,* Vol. 18, No.2, April-June, pp.56-59.

Boyd, M. and Brorsen, B.W. (1986); Dynamic Price Relationship for US and EC Corn Gluten Feed and Related Markets; *European Review of Agricultural Economics,* 13, pp.199-215.

Brown, R.L., Durbin, J. and Evans, J.M. (1975); Technique for Testing the Constancy of Regression Relationships Over Time, *Journal of Royal Statistical* Society, Vol. 37.

Carol, Alexander and Wyeth, John (1994); Cointegration and Market Integration : *The Indonesian Rice Markets*; The Journal of Development Studies, Vol. 30(2), pp. 303-328.

Chakraborthy, R.M. (1968); Marketable Surplus of Foodgrains in Developing Economy, *Arthaniti*, Vol.11, No.1&2, Jan-July, pp. 22-39.

Chand, Ramesh (2004); "*India's National Agricultural Policy: A Critique*", Disucssion Paper Seires No. 85/2004,

Institute of Economic Growth, Delhi University Enclave, Delhi.

Chand, Ramesh and Parmod Kumar (2004); Determinants of Capital Formaion and Agriculture Growth: Some New Explorations, *Economic and Political Weekly,* Vol. xxxix, No. 52, December 25-31, 5611-5616.

Chatterjee, D.R. and Bhattacharya, K. (1986); A note on Marketing of Rice in Burdwan District of West Bengal: An Enquiry of its Spatial and Seasonal Pricing Efficiency; *Indian Journal of Economics;* Vol. 46, No. 2, pp. 125-135.

Chattopadhyay, Manabendu and Sen, Ispita (1988); Marketable Surplus and Size Class of Holdings; *Economic and Political Weekly*, December 24-31; pp. A 151-A 156.

Chauhan, K.K.S. and Singh, R.V. (1971); *Marketing of Wheat in Rajasthan*, University of Udaipur, S.K.N. College of Agricultural Campus.

Chinn, Dennis, L. (1976); The Marketed Surplus of a Subsistence Crop : Paddy Rice in Taiwan, *American Journal of Agricultural Economics*, Vol. 58, No.3, August, pp.583-587.

Cohen, R. (1965); *The Economics of Agriculture*, Cambridge Economic Handbook, Cambridge University Press.

Cummings, Ralph W.J. (1967); Pricing Efficiency in the Indian Wheat Market, *Impex*, India, New Delhi.

Dandekar, V.M. (1964); Prices, Production and Marketed Surplus of Foodgrains, Indian Journal of Agricultural Economics Vol. XIX, No. 3&4, July December, pp.186-195.

Dantwala, M.L. (1937); *Working of the Raw Cotton in India*, Longmans Green & Company, Bombay.

——, (1952); *Report of the Enquiry into the Regulated Markets in the Bombay State*, Government of Bombay, Bombay.

Davidson, R. and Mackinnon, J.G. (1993); *Estimation and Inference in Econometrics*; Oxford University Press, New York.

Dayal, Ram (1963); Some Aspects of the Marketable Surplus of Foodgrains, *Agricultural Situation in India*, Vol.18, No.1, pp.23-25.

Deen, Gaya (1977); Marketing of Potato in Farrukhabad District of Uttar Pradesh, Ph.D. Thesis submitted to the Indian Agricultural Research Institute, New Delhi.

Diakosavvas, Dimitris (1995); How Integrated are World Beef Markets? The case of Australian and US Beef Markets; Agricultural Economics, 12, pp. 37-53.

Dickey, D.A. and Fuller, W.A. (1979); Distribution of the Estimators for Autoregressive Time Series with a Unit Root, *Journal of American Statistics Association*, Vol.74, pp. 427-29.

Dickey, D.A., Jansen, D.W., Thornton, D.L. (1991), A Primer on Cointegration with an Application to Money and Income", Fed. Res. Bank of St. Louis Rev., 73: 58-78.

Diwakar, G.D. and Muralidharan, M.A. (1979); An Analysis of Price Efficiency of Potato in Farrukhabad district of Uttar Pradesh, *Indian Journal of Agricultural Economics,* Vol. 34(4), p. 215.

Dobb, Maurice (1955); *On Economic Theory and Socialism: Collected Paper*, Routledge and Kegan Paul Ltd., London and Boston.

Dries, M.A. and Unnevehr, L.J. (1990); Influence of Trade Policies on Price Integration in the World Beef Market, *Agricultural Economics*, 4. pp. 73-89.

Engle, R.F. (1982); Autoregressive Conditional Heteroscedasticity with Estimates of the Variance of U.K. Inflation, *Econometrica*, Vol. 50, pp. 987-1007.

Engle, R.F. and Granger, C.W.J. (1987); Cointegration and Error-Correction : Representation, Estimation and Testing; *Econometrica,* 55, pp. 251-76.

Engle, R.F. and Yoo, B.S. (1987); Forecasting and Testing in Cointegrated System; *Journal of Econometrics,* 35, pp. 143-159.

Faminow, M. and Benson, B. (1990); Integration of Spatial Markets, *American Journal of Agricultural Economics,* 72, pp. 49-62.

Fan, Shenggen (2002), "Agricultural Research and Urban Poverty in India", International Food Policy Research Institute, EPTD, Discussion Paper No. 94, Sept.

Fuller, W.A. (1976); *Introduction to Statistical Time Series*, New York: Wiley.

Gangwar, A.C. and Pandey, R.N. (1985); Farm Structure of Rice and Producer's Share in Consumer's Price in Haryana, *Indian Journal of Agricultural Economics*, Vol. 40, pp. 358-61.

George, M.V. (1984); Changing Marketing Structure/ Marketing Policies, *Indian Journal of Agricultural Economics*, 39 (4), Oct.-Dec., pp. 586-89.

George, M.V. and Singh, A.J. (1970); Structure, Conduct and Performance of Wholesale Vegetable Markets in Punjab, Proceedings of Second All India Agricultural Marketing Research Conference, Jabalpur, pp.80-82.

Ghosh, Dipak (1987); Theoretical Model of Behaviour of Marketed Surplus in a Partially Monetised Economy, Indian Economic Journal, 34 (4) April-June, pp. 39-54.

Ghosh, Madhusudhan (200), "Cointegration Tests and Spatial Integration of Markets in India", *Indian Journal of Agricultural Economics,* Vol. 55(4), Oct-Dec., pp. 616-26.

Goletti, Francesco and Babu, Suresh (1994); Market Liberalization and Integration of Maize Markets in Malawi; Agricultural Economics, 11, pp. 311-324.

Gonzalez- Rivera, G. and S.M. Helfand (2001), "The Extent, Pattern and Degree of Market Integration: A Multivariate Approach for the Brazilian Rice Market", *American Journal of Agricultural Ecnomics,* Vol. 83 (3), August, 576-592.

Goodwin, Barry, K. and Schroeder, Ted, C. (1991); Cointegration Tests and Spatial Price Linkages in Regional Cattle markets; *American Journal of Agricultural Economics,* 73, pp. 453-464.

Goodwin, Berry K. and Nicholas E. Piggott (2001), "Spatial Market Integration in the Presence of Threshold Effects", *American Journal of Agricultural Economics,* Vol. 83, No. 2, May, pp. 302-317.

Government of India, "*Agricultural Statistics at a Glance*", Directorate of Economics and Statistics, Department of Agriculture and Cooperation, Ministry of Agriculture, New Delhi. Various issues.

——, (1961); *Rice Economy of India*, Economic and Statistical Advisor to the Government, Jan., p. 203.

——, (1976); *National Commission on Agriculture: Abridged Report;* Ministry of Agriculture and Irrigation, Department of Agriculture, New Delhi.

——, (1981); *Marketing of Wheat in Punjab and Haryana,* Directorate of Marketing and Inspection, Ministry of Rural Reconstruction, Faridabad.

——,(1986); *Area and Production of Principal Crops in India*, Dir. of Econ. and Statis., Department of Agriculture and Cooperation, Ministry of Agriculture, 1986-88.

——, (2001); *Agricultural Research Data Book,* Directorate of Economics and Statistics, Department of Agriculture and Cooperation, Ministry of Agriculture, New Delhi.

Granger, C.W.J. (1986); Developments in the Study of Cointegrated Economic Variables; *Oxford Bulletin of Economics and Statistics*, 48, pp. 213-228.

Granger, C.W.J. and Newbold, P. (1974); Spurious Regression in Econometrics, *Journal of Econometrics*, Vol.2, pp. 111-20.

Gulati, Ashok (1999), "*Towards an Agenda for Reforms in Indian Agriculture*", Paper presented at the NCAER-IEG-World Bank Conference on "Reforms in the Agricultural Sector for Growth, Efficiency, Equity and Sustainability, April 15-16, India Habitat Centre, New Delhi.

Gupta, A.P. (1975); *Marketing of Agricultural Produce in India,* Vora & Co. Pub. Pvt. Ltd., Bombay.

Gupta, R.P. (1973); *Agricultural Prices in a Backward Economy*, National Publishing House, Delhi.

Harriss, B. (1979); There is method in my madness : or is it *vice-versa*? Measuring Agricultural Market Performance, Food Research Institute Studies, Vol. XVII, No. 2, pp.197-218.

——, (1982); The Marketed Surplus of Paddy in North Arcot District, T.N.: A Micro Level Causal Model, *Indian Journal of Agricultural Economics,* 37 (2); April-June, pp.145-58.

——, (1984); *Exchange Relations and Poverty in Dryland Agriculture*, Concept Publishing Company, New Delhi.

------, (1996); *A Political Economy of Agricultural Markets in South India: Masters of the Countryside*, Sage Publications, New Delhi.

Hassel, Walter (1975); The Price and Income Elasticities of Home Consumption and Marketed Surplus of Foodgrains, *American Journal of Agricultural Economics,* Vol. 57(1), Feb., (111-115).

Hati, Ashoke (1976); Non-Linear Marketable Surplus Function, *Economic and Political Weekly*, Vol. 6, No. 29, July 17, pp. 1080-1084.

Hays, Jr., H.M. (1975); "The Marketing and Storage of Foodgrains in Northern Nigeria," Miscellaneous Papers No. 50, Institute of Agricultural Research, Samaru, Zaria, p.72.

Heytens, P. (1986); Testing Market Integration, "Food Research Institute Studies, 20, pp. 25-41.

Jain, S.C. (1971); *Problems and Practice of Agricultural Marketing and Price*, Vora & Co. Pvt. Ltd., Bombay.

Janaki, R.R.A., W.L. Adamowicz and M.K. Luckert (1997), "A Cointegration Analysis of Canadian Wood Pulp Prices", *American Journal of Agricultural Economics,* Vol. 79, August, pp. 975-86.

Jasdanwalla, Z.Y. (1966); *Market Efficiency in Indian Agriculture*, Allied Publishers Pvt. Ltd.

Jayaraj, D. (1992); Spatial Pricing Efficiency in Groundnut Markets in Tamil Nadu, *Indian Journal of Agricultural Economics*, Vol.47, No.1, January-March, pp.79-89.

Jairath, M.S. (2002), "Institutional Reforms—A Case Study of Agricultural Markets in India", *Indian Journal of Agricultural Economics,* Vol. 57(3), July-Sept., pp. 535-545.

Jha, Raghbendra and H.K. Nagarajan (1998), "Wholesaler Stocks and Hoarding in Rice Markets in India", *Economic and Political Weekly,* October 10, pp. 2658-61.

Jha, R., K.V. Bhanumurthy, H.K. Nagarajan and A.K. Seth (1997), "Market Integration in Indian Agriculture", *Economic Systems*, Vol. 21(3), pp. 217-34.

Jha, R., K.V. Bhanumurthy, H.K. Nagarajan and A.K. Seth (1999), "Components of the Wholesale Bid—Ask Spread and the Structure of Grain Markets: The Case of Rice in India", *Agricultural Economics,* Vol. 21(2), October, pp. 173-89.

Johansen, S. (1988); Statistical Analysis of Economic Dynamics and Control, *Journal of Economic Dynamics and Control*, Vol. 12, pp. 231-54.

Jones, W.O. (1968); The Structure of Staple Food Marketing in Nigeria as revealed by Price Analysis, "Food Research Institute Studies, Vol.VIII, No. 2, pp. 110-111.

——, (1972); *Marketing Staple Food Crops in Tropical Africa*, Ithaca, New York, Cornell University Press.

Joshi, V.R. (1971); *Regulated Markets in Gujarat;* Kaira District Cooperative Union, Nadiad, Gujarat, p. 7.

Kahlon A.S. and Singh, B. (1968); "Marketing of Groundnut in Punjab, Department of Economics & Sociology, Punjab Agricultural University, Ludhiana.

Kahlon, A.S. and Vashistha, S.D. (1968); A Study of the Factors Governing the Flow of Marketable Surplus of Major Crops in Ludhiana District, *Agricultural Situation in India*, Vol. 23, No. 8, pp. 815-823.

Kainth, G.S. (1982); *Foodgrains Marketing System in India: Its Structure and Performance*, Associated Publishing House, New Delhi.

Krishna, Raj (1965); The Marketable Surplus Function for a Subsistence Crop: An Analysis with Indian Data, *The Economic Weekly*, Vol. 17, No. 6, pp. 309-320.

Krishnaji, N. (1965); The Marketable Surplus Function for a Subsistence Crop: Comments, *The Economic Weekly*, April 17, p. 678.

Kohl, R.L. and Joseph, N.U. (1985); *Marketing of Agricultural Products*; 6th Edition, Macmillan, New York.

Kohlers, D. (1977); 'Niger' in CILSS/Club du Sahel : Marketing Food Policy and Storage of Foodgrains in the Sahel: A Survey No. 2; Country Studies I, Centre for Research on Economic Development, University of Michigan/US Agency for International Development, Ann Arbor, Michigan, USA, pp.35-44.

Krishnan, T.N. (1965); The Marketed Surplus of Foodgrains: Is it inversely related to Price? *The Economic Weekly*, Vol.17, No.5, 6 & 7, Annual Number.

Krishnaswamy, L. (1971); The Degree of Competitiveness in Agricultural Markets; Paper Presented at the International Conference of Agricultural Economics held at Brazil, 1971.

Kulkarni, A.P. (1965); Price Spread for Groundnut in Two Regulated Markets, Seminar on Marketing of Agricultural Commodities, Seminar Series-V, ISAE, Bombay, pp. 147-155.

Kumar P. and Mruthyunjaya (1989); Price Policy and Marketed Supply of Paddy and Wheat in India, *Indian Journal of Agricultural Economics*, 44(4), pp. 430-35.

Kumar, Parmod and R.K. Sharma (2003), "Spatial Price Integration and Pricing Efficiency at the Farm Level: A Study of Paddy in Haryana," *Indian Jaurnal of Agricultural Economics,* 58 (2), 201-217.

Lele, U.J. (1967); Market Integration : A Study of Sorghum Prices in Western India, *Journal of Farm Economics*, 49(1), pp.147-159.

——, (1968); "Working of Grain Markets in Selected States of India 1955-56 to 1965-66", Cornell University, Department of Agricultural Economics, Ithaca, Occasional Paper No.12.

——, (1971); "Foodgrain Marketing in India : Private Performance and Public Policy", Cornell University Press, Ithaca.

Lloyd, T. and Rayner, A. (1993); Cointegration Analysis and the Determinants of Land Prices: Comment, *Journal of Agricultural Economics*, 44(1), pp. 149-51.

Mackinnon, J.G. (1990); "Critical Values for Cointegration tests", Department of Economics, Queen's University, Canada, Mimeo.

Maddala, G.S. (1977); *Econometrics*, International Student Edition, McGraw Hill, Kogakusha Ltd.

Maheshwari, Asha (1998), "Regulation of Markets, Production Growth and Market Arrivals—A State-wise Analysis of Rice", *Indian Journal of Agricultural Economics,* Vol. 53(3), July-Sept. pp. 351-58.

Majid, Abdul (1960); Marketed Surplus of Agricultural Produce in Relation to Size of Cultivated Holdings—Agricultural Situation in India, Vol. XV, No. 3, pp. 259-266.

Majumdar, Manoranjan (1965); The Marketable Surplus Function for a Subsistence Crop : Further Comments; The Economic Weekly, May 15, pp. 820-822.

Mamoria and Joshi (1978); *Principles and Practices of Marketing in India,* Kitab Mahal, Allahabad, pp. 61-69.

Mathur, P.N. (1959); Time Pattern and Quanta of Purchase and Sale of Jowar by Peasants of Vidarbha (Bombay), *Artha Vijanana*, Vol.1.

Mathur, P.N. and Ezekiel (1961); Marketable Surplus of Food and Price Fluctuations in a Developing Economy, *Kyklos,* Vol. 14, No. I, pp. 396-408.

Mathur, P.N. and Kulkarni, A.P. (1965); Some Observations on working of a Regulated Market—In Marketing Agriculture, Seminar Series, Indian Society of Agricultural Economics, Bombay, pp. 83-101.

Mehr, S.C. (1949); Costs of Marketing Cotton in Bombay and Karnatak, *Indian Journal of Agricultural Economics,* Vol. IV, No. I, March, pp. 215-22.

Mirchandani, R.T. and Hirachandani, G.J. (1965); Regulated Markets : Their Impact on Market Structure and Efficiency—In Marketing of Agricultural Commodities, Seminar Series V, Indian Society of Agricultural Economics, Bombay, pp.72-82.

Monke, E. and Petzel, T. (1984); Market Integration : An application to International Trade in Cotton; American Journal of Agricultural Economics, 66(4), pp. 401-487.

Moore, J.R., Johl, S.S. and Khusro, A.M. (1973); *Indian Foodgrains Marketing*, Prentice Hall of India Pvt. Ltd., New Delhi.

Mukherjee, S.K. (1983); *Trends in Cereal Prices, Agricultural Situation in India*, Vol.38(5), pp. 301-304.

Muniyandi, B. (1985); "Pricing Efficiency of Groundnut Marketing System in Tamil Nadu", Ph.D. Thesis submitted to the Faculty of the Post Graduate School, IARI, New Delhi.

Munshi, M.C. (1957); From the Farmers to the Consumer : A Survey of Price Spread, Research Department, Federation of Indian Chamber of Commerce and Industry, New Delhi.

Muthaiah, C. (1964); Marketed Surplus of Foodgrains by Size Level of Holdings and Income, *Agricultural Situation in India*, Vol. 19, No. 2, pp. 95-98.

Nadkarni, M.V. (1980); *Marketable Surplus and Market Dependence in a Millet Region*, Allied Publishers, New Delhi.

Nadkarni, M.V. (1985); *Socio-Economic Conditions in Drought Prone Area*, Concept Publishing Company, New Delhi.

Naik, G. and Arora, V.P.S. (1986); Marketing Pattern and Pricing Efficiency in Indian Arecanut Market, *Indian Journal of Agricultural Economics*, Vol. 41, No. 2, pp. 172-182.

Narain, Dharam (1961); *Distribution of the Marketed Surplus of Agricultural Produce by size level of holdings* : 1950-51; Asia Publishing House, Bombay.

Nasurudeen, P. and Subramanian, S.R. (1995); Price Integration of Oil and Oilseeds, *Indian Journal of Agricultural Economics*, Vol. 50, No. 4, October December, pp. 624-633.

Nayyar, H. and Ramaswamy P. (edited) (1995); *Globalisation and Agricultural Marketing*; Rawat Publication, Jaipur and New Delhi.

NCAER (1990), "*Marketable Surplus Ratios for Agricultural Commodities*", Memio, National Council of Applied Economic Research, New Delhi.

Neal, Barry (1987); Integration and Efficiency of the London and Amsterdam Stock Markets in 18th Century; *Journal of Economic History,* (42), pp. 97-115.

Nelson, C. and Plosser, C. (1982); Trends and Random Walks in Macro-economic Time Series : Some Evidence and Implications; *Journal of Monetary Economics*, 10, pp. 139-162.

Ninan, K.N. (1988); Small Farmers and Commodity Market: An Analysis of Market Participation and Price Discrimination, *Economic and Political Weekly*, December 24-31, pp. A163- A172.

Owen A.D., K. Chowdhury and J.R.R. Garrido (1997), "Price Interrelationships in the Vegetable and Tropical Oils Market", *Applied Economics*, Vol. 29, pp. 119-124.

Palaskas, T.B. and Harris, B. (1993); Testing Market Integration : New Approaches with Case Material from the West Bengal Food Economy, *The Journal of Development Studies,* Vol. 30 (1), p. 1-57.

Pandey, V.K., Gupta, D.D. and Singh, Himmat (1979); A Case Study on Price Spread of Agricultural Commodities in Kurukshetra District (Haryana), *Indian Journal of Agricultural Economics,* Vol.34(4), pp. 205.

Parthasarthy, G. and Rao, B.V. Suba (1964); Production and Marketed Surplus of Rice in the Deltas of the South, *Agricultural Situation in India*, Vol. 19, No. 8, pp. 721-725.

Patnaik K.U.S. (1995), "Factors Affecting the Share of Groundnut Market Arrivals in the Market Yard in Andhra Pradesh", *Indian Journal of Agricultural Economics,* Vol. 50(1), Jan.-Mar., pp. 69-79.

Patnaik, K. and Shankar, U. (1985); Economic Performance of Groundnut Marketing Channels : A Case Study to Rayalaseema Region of Andhra Pradesh; *Indian Journal of Agricultural Economics*; Vol. 40 (1), pp. 26-35.

Patnaik, Utsa (1975); Contribution to the Output and Marketable Surplus of Agricultural Products by Cultivating Groups in India, 1960-61; *Economic and Political Weekly*, Vol. X, No. 52, Review of Agriculture, October-December, pp. A 90-A 100.

Pavaskar, M.G. and Radhakrishnan, V. (1970); Marketing Margins in Cotton, *Economic and Political Weekly*, Vol. V, No. 13, March 28, pp. A 41-A 47.

Pindyck, R. and Rubinfeld, D.L. (1976); Econometric Models and Economic Forecasts; McGraw-Hill, New York.

Prasad, Brahmanand (1965); The Marketable Surplus Function for a Subsistence Crop : Further Comments; *The Economic Weekly*, May 15, pp. 822-823.

Prasad, Jagdish (1989); *Marketable Surplus and Market Performance—A Study with Special Reference to Muzaffarpur Foodgrains Market in Bihar*, Mittal Publications, Delhi.

Raj, D.J. (1980); "Comparison Between Costs and Returns in the Regulated and Unregulated Markets of Groundnuts in South Arcot District (Tamil Nadu)", M.Sc. Thesis Submitted to Indian Agricultural Research Institute, New Delhi.

Rajagopal (1985); Economics of Linseed Marketing in Madhya Pradesh : A Case Study; *Agricultural Situation in India*, Vol. 20, pp. 50-60.

——, (1986); Economic Efficiency of Paddy Marketing System in Madhya Pradesh: A Case Study, *Indian*

Journal of Agricultural Economics, Vol. 41, No. 4 October-December, pp. 583-590.

——, (1988); *Marketing in Peasant Economy*; Mana: Publication, Delhi.

——, (1989); *State and Agriculture Trade*; Renaissance Publishing House, Delhi.

Ramasamy C. (2004), "Constrains to Growth in Indian Agriculture: Needed Technology, Resource Management and Trade Strategies", *Indian Journal of Agricultural Economics,* Vol. 59(1), January March, pp. 1-39.

Ranade, C.G., Singh, R.B. and Hanumantha Rao, K. (1979) "Marketing Channels and Price Spread in Cotton" Centre for Management in Agriculture, Indian Institute of Management, Ahmedabad.

Rao, C.H. Hanumantha (1965); The Marketable Surplus Function for a Subsistence Crop : Comments; *The Economic Weekly*, April 17, pp. 677-678.

Rao, C.H.H. (1997), "Agricultural Growth, Sustainability and Poverty Alleviation in India—Recent Trends and Major Issues of Reforms", IFPRI Lecture Series 5, International Food Policy Research Institute, Washington, D.C., December.

Rao, C.H. Hanumantha and Rao, K. Subba (1976); Marketing of Rice in India : An Analysis of the Impact of Producer's Prices on Small Farmers, *Indian Journal of Agricultural Economics*, Vol. 31(2), pp.1-15.

Rapsomanikis G., D. Hallam and P. Conforti (2004), "Market Integration and Price Transmission in Selected Food and Cash Crop Markets of Developing Countries: Review and Applications", Food and Agricultural Organisation, http://www.fao.org/DOCREP/006/Y5117E/y5117e06.htm

Rastyannikov, V.G. (1975); The Agrarian Evolution of Indian Society in the 50s and 60s of the 20th Century-In Pavlov *et al.*, (ed.), *India : Social and Economic Development-18th to 20th Century*, Progress Publishers, Moscow, pp. 120-121.

Ravallion, M. (1986); Testing Market Integration; *American Journal of Agricultural Economics*, Vol. 68, No. 1, pp. 102-9.

Reddy, M.J.M. (1987); Marketable Surplus in Paddy—A Regression Analysis, *Agricultural Situation in India*, (Jan.).

Reddy, M.J.M., Bhaler, M.M. and Tyagi, V.P. (1985); Producer's Share in the Consumer's Rupee—A Sample Study of Groundnut, *Indian Journal of Agricultural Economics,* Vol. XI, No. 2-3, pp. 398.

Rudra, Ashok (1982); *Indian Agricultural Economics : Myths and Realities*, Allied Publishers Pvt. Ltd., New Delhi.

——, (1992); *Political Economy of Indian Agriculture;* K.P. Bagchi & Co., New Delhi.

Ruttan, V.W. and Hayami, Y. (1971); *Agricultural Development: An International Perspective*, The John Hopkins Press, London.

Sah, D.C., Ranade, C.G., Rao, K.H. (1979); "Cooperative and Private Trade Channels in Groundnut", Centre for Management in Agriculture, Indian Institute of Management, Ahmedabad.

Sahay, S.N. (1980); "Comparative Study on Economics of Product Marketing, Income and Consumption of Tribal and Non-Tribal Forms of Ranchi District (Bihar)", 1980, Ph.D. Thesis submitted to IARI, New Delhi.

Sangwan, S.S.; *Production and Marketing of Potato in India*, Mittal Publications, New Delhi, 1991.

Sarkar, Suman (1981); Marketing of Foodgrains: Analysis of Village Survey, Data for West Bengal and Bihar, *Economic and Political Weekly*, Sept. 26, pp. A 103-A 108.

Sen, Ipsita and H.K. Banerjee (1995), "Behaviour of Marketable Surplus of Some Major and Minor Food Crops in India", *Indian Journal of Agricultural Economics*, Vol. 50, No. 1, January-March, pp. 80-85.

Sexton, R.J., Kling and Gorman, M.F. (1991); Market Integration, Efficiency of Arbitrage and Imperfect Competitor : Methodology and Application to US Colery; *American Journal of Agricultural Economics*, 73, pp. 568-579.

Shah, C.H. (1965); "Shifters of Market Supply of Farm Products"—Seminar on Marketing of Agricultural Commodity; Seminar Series-V, Indian Society of Agricultural Economics, Bombay.

——, (1971); "A Survey of Research in Agricultural Economics in India, Department of Economics, University of Bombay, Bombay.

Sharma, P.S. (1972); Estimation of Marketable Surplus of Foodgrains by Size Classes of Holdings in Rural Cultivating Households—A Physical Approach, *Agricultural Situation in India*, Vol. XXVII, No. 5, August, pp. 327-335.

Sidhu, D.S. (1986); Policies Pertaining to Agricultural Marketing and Input Supply; *Indian Journal of Agricultural Economics*; Vol. 41, No. 3, July-September, pp. 310-24.

Silvapulle, P. and Jayasuriya, S. (1994); Testing for Philippines Rice Market Integration : A Multiple Cointegration Approach, *Journal of Agricultural Economics,* 45(3), pp. 369-380.

Singh, B. and Sidhu, B.S. (1974); Economics of Scale in Groundnut Processing Industry in Punjab, *Agricultural Marketing*, Vol. 15(2), pp. 18-26.

Singh, Jaspal and Dhindsa, K.S. (1983); Marketed Surplus of Wheat and Paddy by Farm Size in Punjab—A Case Study, *Margin*, 2(15), Jan., pp. 81-88.

Singh, Laxman (1962); Marketing Costs and Producer's Share in Consumer's Rupee Two Case Studies of Rice in Madhya Pradesh, *Agricultural Situation in India*, Vol. XVI, No.10, Jan., pp. 1020-24.

Singh, Bhupinder, Singh, A.J. and Dhawan, K.C. (1979); A Study into the Costs and Margins for Wheat and Paddy in the Punjab State, *Indian Journal of Agricultural Economics,* Vol. 34 (4).

Singh, Chhotan and Vasisht, A.K. (1985); A Study of Changes in Producer's Share in Consumer's Rupee of Agricultural Commodity in India, *Indian Journal of Agricultural Economics*, Vol. 40, p. 390.

Singh, R.V., Verma, R.C. and Agarwal, N.L. (1974); Marketing Costs and Margins of Co-operating Marketing Society and a Private Wholesale Trader, *Agricultural Marketing*, Vol. XVII, No. I, April, pp. 14-18.

Sinha, S.P., Kumar, Ajay, Prasad, Jagdish and Pandey, P.C. (1979); A Study of Price Spread of Important Foodgrains in two Agricultural Markets in Bihar, *Indian Journal of Agricultural Economics*, Vol. 34 (4), pp. 136-142.

Sinharoy, S. and Nair, S.R. (1994); International Trade and Pepper Price Variations : A Cointegration Approach; *Indian Journal of Agricultural Economics*, Vol. 49, No. 3, July-September, pp. 418-425.

Sivarama Prasad, A. (1985); *Agricultural Marketing in India: A Case Study of Selected Regulated Markets in Andhra Pradesh*, Mittal Publication, Delhi.

Southworth, V. Roy, Jones, William O. and Pearson, S.R. (1979); "Food Crop Marketing in Atebubu District, Ghana", Food Research Institute Studies, Vol. XVII, No. 2, p. 189.

Stigler, G. and Sherwin, R.A. (1985); The Extent of the Market; *Journal of Law and Economics*, Vol. 28, pp. 555-85.

Subbarao, K. (1978); *Rice Marketing System and Compulsory Levies in Andhra Pradesh—A Study of Public Intervention in Foodgrains Marketing*, Allied Publishers Pvt. Ltd.

——, (1989); "Agricultural Marketing and Credit; Research in Economics"; Second Survey; ICSSR, Monograph 2.

Suryaprakash, S., Venkataram, J.V. and Ramanna, R. (1979); A Comparative Study of Price Spread of Selected Agricultural Commodities in Karnataka, *Indian Journal of Agricultural Economics,* Vol. 34 (4), pp. 142-149.

Talukdar, K.C. (1984); A Study of Efficiency and Equity in Marketing of Major Agricultural Commodities in Assam; Ph.D. Thesis, IARI, New Delhi.

——, (1985); Efficiency and Equity of farm prices in Assam State: A Case Study of Small Farmers, *Indian Journal of Agricultural Economics*, 2 (XL), April-June 1985, pp. 362-68.

Thakur, D.S. (1974); Foodgrains Marketing Efficiency: A Case Study of Gujarat, *Indian Journal of Agricultural Economics,* XXIX, (4), October December, pp. 61- 74.

Thakur, D.S., H. Lal, D.R. Thakur, K.D. Sharma and A.S. Saini (1997), "Market Supply Response and Marketing Problems of Farmers in the Hills", *Indian Jornal of Agricultural Economics,* Vol. 52, No. 1, Jan-Mar, pp. 139-150.

Thodey, Alon R. (1968); Marketing of Staple Foods in Western Nigeria Vol. I : Summary and Conclusions, Stanford Research Institute, Menlo Park, California.

Thomsen, F.L. (1951); *Agricultural Marketing*; McGraw-Hill, New York.

Timmer, P.C. (1974); A Model of Rice Marketing Margins in Indonesia; Food Research Institute Studies, 13(2), pp.145-167.

——, (1984); Corn Markcting and the Balance between Domestic Production and Consumption; Working Paper No.14, BULOG Standard Corn Project.

Tousley, D.R., *et al*., (1968); Principles of Marketing, The MacMillan Company, New York.

Tripathi, R.S., J. Kumar, M.L. Sharma and Chandra Dev (1995), "Marketing of Apples: A Case Study of Chamba-Mussoorie Fruit Belt", *Agricultural Situation in India,* June, pp. 135-39.

Uri, N. and Lin, B.H. (1992); A Note on the Substitutability between Domestically produced Beef and imported United States Beef in Japan; Oxford Agrarian Studies, 20, pp. 89-105.

Verma, A.R. and Nigam, H.K. (1979); Price Spreads in Groundnut Marketing in District Kanpur, U.P. (A Case Study), *Indian Journal of Agricultural Economics*, Vol. 34(4), pp. 208-209.

Vyas, V.S. (1965); Norms and Efficiency in Agricultural Marketing; Seminar Series V, Marketing of Agricultural Commodities, (ISAE), Bombay.

Vyas, V.S. and Maharaja, M.H. (1966); Factors Governing Marketable Surplus and Marketed Surplus: A Study of Two Regions of Gujarat and Rajasthan, *Artha Vikas*, Vol. 2, No. 1, pp. 52-78.

Waite, W.C. and Trelogan, H.C. (1951); *Agricultural Market Price*, John Willy and Sons; New York.

Wilson Edgar J. (2001), "Testing Agricultural Market Integration: Further Conceptual and Empirical Considerations Using Indian Wholesale Prices", in Acharya S.S. and D.P. Chaudhri, "*Indian Agricultural Policy at the Crossroads*", Rawat Publications, New Delhi and Jaipur.

Wyeth, J. (1992); "The Measurement of Market Integration and Application to Food Security Policies", Disc. Pap. 314, Institute of Development Studies, University of Sussex, UK.

INDEX